Primitive Christianity

PRIMITIVE CHRISTIANITY

A Survey of Recent Studies and Some
New Proposals

Gerd Lüdemann

Translated by
John Bowden

T&T CLARK
A Continuum imprint
LONDON • NEW YORK

T&T CLARK

A Continuum imprint

The Tower Building   15 East 26th Street
11 York Road   New York 10010
London SE1 7NX, UK   USA

www.continuumbooks.com

Translated by John Bowden from the German *Das Urchristentum. Eine kritische Bilanz seiner Erforschung*, Frankfurt 2002, with additions by the author

British Library Cataloguing-in-Publication Data
A catalogue record for this book is available from the British Library

ISBN 0 567 08810 3 (Paperback)
0 567 08885 5 (Hardback)

Typeset by YHT Ltd., London
Printed and bound in Great Britain by MPG, Bodmin, Cornwall

Contents

v

Preface

The present book goes back to an account of research into primitive Christianity, 'Das Urchristentum', which appeared in German in *Theologische Rundschau* 65, 2000, 121–79, 285–349, and was then published separately under the title *Das Urchristentum. Eine kritische Bilanz seiner Erforschung*, Frankfurt 2002. The English version is a revised and considerably expanded version of this. In the United States I have been helped to produce it by my friends and colleagues Tom Hall and Eugene TeSelle. In England my friend John Bowden has translated the text into English with his usual skill and he and Margaret Lydamore have relieved me of some of the technical work. I am deeply grateful to all of these.

My report offers a critical review of important literature on primitive Christianity from the last 25 years and is intended to draw a line in a situation in which research has become quite impossible to take account of. If in some cases my verdict proves very harsh, it is because I am not concerned with persons, but solely with the subject-matter. With this report I also want to show that we stand on the shoulders of our fathers, grandfathers and great-grandfathers and not on their tombs. A certain canon of historical criticism must be observed in order to preserve the spirit and legacy of previous research, to examine it in public discussion and thus hand it on to the next generation.

Gerd Lüdemann

Preliminary Remarks

Summary accounts of research into primitive Christianity have been given in the past, especially in *Theologische Rundschau* (Theological Review). This tradition is continued in the account that follows. It should be noted that such abstracts have been published in *Theologische Rundschau* only since 1933.[1] At that time, in the fifth year of the new series (NF), Hans Windisch discussed first of all 'general accounts' (186–200), then the 'role of Jesus and the Baptist in the rise of Christianity' (237–58), then the '"parties" and trends in primitive Christianity' (289–301) and finally the 'leitmotifs' (319–34) which governed primitive Christianity.[2]

After Windisch's premature death in 1935, Werner Georg Kümmel was assigned to writing reviews on research into primitive Christianity.[3] His first report appeared in 1942 (NF 14, 81–95,155–73). In it he first explained his own position with reference to that of his predecessor. He accepted Windisch's definition of primitive Christianity: 'The study of primitive Christianity comprises the origin and earliest history of the Christian religion as well as the relationships of individual figures and forms to one another and to their religious environment in Late Judaism and in Hellenism' (81). However, Kümmel wanted to demarcate and divide the material in a manner rather different from that of his predecessor, since he observed, 'The question of the role of the Baptist and Jesus in the rise of primitive Christianity is too narrow a formulation of the more comprehensive problem of the origin of the apostolic church from the preaching of Jesus' (81). Moreover, the sources of the external history of the primitive church, especially the Acts of the Apostles, had to be a specific topic of discussion. Finally, subjects like the relationship of primitive Christianity to the state, and the history of worship and church order had to be considered. So Kümmel's report consisted of four parts: I. General accounts; II. The pagan and Christian sources; III. The history of the primitive church; IV. The development of the thought-world of primitive Christianity (cf. 82). Accordingly, he first reports on the 'general accounts' (82–95) and then discusses the 'sources for the history of the primitive church' (155–73). The third and fourth parts appeared after the war in 1948/49 (NF 17), namely the reports on the 'history of the primitive church' (3–50) and the 'development of the thought-world of primitive Christianity' (103–42). In 1950 (NF 8), Kümmel rounded off his first overall report with 'Supplements to Parts I-III' (1–53).

In 1983 (NF 48), after more than 30 years, Kümmel resumed the report on primitive Christianity. From then on he limited himself [4] to two main sections: the report on the general accounts (101–28), and the reports on individual problems, which appeared in many issues in subsequent years. Here Kümmel discussed (a) the Easter event, the origin and the history of the primitive community (1985: 132–64); (b) the social history and sociology of the primitive church (1985: 327–63); (c) baptism and worship (1986: 239–68); (d) ministries and the understanding of ministry (1987: 111–54); (e) mission and the attitude to the state (1987: 268–85).

I gratefully base this volume on the work of my predecessors. Like them I begin with the definition of primitive Christianity and the categories of investigation. The general accounts of the history of primitive Christianity form the core of the report. At the end individual problems are discussed from geographical and thematic perspectives. The subject of 'the cross and resurrection of Jesus' will not appear as a major theme in this work since in the meantime an article on it has appeared in *Theologische Rundschau*.[5] However, occasional references to it are unavoidable.

Before beginning the investigation I must also address the question of how it deals with the sometimes obtrusive theological evaluations found in the works to be reported on here. Nor am I myself free from them. I want to approach the question first by referring to my two predecessors as examples. Windisch and Kümmel never discussed this question specifically, but they did evaluate it implicitly. We have to reconstruct their theological judgements from their assessments of the contributions on which they report.

For Windisch it is very important that full justice be done to the role of Jesus, as the first bearer of the spirit, in the origin of primitive Christianity. He states that primitive Christianity '*came into view for the first time with the baptism of Jesus by John*' (though this story may also have been stylized in a Christian way).[6] Furthermore, 'the two main ideas of Jesus' preaching, like that of primitive Christianity, found symbolic expression in the two Aramaic exclamations (viz. 1 Cor. 16.22; Did. 10.6) which have been handed down to us from Palestinian Christianity . . . : 1. belief in the one who comes and brings the community full salvation, and 2. fellowship with the Father . . . Synoptic Christianity is essentially an Abba and Maranatha religion, and primitive Christianity is present wherever both the Abba and the Maranatha are still confessed as the essentials of authentic faith.'[7]

Kümmel, too, makes what amounts almost to a theological confession when he criticizes contributions with an exclusively historical orientation like that found in Helmut Koester and James M. Robinson's *Trajectories through Early Christianity* (Philadelphia 1971). He argues that this programmatic new approach does not yield an overall picture of primitive Christianity, 'especially since the question of the pre-Easter starting point in the figure and fate of the man Jesus is raised only in passing'.[8] Then Kümmel even more directly engages in a fundamentally theological critique. He argues that the work leads 'to a complete relativism, because there is no criterion which would allow one to judge the objective appropriateness of this or that development in respect of the origin'.[9] In other words, the work of Robinson and Koester is both historically *and* theologically inadequate.

In 1987 Kümmel repeats his denunciation of *Trajectories* in the course of a disparaging review of Helmut Koester's *Introduction to the New Testament* (1980).[10] In view of Koester's new overall account of primitive Christianity Kümmel modifies his impression of the earlier work, in particular where historical lines are drawn. But he remains unreconcilable over the lack of a clear theological standpoint.[11]

The intense theological critique of Koester's *Introduction* was not an isolated instance in Kümmel's report on primitive Christianity. The same censure was applied to sociological investigations in New Testament studies, which in Germany are primarily associated with the name of Gerd Theissen. Kümmel thinks that Theissen's remarks in *Social Reality and the Early Christians* (ET 1992) are very important, but on theological grounds he finds Theissen's reconstruction completely inadequate, because 'in Theissen's picture of Palestinian Jewish Christianity the effect of the person and preaching of Jesus and the fundamental significance of the Easter experience' are completely lacking.[12]

Over against Windisch and especially Kümmel, I would want to argue that 'theological' judgements should no longer underlie a report on research into primitive Christianity. My report evaluates the contributions to be discussed solely by: 1. whether they do justice to the criteria of historical criticism; 2. whether and how far they enrich our historical knowledge of primitive Christianity; and 3. whether they can plausibly fit individual elements into the overall picture of primitive Christianity. In other words, my analyses and conclusions strive for objectivity, though of course that can be achieved only to an approximate degree.[13] What I have learned from Windisch's and especially Kümmel's judgements is that I should investigate both overall accounts of primitive Christianity and individual studies also in the context of the theological assessments which guide them. That is a help towards a better understanding of the particular reconstruction of primitive Christianity in accordance with its governing perspective, and thus sheds a more intense light on the subject under investigation.

1

An Overview of the Demarcation
of Primitive Christianity:
The Task and the Method
of Description

Stefan Alkier, in his study *Urchristentum* ('Primitive Christianity', 1993), offers a survey of theories of primitive Christianity from Gottfried Arnold to Ferdinand Christian Baur; it is orientated purely on the history of theology.

Chapter I describes 'The Decline Theory in Eighteenth-Century Church Historiography with Reference to Early Christianity' (5-46); the title of Chapter II is 'The Demystification of the Origin: The Beginnings of Christianity in the Context of a "Purely Natural" View of History' (47–109).[14] Chapter III turns to 'The Renewal of the Idea of the Origin in the Eighteenth and Nineteenth Centuries' (110-72), and Chapter IV discusses 'The History of Primitive Christianity as a Hermeneutical Complex of Relationships in New Testament Studies' (173–254). His Conclusion (255-68) makes the terminological proposal that from now on the term 'early Christianity' should replace 'primitive Christianity', since the latter term a priori suggests the normativity of primitive Christianity as an unrepeatable model. The term early Christianity, it is proposed, contains far fewer preliminary decisions on the results of historical research; it has no idealizing connotations (265).

At this point the question arises whether such a long history of research was needed to arrive at such 'new' results, all the

1

more so since not all the important Anglo-American literature on the subject of Christian origins is discussed. In this connection reference should be made to the book by Jonathan Z. Smith, *Drudgery Divine. On the Comparison of Early Christianities and the Religions of Late Antiquity*, Chicago 1990, the first chapter of which presents an exhaustive account of this subject ('On the Origin of Origins', 1-35).[15]

Further brief reference must be made to the first volume of the *History of New Testament Research* by William Baird (1992). He devotes himself to the period from Deism up to the Tübingen School. He describes the individual schools in a traditional way, orientated on the personalities of scholars (cf. the Introduction, vii), and discusses the period from around 1700 to 1870.

> Within this framework he contributes valuable accounts of the English Deists ('The Attack on Revealed Religion: The English Deists', 31-57), who are completely neglected by Alkier. In this section Baird discusses first of all the champion of revealed religion, Daniel Whitby (1638–1725), then John Locke (1632–1704), John Toland (1669–1722),[16] Matthew Tindal (1657–1733), Anthony Collins (1676–1729), and Thomas Woolston (1669–1733), according to whom the resurrection of Jesus was essentially a deception (47). Then follow the other Deists: Peter Annet (1693–1769), Thomas Morgan (died 1743) and Thomas Chubb (1697–1747). These scholars are presented on the basis of their exegetical work, an approach hitherto absent from the historical study of the New Testament. Only through the careful depiction of the English Deists as forerunners(!) of Reimarus is an essential component of the historical-critical investigation of primitive Christianity opened up, the perception of which I miss in Alkier. At all events Baird's book is a milestone in New Testament research.

In contrast to Alkier, I prefer to retain the old term 'primitive Christianity', although it indeed has the associations that Alkier describes. But the term is still usable if the normative implications are expounded and repudiated. Indeed it is indispensable, because it is a more forceful reminder of the problems inherent in the study of Christian origins than Alkier's more comfortable 'early Christianity'. For at that time normative decisions were made which powerfully influenced the development of the Christian church for the next 1800 years, not only theologically but also historically.

But what should be the chronological demarcation of primitive Christianity? Surprisingly, there are no explicit reflections on this in the work of my predecessors Windisch and Kümmel. Recently Jürgen Becker[17] has proposed that the era of primitive Christianity should be declared closed somewhere between 120 and 130 CE. The period between 120 and 130 is in his view 'the transition ... which indicates the limit for primitive Christianity as *terminus ad quem*' (12). By contrast, Henning Paulsen[18] suggests the years 150–180 CE as the period of transition from primitive Christianity to the early church, because here the end of an old age and the beginning of a new one can be clearly observed in the completion of canonization (210/375).

I have argued elsewhere that the history of primitive Christianity should be understood to represent the historical course of the first two Christian centuries – or more precisely the first phase of church history ushered in by the appearance of Jesus. Its end lies where the process of the consolidation of early Christian groups is complete; where dogmatic and ethical norms of right and wrong, good and bad have been developed; where canonicity has been established; and where with the origin of the monarchical episcopate the early Christian communities or their bishops have developed some power for dealing with their opponents and imposing external sanctions. A further historical justification for this demarcation is that it can be established that towards the end of the second century the oral tradition which is genetically connected with Jesus has fallen silent.[19]

At the same time I pointed out the abiding merit of Walter Bauer's work *Orthodoxy and Heresy in Earliest Christianity* (1934);[20] in 1964 this appeared in a second edition by Georg Strecker and in translation (1971) left its mark on a whole generation of New Testament and patristic scholars in the USA and Canada, above all those around Helmut Koester and James M. Robinson (more on that later).[21] Bauer challenges the view of the relationship between orthodoxy and heresy held by the catholic fathers at the end of the second and beginning of the third centuries CE – namely that pure doctrine comes first, heresies only arise later, and finally the true doctrine becomes established. Bauer reverses the order and, except for the case of Rome, postulates that at the beginning of the second century, in all the spheres of church influence that we know about (Syria, Asia Minor, the Aegean, Egypt), Gnosticism came before orthodoxy.

Now in the meantime it has been recognized that at the end of the second century the teachings which the official church regarded as heretical were not necessarily identical with what particular circles a century earlier had regarded as heretical. Nor are those groups which were condemned as heretics at the end of the second and the end of the first automatically to be identified with one another in their theology. Nevertheless Bauer's work is fruitful. First, by starting from the end of the second century and using the expressions 'heresy' and 'orthodoxy' in a purely formal way for the early period, his approach represents a fruitful heuristic perspective for perceiving the diversity of 'Christianities' in the first two centuries and the struggles between them. When applied to the early period, 'orthodoxy' merely denotes the claim to have the right faith; this denies it to those who deviate and at the same time accuses them of heresy. Secondly, it is beyond doubt that in some areas what was later called heresy preceded 'orthodoxy'. This insight of Bauer's is strikingly verified by the case of the earliest Jewish-Christian community of Jerusalem, the successors of which were declared heretics. But it may also apply to other Christian groups. Thirdly, in connection with Bauer's work the task arises of describing how – whether despite or indeed because of the plurality of Christian groups in the early period – an 'orthodox' catholic church later developed with fixed forms and institutions from which 'heresy' was finally excluded.[22]

However, Bauer's book and its continuation in North America also came under sharp criticism. Thomas A. Robinson's 1988 book derives from a doctoral dissertation at McMaster University in 1985. It was written in the framework of the project being pursued there on 'Jewish and Christian Self-Definition',[23] and addressed Walter Bauer's work, which in the 1970s and 1980s had become almost a classic in

North America on the question of heresy and orthodoxy. Bauer's position was the credo of groups of scholars around Helmut Koester (Harvard University) and James M. Robinson (Claremont Graduate School/Institute for Antiquity and Christianity). It was above all thanks to the latter that in 1977 there first appeared a translation into modern English of all the documents found at Nag Hammadi. This finally presented original sources from the heretics who were expelled from the church in the second and third centuries, and whom Bauer had identified in his book. It is understandable that Bauer's thesis of the chronological reversal of orthodoxy and heresy was found to require a thorough re-examination. Here is Thomas A. Robinson's critique of Bauer and his North American followers:

> To begin with, Thomas A. Robinson states quite rightly that Bauer is a son of the Enlightenment who introduced and established the legacy of the Enlightenment, the historical-critical method, in biblical studies (15). After sketching out the history of the debate over orthodoxy and heresy (Ch. 1, 1-33), in Ch. 2 Robinson looks at the various Christian communities, in part geographically remote from one another, and the theological currents attested for them in the first two centuries (35-91). His conclusion is that the existing sources for the early period of Edessa, Egypt, Corinth, Rome, Jerusalem and Antioch do not offer any support for Bauer's thesis. Unfortunately he does not ask whether Bauer's thesis is not simply a schematic reversal of the orthodox position and precisely for that reason has little prospect of success.
>
> Chs 3-5 (93–205) then turn to the area around Ephesus and western Asia Minor. On the basis of an analysis of relevant sources here Robinson thinks that he can work out decisive arguments against Bauer's view. He comes to the conclusion that Bauer's thesis of an early Gnostic front in Asia does not sufficiently explain the alliance between Palestinian emigrants and anti-Gnostic Paulinists like Polycarp of Smyrna. And because Bauer's thesis does not apply to Western Asia Minor, this also encourages doubt about Bauer's reconstruction of a Gnostic Christianity preceding orthodox Christianity in other localities of the Roman empire. Two appendices on the heretics in the letters of Ignatius (207–10) and the main objections of Ignatius to the schismatics (211–20) round off the work.

Admittedly, since Robinson covers all the works from the 1960s and 1970s which were written in reaction to Walter Bauer's book, his book is indispensable for future research simply as a report. Unfortunately, however, he does not go into possible further developments of Walter Bauer's approach (see p. 4 above), and contents himself with a simple negative reaction to Bauer's work. The logic which guides him, that for example Bauer's inaccurate analysis of *one* complex of texts automatically has negative consequences for his other results, is by no means convincing. In any case, Bauer's analyses continue to be invaluable in that he undermines the orthodox position of Tertullian and Eusebius for the early period of Christianity and puts all future research into primitive Christianity on a new level. In research, it is possible finally to prove a thesis wrong, i.e. to validate negative criticism, only by citing positive reasons. Constructive insights may follow from this and lead to a completely new picture of a particular era. Beyond doubt, Bauer achieved the beginnings of all this. I miss the explicit avowal of this insight in Robinson's critique of Bauer, though it may be inferred from the preface to his book (IX), in which he notes that in the course of his ongoing encounter with Bauer's book, his own approach has evolved and matured. One would be interested to learn what further positive results he has arrived at in studying the pluralism of early Christianity.[24]

2

A Survey and Critique of Recent Conventional Reconstructions of Primitive Christianity

First, mention should be made of Ludger Schenke's 1990 work *Die Urgemeinde* ('The Primitive Community'), which describes one part of primitive Christianity, namely the earliest church (the subtitle is 'Historical and Theological Development'). Schenke sets out to write a history of events, a social history, and a tradition history of the primitive community in one volume and to relate all three aspects to one another. He is concerned above all to base his judgements on the consensus of historical-critical exegesis that he discovers (Preface, 9).

The work is matter-of-fact. It contains 14 chapters, the last of which is specifically called an appendix and discusses the Antiochene community. From this it is evident once again how strictly Schenke restricts himself to the primitive community, i.e. to the Christianity of Jerusalem and its immediate offshoots. According to this programme the theology and history of the Pauline mission are not part of the history of the primitive community or, if they are, only an indirect part.

Since it is generally recognized that this primitive community left behind no sources whatsoever, Schenke must base his findings on source criticism of Acts. Here Acts 6–8 are of primary relevance and the clearly legendary chs 1–5 only secondarily so. Furthermore, although according to Schenke's conception the proclamation and appearance of Jesus are

7

not the subject of the history of the primitive community, he uses later or inauthentic Jesus sayings in order to construct from them situations in expanding Christianity. And time and again he goes back to a particular picture of Jesus in order to depict the development from Jesus' preaching to the preaching about him. The summary description of the message of Jesus on 116f. is noteworthy in this regard. The reasons why Jesus is not discussed are on the one hand practical and on the other methodologically justified since the preaching of Jesus and that of the primitive community are not simply a continuum (12f.). The following impressions arise from a reading of this history of the primitive community:

1. Throughout his work Schenke refers to and quotes a great many texts available to the first disciples: numerous Old Testament documents which in the first period from Easter onwards were read as fulfilment (Ps. 16.9–11; Ps. 118.15–24, 26–8, etc.) and further early Jewish texts which explain the rise of christology (cf. 1 Enoch 102–4; Ps. Sol. 8; 17, etc.). The whole book thus reads almost like a textbook on New Testament history which aims at providing a good explanation of the rise of christology. In this way the description becomes vivid and does justice to the finding that the faith of the first Christians was part of an historical process of reflection on Old Testament expectations, and can be understood only from this perspective.

2. The excessively long quotations from scholarly literature are distracting and superfluous in a work orientated on consensus; quite often half a page is taken up with quotations from the current standard works on particular topics. The cumulative effect of this is quite disruptive (see e.g. the chains of quotations in 56–61, 121–3, etc.).

3. The sparse commentary on the appearances of the 'risen' Christ is striking; these should have been discussed in depth to make the origin of the primitive community plausible. Schenke writes only this: 'But the disciples took up Jesus' *basileia* preaching again only after those events had taken place which they interpreted as the resurrection of Jesus from the dead and the appearances of the Risen One' (17). He continues: 'The resurrection of Jesus from the dead as God's act of the end-time is an event transcending history, which is not yet complete, and about which therefore no historical statements can be made. This is not an evasion by a modern historian. The first Christians also saw it this way. No tradition "narrates" the resurrection. It occurs only in the confession and the kerygma. By contrast, the appearances of the Risen One were events within history and as such have been attested and narrated. Therefore we can make historical statements about them' (ibid.).

Why is this reference to the first Christians an argument for not making any historical statements about the resurrection? Were the first Christians familiar with historical criticism? Schenke's assertions result in a strange mixture of historical and theological perspectives. At any rate, one historical aspect of the resurrection in the history of primitive Christianity could have been clarified by examining the issue of the empty tomb, the facticity of which is increasingly emphasized by the New Testament evangelists as evidence for the resurrection (and the Gospel of Peter gives a vivid account of the resurrection).

4. The clear eschatological interpretation of early Christianity is striking. Schenke *always* understands the resurrection of Jesus in the context of the dawn of the end-time, during which the general resurrection of the dead was expected. That also allows him to understand the outpouring of the Holy Spirit as an event of the end-time, and thus to interpret the history of the primitive community in a plausibly unitary perspective. He also consistently refuses to remove Jesus from the eschatological context.

The strength of Schenke's book lies in its resolute attempt to relate the results of textual analyses of the New Testament Gospels to particular situations of primitive Christianity. Of course in some cases his associations must be described as arbitrary (for example, Matt. 18.18, as a later variant of the saying of Peter in Matt. 16.18f., is supposed to 'reflect the situation of the Jerusalem community after Peter's departure, i.e. after AD 43/44', 245). But it should be emphasized that before the history of primitive Christianity could become a discipline, there had been a long wait for the rich yield of the investigation of the Synoptic tradition. Schenke has carried this through in a promising way over wide stretches, summing up the critical consensus of exegesis. Thus Ch. XII ('Prophecies and Admonitions', 261–87) and Ch. XIII ('Controversy and polemic', 288–316) are brilliant successes. In them traditions from the Gospels are associated in an exemplary way with particular problems of the primitive community.

Two weaknesses of Schenke's approach are that the historical period he portrays is too short, and that he almost completely omits the preaching and activity of the apostle Paul. This latter must be termed a fundamental defect because it is by their position on Paul that scholars in general develop their own view of primitive Christianity in both historical and theological respects. (I do not doubt for a moment that Schenke *has* a view of Paul.)[25] Just as Schenke discusses the Antiochene community in an appendix (Ch. XIV), a section on Paul would also have been welcome. I am thinking above all of the chronology of Paul, and in particular the question of Paul's mission before the Apostolic Council, which Schenke merely touches on at several points in connection with his discussion of the incident in Antioch. Clearly, this mission falls in the early period of the Jerusalem community and the Antiochene church.

On the whole Schenke has produced a very impressive book, which is all of a piece and only rarely shows contradictions in the individual analyses (e.g. on the same page, 337, 1 Cor. 15.3–5 is described as old and not very old, and the end of the primitive community is depicted in contradictory terms, 260/316). However, the book does not really deserve the designation 'history', for the brevity of the period that it discusses does not permit a genuinely historical account. On whole it gives the impression of being a workbook which attempts to relate the texts to post-Easter situations on the basis of a critical analysis of the Synoptic tradition. The analytical acuteness of the findings is beneficial, since as a result most of the Synoptic preaching of Jesus can be seen to be a product of the community.[26] It remains unsatisfactory, however, that the end of the Jerusalem community is put in the year 70. Here a reminder that the era of primitive Christianity in fact extends into the second century would have provided a context for rendering the development of primitive Christianity more understandable. Still, one puts the book down with gratitude and can commend it to a wide circle of readers as an indispensable preliminary study of primitive Christianity.

Whereas exception can be taken to the relative narrowness of Schenke's perspective and the disproportionately short phase of the history of Christianity which he discussed, the same criticism hardly applies to Walter Schmithals' *The Theology of the First Christians* (1997). For his perspective embraces the whole of primitive Christianity including the origin of the New Testament, and his profound knowledge of the exegetical works of the nineteenth century gives the reader great pleasure.

In the preface (ix-xii) Schmithals explains the organization of his work, mainly by distinguishing it from Helmut Koester and James M. Robinson's *Trajectories through Early Christianity* (1971), which had already provoked the criticism of W.G. Kümmel (see above, p. xi). Schmithals finds the 'construction of largely anonymous developmental lines' (ix) a defect in this North American project. His own history of theology is 'focused especially on *basic* theological themes and decisions that are *signposts* of future theological development' (x). Schmithals' purported concentration on essentials (x) is puzzling in view of the very different structure of the individual chapters. Sometimes a 'Conclusion' is sketched at the end (79 et al.); sometimes this is called 'Summary' (118), and other chapters contain nothing of the sort. Here the publisher should have intervened – as in the matter of variation in length and coverage of individual chapters, which as they stand produce a highly incongruous effect, and often are repetitive.[27] It is also extremely unfortunate that in a book intended for students all of Schmithals' idiosyncratic theses should have been presented without substantiation and without taking into account the all too justified criticism from different sides.

A brief abstract of the text will afford an overall view of his analysis.

Ch. 1 ('Jesus, Apocalypticism, and the Origins of Christology' [1–20]) is an excellent account of the apocalyptic background to the message of Jesus. The early Easter confession, it argues, can be understood only in an apocalyptic framework, but in such a way, with a variation on a remark by Ernst Käsemann, that 'the overcoming of apocalypticism in the fulfillment of the apocalyptic expectation of God's imminent activity ... is the mother of all Christian theology' (12). In Ch. 2 ('Jesus and the Son of Man: A Key to Early Christianity's History of Theology and Tradition' [21–43]), Schmithals asserts against the consensus of scholars that the title Son of man was first introduced into the history of early Christianity by Mark. In view of the title Son of man in Q Schmithals resorts to a tenuous expedient: 'It is quite conceivable that the author or redactor of the sayings source Q and the evangelist Mark are identical' (43). Ch. 3 ('Kingdom of God and Kingdom of Christ: A Pre-Pauline Tradition in 1 Cor.15:20–28'

[44–62]) reconstructs a confession of faith behind the Pauline text mentioned (cf. 57–60), and thus confirms that the confession that God had raised Jesus from the dead stood at the beginning of the history of theology. Ch. 4 ('Paul's Conversion Theology' [63–80]) reconstructs a Christianity before Paul to be located in Antioch, which is said to have had contacts with the pre-Johannine tradition. Ch. 5 ('Christology and Soteriology in Hellenistic Churches before Paul' [81–101]) discusses '"Damascene" Christianity' (85ff.), ' "Antiochene" Adoption Christology' (88ff.), and 'Dying and Rising with Christ' – an idea which cannot be located more precisely (99ff.). Ch. 6 ('Paul's Theological Development as a Mirror of the Theological History of Early Christianity' [102–19]) comments on the much-discussed problem of Paul's development, and argues for distinguishing various strata of Pauline theology; here it is argued that the Christianity of Damascus had already completely done away with the difference between Jews and Gentiles and is to be termed a universalist Christianity. Nevertheless, during his activity in Syria and Cilicia Paul continued to carry on his mission to the Gentiles within the institution of the synagogue. The mission outside the synagogue alliance, the formation outside the synagogue of independent Gentile Christian communities not bound by the law, and the separation of the Gentile Christians from the synagogue, took place only *after* the Apostolic Council. But this does not make the difference between two phases of Pauline theology clear.[28] Ch. 7 ('Traditional Teaching Texts in Paul's Letters, with the Example of 1 Cor.1:10– 3:23' [120–35]) sets out to provide an insight into the history of the theology of primitive Christianity by means of the way in which Paul dealt with pre-Pauline traditions. Ch. 8 discusses the topic 'Paul and Greek Philosophy' (136–51); here, however the inner logic of the themes discussed is not clear. The same also applies to the remaining chapters: Ch. 9 ('The Church' [152–79]); Ch. 10 ('Worship in Early Christianity [180–213]); Ch. 11 ('The Origin and Development of the Early Christian Understanding of Baptism' [214–229]); Ch. 12 ('On the Problem of Baptizing Children in Early Christianity' [230–37]); Ch. 13 ('The Origin and Development of the Early Christian Celebratory Meal' [238–57]); Ch. 14 ('The Conflict between Christian Church and Jewish Synagogue' [258–77]); Ch. 15 ('The Old Testament in the New' [278–311]); Ch. 16 ('The Importance of the Gospels in the History of Theology before the Formation of the Canon' [312–34]); Ch. 17 ('The Historicity of Ethics in Early Christianity' [335–56]); and Ch. 18 ('The Origins of the New Testament' [357–69]).

Happily the theological value-judgements in the account are restrained and at some points only indirectly present. Yet unless appearances deceive, theological value-judgement becomes particularly clear at the end, where Schmithals writes: 'The formation of the New Testament did not bring about a new truth; rather, the churches joined together in a common defense against untruth by bringing together the various individually familiar documents of truth and making them a common possession' (369). Then follows the appeal to readers: 'We should also regard the New Testament in the same way today. For whatever distinguishes or even separates Christians from each other in the various confessions, the New Testament joins them, and when they are joined by the New Testament, they are joined in the truth' (ibid.). After these remarks one asks oneself why *historical* research should still be carried on at all today.

The concentration on the New Testament, which Schmithals defends with theological arguments, correlates with his critical remarks about the use of the apocryphal Gospels for the history of early Christian theology (331f.). He says that in any case they had no significance in the history of theology. But here once again he rather arbitrarily dismisses the significance of any newly-discovered sources.

The guiding principle of this history of primitive Christian theology is unclear. Despite an abundance of detailed information and the presentation of a wealth of material, this account of the problems in the history of the theology of primitive Christianity cannot be said to be either original[29] or convincingly presented. Moreover it is haphazardly constructed, difficult to read, and – most important – many of its theses have little to support them.[30] The remarks on the back cover of this book by M. Eugene Boring recommending it 'to students of the New Testament whose studies have been carried on within the horizon of recent North American scholarship' for its 'combination of theological passion and historical intensity that has become rare in current biblical studies' are therefore out of place.

Klaus Berger's *Theologiegeschichte des Urchristentums* ('History of the Theology of Primitive Christianity') is such an enormous volume (746 pages with 569 numbered sections), that it has the outward appearance of a lexicon. The book is the 'expression of a hermeneutics which understands itself to be consistently historical' (Preface); it follows 'that this book does not provide any applications but rather deliberately leaves these to a more open field' (ibid.). For Berger the modern age is an age of decline. But here of course one may justifiably object that the historical method he applies has been possible only in modern times.

There is a further problem. Berger understands his agenda to be the implementation of that of William Wrede ('The Task and Methods of "New Testament Theology"', in *The Nature of New Testament Theology: The Contribution of William Wrede and Adolf Schlatter*, ed., trs. and with an introduction by Robert Morgan, SBT II/25, London and Naperville, Ill. 1973, 68–166 [text], 182–93 [notes]). But here it must be recalled that Wrede was utterly imprisoned in the historicism of modern times and thought any theology of the New Testament impossible. What, for example, do Wrede and Berger have in common on the issue of miracle?[31] Until the opposite is proven, with his appeal to Wrede's programme, which again has received international plaudits,[32] Berger is dressing himself in false feathers. At the opposite pole, of course, there is Rudolf Bultmann, against whom a respectful polemic is scattered throughout the work. But the striking thing is that right in the foreword Berger attributes to Bultmann, without giving any reference, the view that 'for substantive reasons there cannot be a history of the theology of early Christianity' (v). As far as I know, Bultmann never said anything on this question, although for substantive reasons he did regard a *history of the literature* of early Christianity as impossible.[33] If in his preface Berger is already confusing the history of theology with the history of literature, this lapse would hardly reinforce trust in his mammoth work.

Immediately after its appearance, Berger's book was described by Kurt Flasch[34] in the *Frankfurter Allgemeine Zeitung* of 4 October 1994 as 'a great success which takes its place in claim and execution alongside Harnack and Bultmann' (L 24). By way of anticipation it must be said that the comparison with Harnack and Bultmann is an insult to the two great theologians of the last century. Berger's book is imposing only in extent and aim, and is unconvincing both as a whole and in details.

From the outset it is difficult to understand the structure of the book. To explain his principle of division, Berger uses the image of a tree. There is a trunk which has many twigs, branches and leaves (5). So starting from this organic picture, Berger first of all recounts what is common to all the theological positions of primitive Christianity from the beginning, and after that describes the dynamic unfolding of differing theologies in their various locales.

Essentially there were two geographical centres of primitive Christianity, Antioch (to which more than half the book is devoted) and to a far lesser degree Ephesus. To Antiochene theology belong all the writings 'which are orientated on the two apostles Peter and Paul or are very closely connected with such writings' (150); thus along with the authentic letters of Paul, 2 Thessalonians and Jude, would be included the Gospels of Mark and Matthew and the Johannine writings, together with Hebrews and 1 Peter, which are to be described as Pauline-related, and also the letters of Ignatius and the Gospel of Thomas.

In the other centre, Ephesus, there was a dispute over the legacy of Paul, which had fallen apart ('The synthesis between Jewish and Gentile Christians, which the apostle had attempted lastly in Romans, would not hold' [512]). Berger assigns Ephesians, Colossians, the Pastorals and the Apocalypse of John to Ephesus (511–76, 695–707). Egypt is also introduced as another focal point (709–15), but extremely briefly. Only two primitive Christian writings, James and Hermas, are not assigned to any of these centres but covered under the significant heading 'Outside Antioch' (157–75).

It would take me too long to list the 19 parts and 569 sections in detail. Instead, I wish to raise two fundamental questions of method. Most individual analyses are based on Berger's unexplained trust in the historical reliability of Acts. According to him plausibility 'is the only criterion for a historical reconstruction' (133). But on that basis one could also prove the historicity of the stories of the novelist Karl May (as Hans Conzelmann pointed out). And precisely what does Berger mean when he says, 'We trust ... the Lukan accounts but by no means in a naive way' (141)?

In this context mention should be made of Berger's questionable analysis of Acts 8.4–24.[35] His conclusion is: 'What has hitherto been regarded as an exotic heresy (the "Gnosis" of Simon Magus) is in origin a schism among Samaritan Christians. Luke merely states that there are non-apostolic Christians there' (162). Later, he claims, 'the further course of the schismatic Samaritan Christians led into Gnosis' (ibid.). Berger's analysis of Acts 8 is written without asking any redaction-critical questions and in sovereign disregard of the history of the tradition of Simonian gnosis which – according to the consensus of scholars – assimilated Christian features only at a secondary stage. Furthermore, there can hardly be serious dispute that the statement about Simon's baptism (Acts 8.13) derives from his opponents, who in this way wanted to emphasize his subordination to Christian missionaries like Philip. Equally fantastic is Berger's thesis that Acts 8.14 is 'a reflection of the events which are evidently closely connected with the origin and dissemination of the Gospel of John itself. Acts 8.14f. and the establishment of the Gospel of John therefore relate to the same event' (669). Just as improbable are the chronological placing of the Gospel of John (chs 1–21) in 68 CE (653–7) and the view of Q as an appendix to the Gospel of Mark (643f.) – not to mention the early dating of the Apocalypse of John in 68/69 CE (569–71).

The breadth of knowledge and tremendous diligence evident in the writing of this ambitious 'history of theology' are of no help at all. The foundations are rotten. Students will find Berger's book quite unusable, and for the specialist it is a mere curiosity with a score of 1 out of 20. And that is too low. Within the history of research this work seems to be a vain attempt to turn back the wheel of history to the pre-modern period.[36]

François Vouga presents a far briefer (284 pages) but no less ambitious *Geschichte des frühen Christentums* ('History of Early Christianity'). After an introduction (1–19) which clarifies the literary sources, the principles of the account, and its presuppositions, the task is carried out in three main sections. Each of these is divided into three sub-sections which sketch out first the persons and groups involved, then controversies and trends, and finally persons and works. Part I is 'The Perceptible Beginnings of Early Christianity' (21–77), Part II is headed 'From the Pauline Mission to the Gentiles to the Jewish War: The Time of the Apostles' (79–193), and Part III is entitled 'The End of the Apostolic Age: The Time of the Apostolic Literature' (195–284).

A wealth of information is given in a relatively small space, but the book is not easy to use because the author deliberately goes his own ways. The style at times shows signs of Vouga's native French, and his repetitive use of 'in short' often mars the argument. The final theses (274–84), which are attached to Part III, make it clear that the author really needed at least three times as much space for his presentation. First, they are in the wrong place – they round off the whole work and not, as their present position and context suggest, the third part. Secondly, in them it becomes symptomatically clear that the material should have been examined much more thoroughly. And finally, these closing theses are so much open to dispute that they urgently need examination. I shall quote only the closing sentences.

> The dialogue form, which is carried on in the perspective of the continuation of the dialogue, is the orthodox form of the unity of Christianity, which in this way also defines itself as open society. The presuppositions of the dialogue are the existential quest for the truth and the mutual recognition of the rival interpreters as conversation partners. The result of the dialogue, which is always provisional, consists in the further search for the understanding of the Jesus event which forms its basis and its significance for human existence (283f.).

Just two questions: 1. Does this portray the first century or an ideal visible at the end of the twentieth century of the Christian churches? 2. What does 'Jesus event' mean here, especially since the common denominator, i.e. the historical person of Jesus, remains unattainable for Vouga (thus 283)? For the same reason, namely that Jesus is historically unattainable, Vouga also brackets the person and preaching of Jesus out of the history of early Christianity (cf. 4).

Vouga states his presuppositions, the delimitation of the subject, and the literary sources very briefly (1–19). At the outset he confirms that 'Despite the relative wealth of documents for a chronologically and geographically restricted framework – the New Testament and the extra-canonical literature of early Christianity – we know only a little about the beginnings and the development of early Christianity and the life of the first Christians' (1f.). The theological presupposition for the present account of early Christianity (with a reference to Kierkegaard and Pascal) is said to be 'that faith can be questioned and examined in freedom in an unpreju-

diced and critical way ... Criticism cannot endanger faith –
quite the contrary' (2).

A further presupposition of his account is a very low esti-
mate of the historical value of Acts (2f.); one gains this
impression from even a quick reading of his work. For
example, Vouga thinks that the chronology of Acts and the
details of the missionary journeys in Acts are directly dependent (!) on the letters of Paul (83), and the same goes for the
relationship between Acts 15 and Gal. 2 (152). Now one can
have considerable reservations about the historical reliability
of Acts, but the question is whether in his reconstruction
Vouga is not replacing tradition (Acts) with wandering imagination (e.g. that of non-apocalyptic Galilean followers of
Jesus) (see below).

In terms of content, Vouga refuses to reduce the history of
early Christianity to the history of canonical or orthodox
Christianity, and says that he will take note of the Nag Hammadi texts, discovered in 1945 and for 20 years available for
the reconstruction of the history of early Christianity in a
complete English translation (3). That is extremely praiseworthy, although the author cites only a small part of the
writings mentioned. But at least it is a beginning! Attention
should be drawn to the following sections, each of which is
supported by relevant passages from the Nag Hammadi
library: 'Mary Magdalene' (190–3), 'Syria: The School of
Thomas and the Communities of the Redeemer' (211f.);
'James as Apostle and Author of a Letter' (266–8); 'The
Revelations of the Gnostic Peter' (271–2); 'Orthodoxy and
Heresy under the Name of Peter' (272–3).

In the last mentioned section, Vouga, starting from the
'Letter of James' (NHC I, 2) and the 'Letter of Peter to Philip'
(NHC VIII, 2) as illustrations of the Gnostic group attacked by
the author of 2 Peter, offers some profound comments which
are a fine illustration of the nature and content of the dispute
between orthodox and Gnostic Christians. Vouga writes:

> The somewhat perplexing argumentation of 2 Peter makes
> it clear that the Gnostics appealed to the apostolic
> authority of Peter even before the anti-Gnostic polemic.

The first surprise is the reference to the account of the Transfiguration in the Gospels (2 Peter 1.16–18; cf. Mark 9.2–10), which is meant to demonstrate Peter's quality as an eyewitness to the glory of Jesus. The only explanation of this reference is that the *sesophismenoi mythoi* of the 'heretics' (2 Peter 1.16) have a similar hermeneutic structure like the apocryphal letter of James (NHC I, 2) and the letter of Peter to Philip (NHC VIII, 2) and that they used the tradition of the Easter appearances (1 Cor. 15.5) and the conversations of the risen Christ as a framework for the Gnostic revelation discourses and dialogues. In opposition to the Gnostics, who 'invent' special instructions given by the semi-exalted Christ (cf. John 20.17), 'orthodoxy' refers back to the history of the historical Jesus or the pre-Easter Jesus to emphasize its own continuity with the apostolic tradition (272).

In conclusion Vouga describes the opposition between the two ways of thinking as follows:

Two consistent and plausible views of Christianity are in conflict in the name of the apostle. For one the world has become something that is impossible to survey, which can no longer be understood, far less be guided. Any hope for a future is given up, and knowledge of redemption offers a way to rescue the spiritual life of the individual by its finding its authentic home. For the others the world may indeed also have become incomprehensible and an apparently motionless system. But this is also the justification for not giving up hope, since God guides history from the beginning to its end (2 Peter 3.3f.). For some the world has its autonomy and is controlled by its own laws. God or his messenger has indeed revealed himself in the world, but the revelation does not belong to the world. The world remains the world and behaves in accordance with its own logic, as is finally attested by the event of the cross. For the others this perspective arises from superficial notions. One element of the confession is that God has created the world, that his word guides world history, as is shown by his

acts of salvation and punishments (the story of the flood).
Certainly the world seems to be guided by its own logic, but
one can only interpret this provisionally as meaning that
God is preparing his judgement (2 Peter 3.5–7). For some
the idea of the judgement is quite relevant, but only
metaphorical and in connection with the redemption. God
is not judge but the heavenly Father and the spiritual home
of the redeemed. He has sent his son into the world
because its history continues and is guiding it towards its
self-destruction, and so that the redeemer brings eternal
life to those who believe by bringing them back to their
heavenly origin. For others there is no salvation history
other than the time that is given by God on earth. It should
be noted, first, that the divine understanding deviates from
the human and secondly, that the delay of the parousia is
not a delay but proof of the patience of God who does not
want to destroy men and women and awaits their conversion (2 Peter 3.8f.) (273).

Here Vouga has hit the nail on the head and has demonstrated in connection with one point how important the Nag
Hammadi texts can be for research into early Christianity.

On the the chronological demarcation Vouga remarks:

If we define early Christianity by the transition from the
apostolic to the post-apostolic writings, the definition of
early Christianity chronologically coincides with the history
of the origin of the New Testament writings. This is not a
coincidence, although the connection is only an indirect
one. But it does indicate that a certain break in the definition of the canon has been perceived (5).

The dividing line between the apostolic writings (i.e. the
writings under the pseudepigraphical names of the apostles) and the post-apostolic writings (i.e. the writings of the
'apostolic fathers') therefore seems to make possible a
demarcation of 'early' Christianity which itself follows from
the historical self-understanding of Christian faith (5).

That accords with the principles which are given later (12), where it is said that the description of early Christianity will take place in two main parts: the first deals with the time of the apostles (i.e. up to the beginning of the 60s), and the second with the period of the apostolic writings (thus from the end of the 60s to around 150 CE). But objections must immediately be made to these principles, too: 1. 'the time of the apostles' comes from the perspective of the second or third generation (namely 'Luke', whose work Vouga disparages historically); 2. the so-called apostolic writings cannot be strictly limited to the time before 150, since the apostolic fiction is also maintained after the middle of the second century (we need think only of 3 Corinthians[37] and the opening letters to the Pseudo-Clementine Homilies).[38]

I fail to understand the remarks about the history of early Christianity as the evolution of a deterministic chaos (13–19), so I shall pass over them here. But here again reference should be made to a clearly false historical judgement. Vouga writes: 'The presupposition for Christianity not remaining a sect within Judaism – which probably would have disappeared with the retreat of Judaism after 70 CE – lies largely in the radical nature of the theology which Paul formulated' (17). That can hardly be the case since from an historical perspective Paul's radical theology had no influence at all. This can be demonstrated from the disciples of Paul who did not understand the doctrine of justification. Paul's radical nature then appears again only in Marcion, whom Vouga curiously omits from his account.

The investigations into the origins of Christianity (23–8) suffer from an inadequate analysis of key texts. Vouga translates 1 Cor. 15.3 'Christ has died for our sins . . .' (23), although the chief point is that Paul here uses the aorist ('died'), because immediately afterwards he emphasizes the statement about the resurrection in the perfect ('has been raised').[39] Moreover the stratification of the text 1 Cor. 15.3–5 is not sufficiently recognized, since Vouga speaks without differentiation of the confessional formula 'which Paul quotes in 1 Cor. 15.3–7' (23). But the mention of the 'appearances of the Risen Christ as an interpretation of his death' (24) is clearly a modernization by a late twentieth-century scholar; for in the first century the appearances of the Risen Christ were taken to be real and in no way an interpretation of the death. Vouga's further thesis runs: 'the first chain (vv. 5–6: Cephas, the

Twelve, the 500 brethren) hands on the tradition of appearances of the Risen Christ in Galilee, the second (v. 7: James and all the apostles) traditions of appearances of the Risen Christ in Jerusalem' (25).

If Vouga then rightly maintains that the group of Twelve is a creation of Jesus (26: however, he says that it is not to be limited to twelve persons), one cannot quite see how in his later remarks about the itinerant preaching of Jesus' Galilean comrades he can ignore a future expectation. In other words, if the Twelve are symbols of the twelve tribes of Israel, then a hope of Jesus for the imminent restoration of the twelve tribes of Israel is bound up with them. And this insight hardly allows the assumption of an itinerant preaching by Jesus' followers and communities in Galilee based purely on wisdom and having no vision of the future (but thus 33–7), quite apart from the fact that there is no external evidence at all for Galilean communities whose ethos reflects the wisdom tradition. At all events, one could see Acts 9.31 as an indication of the existence of communities in Galilee, even if Vouga is decidedly of another opinion and writes: 'Acts, *which knows no Christianity in Galilee,* gives extensive information about the first community *in Jerusalem'* (37, my italics).

Furthermore, I cannot help seeing Vouga's remarks about the early Christian apostolate or the apostles as wrong. Perhaps they are grounded in an overly strict reading of Acts, which identifies the Twelve with the apostles. Vouga writes: 'If we want to avoid anachronisms, then the term apostle fits only the early Christian group which Acts calls the Hellenists (Acts 6.1; 9.29; cf. 11.20)' (28). That confuses all our apparently solid facts about early Christianity; we can hardly dismiss the fact that Paul himself understands the apostolate to be rooted in Jerusalem. For example, he writes that after his conversion he did not go to Jerusalem, to those who were apostles before him (Gal. 1.17–19), and in the same connection counts James among the apostles. At the time of his visit to Jerusalem, which was the first in his Christian period, the Hellenists had already been driven out of Jerusalem. In other words, one can only describe as misleading Vouga's remarks about the apostolate, which attempt to reverse relatively certain knowledge by a few sentences thrown together.

And Vouga goes on fantasizing: 'Peter and probably others continued their itinerant existence in a new form, among other things within the framework of the missionary organization of the Hellenists' (33). He then turns his attention to the Hellenists (40–6). His remarks are historically misleading and theologically modernizing. He writes that the Jesus event 'meant for these Hellenized Jews a revision of their understanding of God and his Law, which led them into open conflicts with other, perhaps "conservative" Hellenized Jews' (43). Jesus is said to have met these Jews in Jerusalem.

'What they experienced were the last days of Jesus. They were witnesses to his last controversies with the Pharisees and other preachers in Jerusalem, the last days of table-fellowship, his violent death and the Easter events. They then went home and brought the message of the saving events, i.e. the forgiveness of sins which had taken place in death and resurrection, into their synagogues' (45).

One does not have to read these sentences several times to recognize that they are quite unfounded. What sources does Vouga have in mind when he writes about the last controversies of Jesus with Pharisees (?) and other preachers (?) in Jerusalem?

These soundings into Vouga's ambitious history of early Christianity may be enough to recommend general mistrust of it. It is a pity that his praiseworthy use of the Nag Hammadi library is embedded in a mishmash of almost incomprehensible new conjectures and not in solid historical explanations. I cannot recognize this collection of new proposals, discoveries and confusions as a history of early Christianity.[40]

In 1988, the Freiburg doyen of New Testament exegesis, Anton Vögtle,[41] produced a history of early Christianity written in a popular style and orientated on historical consensus, under the title of *Die Dynamik des Anfangs. Leben und Fragen der jungen Kirche* ('The Dynamic of the Beginning: The Life and Questions of the Early Church'). At another point he calls his work 'The Church of the Beginning' (199). His view is that the question of the early church is of central importance in present-day exegetical and theological discussion because 'the church of all times must measure itself by its "original form"' (5). His interests in composing the work relate to the present situation of the church (see e.g. 43: 'The primitive community provides ... a good example for present-day communities and parish councils in which groups with different views confront one another'). At other points he encourages his readers to achieve ecumenical unity and complete church fellowship by shared urgent prayer (135). All these remarks, focused on the present and derived from a commitment to present-day questions of the church, do not alter the fact that Vögtle has composed a significant short history of the early church, reflective of the critical consensus and yet easy to understand. (It does not cover the whole of primitive Christianity but ends in the so-called post-apostolic period; i.e. it covers the whole New Testament, including such late writings as 2 Peter.)

Ch. I ('The New Beginning through the Exalted Lord' [11–24]) discusses the total resignation of Jesus' closest followers and the various appearances. Here Vögtle bases himself exegetically on his own earlier works and those of his pupils.[42] He writes: 'Without a revelation event following Good Friday, the Twelve would hardly have arrived at the idea of also going on to proclaim under their own control and on their own authority the message of the dawning kingdom of God which had been proclaimed by their master to the last' (11). To be sure, the term 'revelation' does not have an objective referent. Nevertheless it helps the author on the one hand to take full account of historical criticism and on the other to be in a position to remain a theologian and on occasion also refer to the purported revelatory event. Ch. II ('The Primitive Jerusalem Community' [25–48]) reports the critical consensus on the primitive Jerusalem community based on an analysis of Acts with special reference to the letters of Paul. Ch. III ('Providential Steps towards the Church of the Nations' [49–69]) depicts the further development of the primitive Jerusalem community, starting from the split between the Aramaic-speaking primitive community and Hellenistic Jewish Christianity and proceeding to the conversion of Paul and his significance for the development of the mission to the Gentiles. 'The decision of the apostolic council which finally gave the green light to Paul's mission to the Gentiles free of the law was beyond doubt theologically the most important decision of the early church alongside and before the formation of the canon of the New Testament writings' (63). That might be an exaggeration if we consider what the apostolic council specifically was: a meeting provoked (?) by Paul (and Barnabas) to which the apostle to the Gentiles attached great importance when writing to the Galatians. Ch. IV ('A Young Big-City Community – Its Life and Its Problems' [70–96]) draws a lively picture of Corinthian Christianity. Ch. V ('Organization and Ministries' [97–135]) deals with the problem of ministries in the early church.

Ch. VI ('Women and Ecclesial Functions' [130–66]) works out the new consensus in the reconstruction of the significance of women in early Christianity. This section is better than some that have been written in more recent feminist books (see below, pp. 83–93), and also in some anti-critiques. On the one hand note his remarks on the group of the Twelve: 'By having twelve followers constantly surrounding him and confessing him, Jesus wanted symbolically to indicate that he was maintaining his offer of salvation to prepare for the Israel of the end time, even in the face of the conflict which he experienced and the lack of a readiness to believe him. The meaning and purpose of the symbolic action intended by Jesus could only be recognized and prove enlightening in the public life of Israel if the group of the Twelve consisted exclusively of men' (138). On the other hand, it is said to derive from the example of Nympha in Laodicea (Col. 4.15) that women ran households and 'presided at the eucharist' (148). Likewise there is no dispute that Junia (Rom. 16.7) belonged to the circle of the apostles as a woman before the conversion of Paul (149–51). The author also depicts the post-apostolic period and its withdrawal of women's privileges with great clarity (153–8). Ch. VII ('Church and World in the Apostolic and Post-Apostolic Age' [167–200]) contains a noteworthy survey of the problem indicated in the chapter heading. But unfortunately the conclusion descends into sermonic edification: 'The mission of the church of Jesus Christ cannot be stopped!'

The Catholic dogmatic theologian Walter Simonis has produced a history of the primitive community under the title *Jesus von Nazareth. Seine Botschaft vom Reich Gottes und der Glaube der Urgemeinde* ('Jesus of Nazareth. His Message of the Kingdom of God and the Faith of the Primitive Community. A Historical-Critical Clarification of the Origins of Christianity'). While both popular and of high quality, this history of the primitive community is really only the prelude to a reconstruction of the historical Jesus (203–68).

After an introduction which sketches out the main problems of the quest for the historical Jesus and in terms of method champions the principle of difference,[43] the first part presents the history of the primitive church and its christology (35–202). This part is relevant for an overview of research into primitive Christianity.

Since Simonis' picture of Jesus decisively determines – I suspect in advance – his reconstruction of primitive Christianity, we need first to consider the view of the preaching of Jesus which guides him. Fundamental here is the thesis that Jesus did not expect the imminent action of God (cf. 203–68).

Simonis has deepened this view in a later publication in 1986 which under the title *Das Reich Gottes ist mitten unter euch. Neuorientierung an Jesu Lehre und Leben* ('The Kingdom of God is in Your Midst: A New Orientation on Jesus' Teaching and Life') repeats his remarks in the previous book word for word.[44] The two books also correspond theologically in their sections on Jesus in that Simonis thinks that present theological statements can be made only if they are orientated on Jesus. We read in the introduction to the latter book: 'It is precisely the little that we can assume with certainty to be his own words or to maintain the characteristic features of his own activity that throughout gives the impression of being fresh and unworn' (7).

Back to Simonis' reconstruction of primitive Christianity: Chapter 3 ('The Beginnings of Post-Easter Christology' [35–92] is devoted to the texts taken from the Easter accounts. They are discussed under a series of key phrases: flight of the disciples, Galilee or Jerusalem, 'The Lord has appeared to Simon', 'Simon, when you are converted, strengthen your brothers', the return to Jerusalem, the group of twelve and the betrayal of Judas, a christophany before the twelve, etc.

According to Simonis the group of twelve was constituted only after Easter and was connected with the hope for the restoration of the twelve tribes of Israel. Those first believers expected that this restoration would fulfil what Jesus in his preaching before Easter had called the kingdom of God. Furthermore, contrary to Jesus' proclamation that the rule of God had already arrived, the disciples made the all too understandable mistake of expecting its arrival only in the future (92). But finally the original first Easter expectation – that the Jesus who had appeared to Simon would now arrive in Jerusalem and bring about the restoration of the old people of the twelve tribes – proved to be a mistake. Then, Simonis argues, the following happened:

> Under the leadership of James the brother of the Lord ... a community formed which had its institutions and its liturgical practice and promoted itself. The basis of its faith certainly continued to be the conviction that Jesus was

alive. But the certainty that his return was imminent and
that he would then establish the kingdom of God in Israel
became the hope that, having been raised by God after his
death, he would come again in power and glory. This
conviction found concrete expression in the ... Son of man
christology (128).

With good reason, Simonis regards this Son of man christology as secondary (129–63). First, there is no text according to which Jesus requires
and expects a confession of his own person or the one whom he proclaims
(except the very doubtful Luke 12.8f.). Secondly, it remains incomprehensible that the disciples' pre-Easter attitude towards Jesus should be
related to a future attitude towards the Son of man without further
explanation (cf. Luke 12.8f.; Matt.10.32f.). Thirdly, assuming that Jesus
was thinking of the apocalyptic Son of man, it remains inexplicable that
elsewhere Jesus shows no signs of apocalyptic thought. (Yet this argument
is the weakest of the three.)

    In the remaining chapters, which I shall not be describing further,
Simonis eruditely describes the christology of the Synoptic Gospels and
here, as in all other analyses, shows himself well informed about the state
of scholarship. As a curiosity, it should be mentioned that according to
Simonis, Jesus was not baptized by John (124).

This historical-critical clarification of the origins of Christianity by Simonis is one-sidedly orientated on christology, and
as a consequence separates the historical Jesus and the early
church. That seems to be a priori a historical improbability,
especially as the group of Twelve must go back to Jesus (see
below, p. 38). The analyses are all hypercritical and to my
mind do not lead to an understanding of the historical
development. So this clarification of the origins of Christianity
must be read above all as crypto-dogmatics which makes use of
acute analysis to the point of absurdity and then ends with a
Jesuology. A real reconstruction and a real understanding of
primitive Christianity can hardly be achieved in that way.

Under the title *The Defence of the Gospel in the New Testament*,
F. F. Bruce's popular book sets out to explore the proclamation of the gospel in the first century. This book, in which
Bruce puts forward an evangelical standpoint – e.g. for him all
the details about the authorship of the New Testament writings are authentic – is committed to making the gospel useful

in our time (cf. 49, 89f etc.). Against this background Bruce depicts the proclamation of the gospel to the Jews ('The gospel confronts the "Jews"', 14–31); to the Gentiles ('The gospel confronts paganism', 32–49); to the Roman Empire ('The gospel confronts the Roman Empire', 50–69) and to the Christian false teachers ('The gospel confronts "Christian deviations"', 70–88); then in a last chapter consisting of sections on Hebrews and the Gospel of John he describes the consummation of the ages ('The finality of the gospel', 89–103).

However, Bruce's remarks lack any critical evaluation of the sources, and essentially consist of paraphrases of selected New Testament passages which are regarded as accurate reports: thus he claims that Stephen's defence speech (Acts 7.2–53) is authentic (23–7) and that Paul actually delivered the speech before the Areopagus (Acts 17.22–31, 39–49). I do not know how an historical-critical reconstruction can be based on such assumptions. Of course, according to Bruce, the author of 1 Peter is also Peter the Lord's disciple (53), and the historical Peter spoke in Jerusalem the words which appear in Acts 2.32: 'This Jesus God raised up, and of that we are all witnesses' (17). Present-day Christians are therefore told that 'the evidence for Christ's resurrection' could become 'a most potent argument for the truth of Christianity' (18). One puts the book down regretting that it had not been better.[45]

One gains quite a different impression from the richly illustrated *The Roots of Christianity* by Michael Walsh (the US title is *The Triumph of the Meek: Why Early Christianity Succeeded*), which describes the history of Christianity from the appearance of Jesus to Constantine. Under this rubric Walsh describes the Christian churches of the second to fourth centuries before concluding with sections on 'Ritual and Worship' (188–203) and 'Christian Attitudes' (204–23). Primitive Christianity is the content of the greater part of the book, and appears through the eyes of an historian who cannot and will not hide his sympathies, who has no apparent theological interest, and who develops his material in a vivid and sensitive way, supported by many passages of texts and admirably chosen illustrations.

Ch. 1 ('Introduction' [11–23]) gives as the aim of the book 'to present evidence about the ways in which the early Christians thought of themselves' (17); Ch. 2 ('Palestine at the Time of Jesus' [24–47]) then gives a description essentially orientated on standard works. Ch. 3 ('The Message of Jesus' [48–69]) emphasizes that Jesus' announcement 'that the kingdom of heaven was at hand' (52) was a more important teaching for his disciples than the ethical principles of the Sermon on the Mount. ('Because the "last things", the " end times", have not arrived after two thousand years of Christianity, the eschatological element of Jesus' teaching has been overlooked' [ibid.].) The resurrection of Jesus, the literalness and physical aspect of which is rightly emphasized ('empty tomb'), does not fall within the competence of the historian. 'But were the resurrection true, there is nothing with which to make a comparison' (68). Ch. 4 ('The New Scriptures') [70–89] falls below the level previously reached. Neither is there scholarly agreement that the Gospel of Mark 'was written for a Roman audience by John Mark, a disciple of St Peter' (73), nor can one say that the (apocryphal) Gospel of the Hebrews 'may, just possibly, have been composed' before Mark (thus 76). Walsh asserts the authenticity of Colossians and 2 Thessalonians without offering any evidence (78) and neglects to date the letters of Paul and his travels. Ch. 5 ('The First Christians' [90–117]) relates the history of the primitive community using a number of unsubstantiated assertions. For example, James the brother of the Lord is said to have gone to Jerusalem from Galilee in 40 CE (93), and the Hellenists of Acts 6f. are said to have believed that the end time had already begun with Jesus' death and resurrection – and for this thesis Walsh does not even refer to the pre-Pauline traditions in Paul's letters but to Acts. Otherwise the whole narrative is exciting and sometimes not without its own independent criticism (e.g. 110f., which questions the historicity of the flight of the primitive community to Pella). Ch. 6 ('Christians of the East' [118–45]) depicts the Christian life in the East under headings like 'The Churches of the Apocalypse' (118–20), 'Ignatius and Polycarp' (120–4), 'Christian Origins in Syria' (124–7), 'Marcion and the Problem of the Canon' (127–30), 'Montanus and the Prophetesses' (130–3), 'Mani and the Lure of Gnosticism' (133–6), 'Problems with the Calendar' (136–40), 'Dura Europos' (140–5). There follow Chs 7 ('The North African Experience' [146–63]) and 8 ('Rome and the West' [164–87]), and then Chs 9 ('Ritual and Worship' [188–203]) and 10 ('Christian Attitudes' [204–23]), which have already been mentioned above. The closing sentences of the last chapter, 11 ('The Final Challenge' [224–49]), answer with a clear 'Yes' the question whether the Christian church to which Constantine gave freedom of religion in 313 CE 'despite all the changes in its structures and all the development of its theology ... believed itself identical with the Church

Jesus had founded' (249). The bibliography (250–2) shows that Walsh is
thoroughly acquainted with scholarly literature in the field.

Walsh's book contains a wealth of information, yet it cannot
be used as a textbook. Certainly the maps included, which like
the more valuable pictures give the book a markedly academic
look, could lead the reader to assume that it could be. However, the work lacks any systematic criticism of the sources.
The admitted power of its gripping narrative does not contribute to the requirement to seek out the truth. Moreover,
the book is not very suitable for students, since it does not
encourage independent judgements, though it may engage
the attention of interested lay people in early Christianity.
And finally the work has no reflection on the principles on
which any history of early Christianity can be written. It is
hardly enough to say that the book's aim is to examine the
truth of the statement that 'Jesus preached the kingdom, but
it was the Church which arrived' (17, quoting A. Loisy).

The book edited by Jürgen Becker, *Christian Beginnings: Word
and Community from Jesus to Post-Apostolic Times,* which was originally conceived of as Volume I of a series on church history
entitled 'Christianity and Society' and is now published as the
only finished work in this series, is an ambitious one. In the
Preface Becker rightly expresses doubts 'whether it is at all
possible at this time for a single author to respond to this
inquiry with a comprehensive presentation of early Christianity' (7). The authors of the individual contributions were
asked to write on 'the question of how early Christianity is
intertwined with antiquity on such levels as governmental
institutions, social reality, culture and religious phenomena...' (7). According to Becker this aspect 'cannot be
neglected if New Testament studies are not to lose sight of the
concrete historical dimension of early Christianity' (ibid).

Becker's introduction (9–11) mentions three periods in
early Christian history: 'the time of Jesus, the generation of
the apostles (the first early Christian generation), and the
postapostolic period, a time of transition that would even-
tually evolve into the early Catholic church (second and third
early Christian generations)' (11). He says that this division

determines the organization of the present work. This division 'sketches the outline of the task at hand. While each of the three periods has its own makeup, the interconnections of early Christianity with the ancient world have to be indicated separately for each period' (ibid.).

At this point the critical observation should immediately be made that here Becker (as also in his own writing on primitive Christianity as an era with different periods, see p. 3 above) reflects the Lukan scheme rather than the historical phenomenon of primitive Christianity, which requires a much later external demarcation – namely the conclusion of the formation of the canon. Indeed the apostolic generation existed only on paper, and then from 'Luke's' later perspective.

Christoph Burchard's contribution to Becker's anthology is an extremely knowledgeable and sensitive article on Jesus of Nazareth (15–72). He aptly defines the problem of the present and future kingdom of God as follows: 'Jesus talked of the present kingly rule of God as if nothing else was to follow and of the rule to come as if it had not yet arrived. How to explain that is a perpetual problem of scholars' (29). On Jesus' relationship to John the Baptist he rightly says that Jesus not only retained friendly memories of him but also built on him. 'One does not always remember that the Baptist did not influence only Jesus and his disciples but also many other people whom Jesus addressed later on. Jesus could presuppose their familiarity with John, and without John's preparatory work they might have received Jesus differently' (25). Not only is Burchard's account of Jesus[46] written in a compelling way, but its balanced critical judgements can confidently be trusted.[47]

In another admirable article Carsten Colpe discusses 'The Oldest Jewish-Christian Community' (75–102); one can give depth to his remarks by referring to the chapter with the same title in his earlier work *Das Siegel der Propheten* ('The Seal of the Prophets', 1990), 59–89. This also contains important remarks on 'Jesus and the Sealing of Prophecy' (15–37) and 'The German Word "Judenchristen" and the Historical Circumstances which Correspond with it' (38–58).

Colpe describes the earliest Jewish-Christian community with the term 'Nazaraeans' and begins with the apt remark that the earliest community doubtless had its origins in pneumatic experiences after Jesus' death (76). He carefully reconstructs a small chain of facts between the death of Jesus on the cross and the formation of the first community in Jerusalem, also sensitively investigating the hermeneutical presuppositions for the shaping of the statements about Jesus' resurrection or exaltation (76–8). Colpe calls the restoration of the group of twelve on Peter's urging an institutionalization, but like the first period generally, this had an eschatological stamp. For 'it was meaningful only if, as according to Jesus, the twelve tribes of Israel were to be fully represented at the arrival of the kingdom of God' (83). Colpe calls 'the introduction of baptism' (83) and the celebration of the Lord's supper (85) further important pieces of institutionalization. He distinguishes the theocratic leadership of the Nazaraeans from the eschatological assembly and argues that it finds expression in the triumvirate which Paul faces at the apostolic council (47/48 CE). But that is still not enough: the community of the Nazaraeans in Jerusalem developed further and formed the caliphate of James, who, as the brother of Jesus, was the born representative (94f.). 'Since centuries later the charismatic milieu of Mecca will resemble that of Jerusalem, it is better to speak in Semitic areas of a caliphate' (98). All in all, Colpe succeeds in developing in a short space new insights into the development of the primitive Jerusalem community up to the Jewish war – perceptions which beyond doubt will be fruitful for research.

Next, Karl Löning discusses 'The Circle of Stephen and its Mission' (103–31). He offers a careful analysis of Acts 6–8 and works hard to combine the elements of tradition which become visible here with the letters of Paul. He takes up Lüdemann's thesis that Gal. 2.7 is a reference to Paul's first visit to Jerusalem (Gal. 1.18) and that thus the independence of the Pauline conception of mission is again recognized. The agreement at the council mentioned in Gal.2.9 is to be distinguished from this. He follows Lüdemann also in arguing that the incident which Gal. 2.11ff. sets in Antioch actually took place before the council.[48]

The longest contribution to the anthology comes from Becker himself, who discusses the topic 'Paul and His Churches' (132–210). This is basically the short form of a monograph on the apostle Paul which was published in English in the same year.[49] In his contribution Becker discusses (a) 'Paul as Pharisee and as Apostle to the Gentiles' (132–44); (b) 'Paul and Antioch' (144–55); (c) 'The Apostle to the Gentiles and the New Churches He Founded' (155–63); (d) 'The General Situation of the Churches from the Perspective of Social History' (163–72); (e) 'The Integrative Power of the Churches' (172–7); (f) 'Ways of Easing Specific Tensions within the Churches' (177–96); and (g) 'Christians and Their Former World' (196–209). He ends with bibliographical references (209–10), though these are limited to essentials.

It is striking that Becker rejects the chronological reversal of the incident at Antioch and the Apostolic Council asserted by Löning's previous article in the collection, and repudiates the derivation of vv. 7–8 from the occasion of Cephas's visit (Gal. 1.18). He writes:

> What would have forced Paul to declare the agreement, which was actually reached in the context of Gal. 1:18, to be a result of the Apostolic Council, thereby contradicting the historical facts that the Galatians knew or were able to check? It also remains unclear how it would be

possible to break up the single complex sentence in Gal. 2:6–9, declaring just vs. 7–8 to be an already existing tradition (117).

However, any analysis of Gal. 2.7–9 has to begin from the tension in language and content between vv. 7–8 and v. 9. Whereas the 'formula of union' achieved at the conference appears in v. 9, in vv. 7–8 there is a personal tradition recognized at that time, which can most naturally be derived from Cephas's visit (Gal. 1.18).

Moreover Becker hardly has an accurate understanding of the 'Apostolic Council'. This emerges from the fact that he regards the agreement made over the collection there as a voluntary one, separate from the agreement proper made at the convention of the apostles (179f.). Here he clearly succumbs to Paul's effort to declare to his readers in Galatia that this collection was a voluntary, loving gift.[50] Granted, as Becker writes, 'The gift is based neither on a right Jerusalem might have (a possible analogy: the Jewish temple tax) nor an obligation imposed on Paul at the Apostolic Council, which would be binding for his post-Antiochene period. Rather, even the members of the church in Jerusalem consider it an act of love to which they have no claim' (180). But after all, Paul says precisely the opposite in Rom. 15.27a, in which he remarks that Macedonia and Achaea are *in debt* to the Jerusalem community. The apostle continues: 'For if the Gentiles have come to share in their spiritual blessings, they ought also to be of service to them in material blessings' (Rom. 15.27b).[51]

All in all, however, Becker's article best serves the aim of the composite volume, namely to sketch out the social dimension of early Christianity. Still, it is surprising that he adorns his account with Ernst Troeltsch's alleged description of Paul's attitude as 'the early Christian patriarchalism of love' (195) but does not even mention Troeltsch's work *The Social Teachings of the Christian Churches* (1912) in the bibliography.[52]

John K. Riches discusses 'The Synoptic Evangelists and Their Communities' (213–41), paying separate attention to Mark, Matthew and Luke. He considers the social function of the Synoptics and discusses in a knowledgeable way the reciprocal interaction between the individual Synoptic Gospels and the surrounding culture. What is completely lacking from his contribution is recognition of the fact not only that Jesus was a condemned criminal who had argued for certain social and ethical values but that the Gospels were composed only because their authors believed that this criminal had been elevated to become the Lord of the Universe, i.e. the Son of God. In other words, I miss in Riches' work any reflection of this Easter perspective of the three Synoptics. He manifestly overlooks the cause which motivated the three Synoptics when he remarks that the publication (!) of these traditions (of Jesus) in book form made a special claim to this socio-cultural significance. Was it primarily a matter of socio-cultural significance, or of a gospel proclamation grounded in a new religious life?

In his discussion of the Gospel of Matthew, Riches begins from the Synod of Jamnia (223, cf. 234) – something which has long been recognized as a fiction.[53] He seriously thinks that Luke has to be regarded more as 'a universal historian rather than simply ... a salvation historian' (238), for 'to stress too much the element of salvation history in Luke is to overlook the way in which his Gospel attempts to create a – historical – social world for the church as it cuts its moorings in Judaism and emerges as a distinct entity, even with all its Jewish heritage' (ibid.). I fail to see why this makes Luke a universal historian. This contribution sheds some light on subsidiary aspects of the three Synoptic Gospels, but because there is no indication of a religious or theological motive force behind them, even by historical standards, they are brought too much into the foreground.

The next contribution, by Peter Lampe and Ulrich Luz, is the richest of the whole volume. It discusses the topic of 'Post-Pauline Christianity and Pagan Society' (242–80) and demonstrates with equal competence the social roots of Christianity and the theological claims of the individual communities.

The authors give an impressive account of the circumstances in which Christians were put on trial (255–60: all in all, the unplanned nature of the persecution is striking) and set forth in detail both the hostile environment (260f.) and Christian reactions (263–74). This is carefully demonstrated at individual points, so that one derives great profit from reading this contribution. The conclusion contains among other things an account of 'Mission methods' (276–8), and a brief section on 'Success and failure' (278–9) rounds off the piece.

The contribution by Ulrich B. Müller is devoted to the study of 'Apocalyptic Currents' (281–329).[54] He takes strong issue with the argument that Jesus and Paul are to be regarded as apocalyptists or apocalyptic theologians. The basis for his approach is to designate as apocalyptists only such persons as have composed a particular genre of revelation literature, namely an apocalypse (282). It is clear that neither Jesus (cf. 288: Luke 10.18 is isolated) nor the first Christians can be regarded as apocalyptists in Müller's sense, since initially he thinks they did not interpret the resurrection of Jesus as the beginning of the general resurrection of the dead (but this is the case in 1 Cor. 15.20; Col. 1.18; 1 Peter 1.3; Rev. 1.5). Nor is Paul to be called an apocalyptist, since his remarks on the fate of the dead (1 Thess. 4.13–17) rest on a reduction of elements of apocalyptic ideas. In my view one can say all of this only if one knows in advance that Paul was not an apocalyptist.[55] Moreover, according to Müller, Käsemann's thesis that apocalyptic is the mother of Christian theology would come to grief on the fact that his concept of apocalyptic cannot be verified in the history of religion (289).

Now it must be clear that if one starts from a problematical definition, one cannot arrive at a reasonable understanding of historical facts. As Jacob Burckhardt once remarked, 'Clear-cut concepts belong to logic, not to history, where everything is in a state of flux, of perpetual transition and combination. Philosophical and historical ideas differ in essence and origin; the former must be as firm and exclusive as possible, the latter as fluid and open.'[56] At all events a study of the phenomena must precede definitions, just as reflections on method always follow methods which work organically. And here in view of Paul's expectation of an imminent end – manifestly he reckoned that he would survive to the parousia – the simple question arises whether the apocalyptic scenario was not something he took for granted. All this can be avoided only by artificial definitions of concepts, but these would ignore the historical situation. In short, many if not most of the first Christians regarded themselves as the last Christians and had a passionate expectation of an imminent end (see Paul). The further question is whether Jesus also expected an imminent end or whether this expectation first arose in connection with the 'resurrection' of Jesus. In that case the problem of apocalyptic is to be decided in connection with Jesus and the first Christians and not by artificial conceptual definitions. In other words, on the basis of a consideration of the phenom enon I regard the starting point from the literary genre of apocalyptic as being too narrow. Unlike Müller (281f.), I would use criteria of content (e.g. the two-ages doctrine, the imminent expectation) to decide what apocalyptic is and not base criticism on the definition of a genre.

Reference may be made here to some more recent works on apocalyptic, none of which seek to limit apocalyptic exclusively to literary genres, but which see in it a basic spiritual and religious orientation.

In *Begriff und Wertung der Apokalyptik* ('The Concept and Evaluation of Apocalyptic in NT Research', 1989), Werner Zager examines research into apocalyptic from 1832 to around 1960 (from Friedrich Lücke's Commentary on the Apocalypse to Werner Georg Kümmel) and with his very first book (a Mainz theological dissertation from 1987/8) offers a standard work which all future works on apocalyptic will have to take into account. His Bochum Habilitationsschrift of 1995/6 (*Gottesherrschaft und Endgericht in der Verkündigung Jesu. Eine Untersuchung zur markinischen Jesusüberlieferung einschliesslich der Q-Parallelen*, BZNW 82, 1996 ('The Rule of God and the Last Judgement in the Preaching of Jesus: An Investigation of the Markan Jesus Tradition including the Q Parallels') takes his work on apocalyptic further, since here (51–113) he offers individual analyses of various Jewish texts understood in apocalyptic terms.

In his *Studien zur frühjüdischen Apokalyptik* ('Studies on Early Jewish Apocalyptic'), 1991, Karlheinz Müller has reprinted earlier works on the topic including his original article on early Jewish apocalyptic from *Theologische Realenzyklopädie* III, which here at last appears in full (i.e. three times as long). In the preface he confirms 'that the apocalyptic world-view which gradually developed in early Judaism offered the earliest primitive Christian confessors and communities the indispensable and obvious presuppositions for grasping and describing the significance of Jesus of Nazareth after "God" had "raised him from the dead"' (15). In apocalyptic, Müller argues, attention was focused on future salvation and not orientated on the salvific relevance of the past.

In 1992 Christfried Böttrich turned to a Cinderella of apocalyptic literature, the Slavonic book of Enoch. In his book *Weltweisheit* ('The Wisdom of the World. The Ethics of Humankind. The Original Cult. Studies on Slavonic Enoch') he sees the author of Slavonic Enoch as a representative of Alexandrian Diaspora Judaism before 70 CE, a group which 'to a quite special degree was concerned with the integration of traditional early Jewish and Greek Hellenistic thought. Thus it followed an overall feature of its time' (225).[57]

In a further work (*Adam als Mikrokosmos. Eine Untersuchung zum slavischen Henochbuch*, Judentum und Umwelt 59, 1995 ['Adam as Microcosm: An Investigation of the Slavonic Book of Enoch']), Böttrich turns to Slavonic Enoch 30.8–14 and after a survey of previous commentaries attempts 'to explain the passage above all from the context of contemporary Hellenistic literature' (3). He conclusively demonstrates 'that it is extremely probable that the traditions of Adam being given names from the four points of the compass and his creation from seven elements of the world came into being in Hellenistic Diaspora Judaism' (55).

In connection with his remarks on early Christianity and Paul (289–94), U. B. Müller in Becker's anthology expertly examines '(T)he apocalyptic starting point in Palestinian Christianity' (294–97) and discusses the relevant texts: Mark 13 (297–306; this passage is the first Christian text rightly to bear the label 'apocalyptic' [297]); 2 Thess. 2 (306–11); Revelation of John (311–23). Here the absence of a discussion of whether the name of the author of the Apocalypse is reliable (apocalypses were normally pseudonymous writings) is striking (cf. 313: 'John writes not under the name and the borrowed authority of a great figure of the past but under his own'). Müller's work concludes with discussions of 'Apocalyptic chiliasm in John and the so-called presbyters' (320–3) and 'The Changed Character of Apocalyptic Thought at the Turn of the First Century' (323–6).

The last contribution ('Johannine Christianity') is by Charles Kingsley Barrett (330–58), himself the author of an extensive commentary on John.[58] Barrett offers a careful introduction to the Johannine literature and cautiously discusses the relationship of the Fourth Gospel and the Johannine letters to society. There are remarks at the end of the contribution on 'Tensions in the Johannine Community' (353–6).

The composite volume edited by J. Becker still bears too many traces of its origin. As I have mentioned, it was originally conceived of as a contribution to the wider topic of 'Christianity and Society', and in the individual articles this is reflected in a great variety of ways – although occasionally, as in Löning's contribution, not at all. It is impossible to detect a single common theme in the articles apart from the fact that they refer to the same corpus of writings. So one may assume that the motto of the whole volume – taking up the editor's preface – is that the contributions 'provide an incentive to look further for the truth' (7). The volume seems to me a hotchpotch of the most varied contributions which because of their disparate nature, diversity of content and contradictions are likely to make readers throw up their hands in despair. The usefulness of the volume is further impaired by the lack of an index.

The 1988 book *'Sie aber hielten fest an der Gemeinschaft ...'* ('And they devoted themselves to the fellowship ...') is the result of an interconfessional conversation between professors and students of the universities of Bern and Fribourg, written up by three members of the group: Christian Link, Ulrich Luz and Lukas Vischer. The contributions by Vischer (17–40) and Link (187–271) belong with systematic theology and will occupy us only peripherally here. But the second part, edited by Luz in conjunction with individual collaborators, each of whom is mentioned (43–183), is basically an outline of the theology of primitive Christianity with special emphasis on the importance of community during the church's first two centuries.

After an 'Introduction' (43–59), there is a non-technical but quite critical discussion – though it is based on early Catholic terminology – of 'The Apostolic Age' (60–116) and 'The Post-Apostolic Age' (117–83).

In the section 'Jesus – origin of the fellowship of the church' (49–59), Luz resolutely opposes the 'radical thesis' that the church derives from the risen Christ. He argues that this thesis is historically false: 'Jesus did not found the church if by that we understand the sociological entity "church" distinct from Israel and composed of Jews and Gentiles; what Jesus did found was a new fellowship in and for Israel' (52). Fine, but what does Luz mean when he introduces the risen Christ (51)? (Cf. 123: 'The risen Lord spoke time and again anew through his prophets'; cf. 204.) Luz can hardly mean the risen Christ himself; he refers only to interpretations of the crucified Jesus (in the form of a vision). And in that case talk of the earthly *and* the risen Christ is open to misunderstanding, for the first element is a fact and the second its interpretation.

Luz convincingly argues for the historicity of the group of twelve founded by Jesus (53: 'How could this group first have come into being after Easter? After all, at that point – as a result of Judas' betrayal – it was no longer complete'). Referring to Mark 15.40f. and Luke 8.1–3, Luz is positive that Jesus had women followers and says that this is a central issue for the unity of the church today (54 n. 12). But not only the historicity of the information here is questionable (see below, pp. 91ff); if I may be allowed the observation, no one in the Protestant world today would judge that women should be excluded from leading church services even if the question was answered in the negative.

As for Jesus' end, Luz thinks that he wanted the fellowship of his disciples to continue after his death: to be specific, 'Thus Jesus wanted his community of disciples to go on beyond his death' (56). In my view that is a hopeless modernization which contradicts the insight formulated on the same page that the saying Mark 14.25 refers to a community in the kingdom of God which is to dawn in the near future.

In the section on 'The Apostolic Age' (60ff.), the second subsection offers an excellent discussion of 'The Beginnings of the Church after Easter' (60–73). Since the whole church had been something real from the beginning, Luz asks why after Easter the baptism of John was taken over by the whole Jesus movement. He gives the plausible answer: 'One of the reasons which were decisive here is the reference of the baptism of John to Israel. It is the sign and seal of those who belong to the end-time people of God. In taking over the baptism of John, the followers of Jesus claimed to be the people of God called by John and gathered together by Jesus. Thus the general acceptance of baptism presupposes something like an awareness of being the people of God' (66). At the same time, 'There are no reasons for concluding that there was ever a Christianity without formulated confessions. The diversity of the confessions that have been preserved and their common reference to the risen Lord Jesus speak a clear language here' (67).

In view of the emphasis on the church as the unified people of God from Israel, the composite volume cannot fail to take note of the so-called apostolic council. For here the direction is set for the future unity of the church; and both parties, Paul and his Jewish-Christian opponents, had a vital interest in resolving the dispute which had broken out (76–8). So the question arises how the two conversation partners, James and Paul, understood the unity of the church and its relation to Israel. It is surprising what optimistic remarks are made concerning the attitude of James, although the authors know that James did not leave any writings. Moreover, it is striking that in forming their judgement they take no account of the evidence that James had no religious relationship with his brother during Jesus' lifetime, but evidently rejected him (cf. Mark 3.21).[59] Despite that, the conclusion on James reads thus:

James 'understands "the church" as the people of God, gathered anew by the message of Jesus. For him it consists of two concentric circles: first of all there is the real Israel, the completion of which is to be achieved by the gathering of the "apostolate to the circumcision" (Gal. 2.8), for which Peter in particular is responsible. In addition, as a second group there are the godfearing Gentiles, whom Paul is to win for the people of God. Here James is perhaps thinking of prophecies (Isa. 2), and sees the place of these Gentiles within Israel as the end-time people of God. Therefore they are to observe parts of the Torah of Moses. Thus the unity of the church is possible only as unity *in* Israel' (82).

The section on Paul ('Paul and the Unity of the Church with Israel') is of course longer because of the greater number of available sources (83–97). Among the individual themes discussed are the conflict at Antioch, the conflict between the strong and the weak in Rome (both by Peter Lampe), Paul and his opponents (they pursued him virtually without a pause [89]) and the collection, the acceptance of which by the Jerusalem church is rightly doubted (cf. 94).

The next section is headed 'The Church as the Reality of Christ in Paul' (98–116). By way of summary it is stated that: 'The fellowship of the whole church is emphasized extraordinarily strongly in the Pauline mission, in the life of the communities and in the letters of Paul. For Paul, the community at a world-wide level is not a mere idea but a practice which is lived out' (106).

The following section, 'The Post-Apostolic Age' (117–83), reconstructs developments in the church after the death of the apostles, events which caused difficult and unexpected problems for the Christian community (cf. e.g. John 21.21f.). Nevertheless the post-apostolic age was marked by reinforced orientation on the tradition. The pseudo-apostolic letters are said to be the key to the post-apostolic period: 'they are all pseudo-apostolic. It is also striking that these pseudonymous writings are letters. Ultimately most pseudo-apostolic letters have an ecumenical character or at least extend beyond a region' (125f.). The authors infer the ecumenical character of the pseudo-apostolic letters from the Pastorals, which are said to be addressed to the whole sphere of the Pauline churches. The apostles are said to be 'fundamental figures of unity' (131). That is initially demonstrated from James (132f.: as the basic figure of unity he is said to reflect the diminished significance of Jewish Christianity in the church as a whole and to be the chief unifying figure of a marginal group).

Peter is also discussed in a very knowledgeable way (133–8), and after this Paul is given due attention (138–44). In the section 'the ministries as a power which furthers unity' (145–56), there follow remarks on the first ecclesiological schemes of church unity (Ephesians, 157ff.; Revelation, 160ff.; Acts, 163ff.). Then comes a discussion of the unity of the church in the Gospel of John (165–72) and following the theme of 'church fellowship in the Gnostic conflict' (172–83). Here in conclusion it is said: 'It may have been the case that the confession or dogma set limits to the Christ whom it confesses, and thus made it impossible for him to become effective as a guideline and a power for unity' (183).

The collective effort of these authors has produced an extremely noteworthy reconstruction of early theology and church history from the specific perspective of the unity of Christianity. If one reads the whole work through at a sitting, the great relevance of the historical perspective for questions of the present also becomes clear. This is a remarkable volume with many apt observations, but one would like it to be continued in a work with an exclusively scholarly orientation.

Due to its thematic similarity, reference should here be made to the book *Einheit der Kirche* ('Unity of the Church') by Ferdinand Hahn, Karl Kertelge and Rudolf Schnackenburg from 1979, the sub-title of which is *Grundlegung im Neuen Testament* ('Foundations in the New Testament').

Hahn discusses the 'unity of the church and church fellowship from a New Testament perspective' (9–51), Schnackenburg the 'unity of the church in the light of the notion of koinonia' (52–93) and Kertelge 'eucharistic fellowship and church fellowship in the New Testament and the early church' (94–132). All three contributions display strong theological interests. For them 'the concern to achieve a theological understanding remains a guiding principle' (12 n. 6), and likewise the interpretation of the New Testament documents 'which are recognized by all the churches and church fellowships' (5).

Hahn points out that both Jesus' call to discipleship and the (pre-Easter) community of the disciples as the eschatological people of God precedes the earliest post-Easter Christianity (26f.). The question of church fellowship cannot be detached from this unassailable axiom.

On the basis of a study of the Johannine writings, along with the Paulines and Deutero-Paulines, Schnackenburg emphasizes the dimension of koinonia which is expressed in baptism and eucharist. This is not to be detached from the preaching of the gospel (cf. the summary and prospect, 90–3).

Kertelge points out that in Paul there is 'a deep inner parallel between community and eucharistic meal, between church fellowship and eucharistic fellowship' (109), and suggests, following Paul (1 Cor. 11.26), that there is a need to strive for unity in the fellowship of the church and the eucharist, a goal as yet still unfulfilled from an eschatological perspective, namely in the expectation of the coming Lord (131).

Perhaps I may be allowed here the critical comment that the failure to achieve eucharistic fellowship right down to the present can be explained primarily by sociological, psychological and political factors (like e.g. the ongoing conflict between Protestants and Catholics in Northern Ireland) rather than by a purely theological concern such as that presented by the authors. For theologically, Protestant and Catholic New Testament scholars are largely agreed on the meaning of the eucharist in the New Testament.

Contrary to the blurb on the back of the book, the work by Adalbert Hamman entitled *Die ersten Christen* ('The First Christians') is not devoted to the first two centuries of the expansion of Christianity; it is above all devoted to the second century. The title of the original French edition, *La vie quotidienne des premiers chrétiens, 95–197* ('The Everyday Life of the First Christians, 95–197') both avoids such a misrepresentation and signals Hamman's concern to provide an introduction to the world of the second-century Christians by giving specific details.

After an introduction (9–12), the first part begins with the heading 'The Environment' (13–66); then follows the second under the heading 'The Presence in the World' (67–119); after that there are two further sections, the third with the heading 'The Face of the Church' (121–80) and the fourth entitled 'Everyday Heroism' (181–227). The conclusion, 'From Dream to Reality' (229–32), rounds off the contents; here the closing sentence says a great deal about the general orientation of the work: 'God discloses to those who are watchful and wait for him the bright dawn of a new day' (232). But such edifying flourishes should not prevent us from noting that Hamman has written a solid work, the strength of which lies in its clearly detailed descriptions and the extremely vivid individual images, which are drawn very precisely. He arranges little mosaic stones which together create an impressive picture of social relationships in the daily life of Christians of the second century.

Among the attractive features of Hamman's book are the endnotes (235–69), which give detailed and precise references to the phenomena discussed in the text, and two charts (282–5) presenting the Christian writers and the churches of the second century. We get the impression of an author who is thoroughly familiar with the material outlining his own picture of the Christianity of the second century and doing so with great vividness and precision. The family portraits of Ignatius of Antioch, Justin, the slave girl Blandina from Lyons, Irenaeus, and the young mother Perpetua from Africa constitute the high point of the book (162–80). Twenty plates make it even more vivid and round off the positive expression.

But there are also criticisms to be made:

1. Throughout the book, the views about the authorship of the New Testament writings put forward by Hamman are too conservative. Thus the Pastorals seem to him to be authentic (216), as does Ephesians (217). The reports of Acts are regarded throughout as reliable (cf. 47). And these weaknesses relate not only to the New Testament but also to the authors and persons of the second century, when for example Marcion's pupil Apelles is said to have turned a woman's (Philoumene's) head (63),[60] or when Justin's dialogue with the Jew Trypho is presented as a 'tribute to Israel' (70). One also asks why in this 'tribute' the Jew Trypho, a construct of Justin's, is allowed so small a say.

2. Hamman's treatment of the martyrs, which becomes almost a veneration (cf. 154f.), arouses mixed feelings, all the more so since no note is taken of the fact that Christianity could spread undisturbed in the first three centuries over wide areas. According to the most recent estimates, of a total of seven million Christians up to the beginning of the fourth century, fewer than a thousand suffered martyrs' deaths.[61]

3. Hamman maintains the old thesis that the Gnostics were morally degenerate. Even Marcion is condemned because of a moral lapse in the East, 'before he confused the faith in Rome' (108). But now the Nag Hammadi texts have demonstrated ascetic efforts by some Gnostic groups,[62] and given Marcion's own ascetic doctrinal system, we can no longer trust the remark by the church fathers that Marcion was expelled

from the church for seducing a virgin. ('Virgin' here, as in other early Christian sources, symbolizes the non-defiled church.)[63] In other words, here Hamman is basing his work on old prejudices which have long been superseded in scholarship. So while one is grateful for this book, it provokes mixed feelings.

W. H. C. Frend's monumental work *The Rise of Christianity* deals with the first 600 years of the expansion of Christianity; the present report is exclusively concerned with Part I (11–270), which is devoted to 'Jews and Christians'. This first of four parts is sub-divided into seven chapters and discusses 1. The Jewish background (11–52); 2. Jesus of Nazareth (53–84); 3. Paul and the first expansion in 30–65 CE (85–118); 4. The Christian synagogue in the years 70–135 (119–60); 5. Opposition cult in the years 135–180 (161–92); 6. Acute Hellenization in the years 135–193 (193–228); and 7. The emergence of orthodoxy in the years 135–193 (229–66).

The chapters are constructed in such a way that the text is immediately followed by an introduction to the sources and a brief sketch of the main scholarly works; this is then followed by the notes. As might be expected from Frend, the description is marked by a profound knowledge and command of the material.[64] Frend writes that the inspiration for his work was Adolf von Harnack's classic *Mission and Expansion of Christianity in the First Three Centuries* (1).

As the heading of the first part ('Jews and Christians') shows, the account is generally orientated on the question of how closely the Christian religion is related to its mother religion, and to what degree it became a distinct entity in the formation of the thought of the third generation. Frend's approach is chronological and 'old-fashioned'. He works from the extant texts, which he mostly trusts, and attempts to highlight important elements. The account is richly illustrated and contains a synopsis of events (912ff.) and various maps; the map on the inside cover, following Adolf Deissmann, shows the Jewish settlements in the central and eastern Mediterranean.

In general, it can be said that in this first part (and also in the following three) practically no new inscription, no new discovery, no new insight has escaped Frend's eye. But in his judgement on introductory questions relating to the New Testament he largely follows conservative British authors, as may be demonstrated from Chapter 2, on Jesus of Nazareth.

> Unfortunately the writing in this chapter is completely uncritical; it takes no account of form criticism and accepts New Testament texts largely at face value: for example, it begins by recognizing Bethlehem as the birth-place of Jesus (54). Moreover Frend regards the cross as the culmination of Jesus' mission (ibid.), and argues that the Easter story is grounded in the unique personality of Jesus during his lifetime (55), and that Jesus' family emigrated only briefly to Galilee (57). He attributes Luke 3.10–13, the Baptist's sermon – which the scholarly consensus sees as a Lukan summary – to John the Baptist himself (59), and thinks that Jesus' baptism by John constitutes Jesus' call (60). Declaring himself Messiah before Caiaphas (Mark 14.62) was what sealed his fate (73). The Gethsemane scene is historical,[65] as is the reconciliation of Jesus with his mother at the cross reported in John 19.25–7 (74). Frend ends Ch. 2 with a statement which could easily be misunderstood to be anti-Jewish: 'The new wine of Jesus' teaching could not, after all, be contained within the old wineskins of Judaism' (74).
>
> Ch. 3 deals with Paul and the initial growth during the years 30–65 CE, and shows how Frend imagines the expansion of Christianity in the first four decades. He follows Hans von Campenhausen's theory on the origin of the Easter faith, namely that finding the empty tomb gave rise to the Easter events. (See Hans von Campenhausen, 'The Events of Easter and the Empty Tomb', in *Tradition and Life in the Church: Essays and Lectures in Church History*, London 1968, 42–89.) Peter's decision to return to Jerusalem was one of the most important decisions in the early history of the church (86). Frend uses the narrative of Acts throughout his reconstruction of the history of the primitive Jerusalem community and here is influenced by British research into Acts. The result of the Pauline mission, he sees, was that Paul 'opened the way for the religion of Jesus to become the religion of the nations' (92). But here one asks whether he has adequately identified the historical Jesus with the Christ of Paul's preaching.
>
> Of course he thinks that Colossians and Ephesians are Pauline, and likewise the three-month stay in Corinth is historical on the basis of Acts 20.2 (even though it is well known that 'three' is a favourite number of Luke's). The reconciliation between Paul and James is related in close conformance with Acts 21 (106), and the composition of Acts is dated to the end of 62 – Paul was allowed to preach in Rome unhindered (109) – although a few pages later (122) Frend argues for 75–80 CE as the date of the final version of Luke-Acts.
>
> Ch. 4, on the Christian synagogue in the years 70–135 (119–60), discusses Christianity in this period: generally speaking it is to be designated 'Jewish Christianity' or 'Israel with a difference' (123). Frend repeatedly

calls this period 'sub-apostolic' (120f. etc.). With this designation, he like many of his predecessors commits himself to the Lukan historical picture of an apostolic era.

Furthermore, he subdivides the period into two sections, extending from 65 to 100 and from 100 to 135 (121). Frend senses differences in the Christian documents of the period: 'It is difficult to conceive of the book of Revelation and I Clement, both written, it would seem, near the end of the first century A.D., as products of adherents of the same religion' (120). However, it is harder to understand that for the church, the periods between 65 and 100 and between 100 and 135 together comprised the era of Paul, as Frend seems to think.

Generally speaking, due to the number of parallel threads in this chapter, the reader finds it difficult to understand what goal Frend is pursuing. Is he concerned to depict the first beginnings of Christian orthodoxy or to demonstrate the origin of the Christian churches in the various geographical areas? Or is he merely following closely Jean Danié-lou's *Théologie du Judéo-Christianisme*, Paris 1958 (ET *Theology of Jewish Christianity*, London 1977), which he presents as a 'classic' (151), in order to demonstrate the phenomenon of a Jewish Christianity understood unhistorically?[66] Nor do I know what to make of the reference (152) to Walter Bauer's *Orthodoxy and Heresy in Early Christianity* (ET London 1971), when Frend writes that this book should be referred to 'for the rise of sectarian tendencies and differences of interpretation in the faith' (152). For that was not the purpose of Bauer's book; rather, it set out to demonstrate that – by the standards of the orthodox view of the late-second century – Gnostic Christianity chronologically came first in all areas outside Rome. Frend's remark gives the impression that as an afterthought he has borrowed here and there from the Bauer school in America without grasping the overall significance of the work and understanding its further development by American New Testament scholars. That also seems to be the case in the seventh and last chapter of the first part of his work, where H. E. W. Turner's *The Pattern of Christian Truth: A Study in the Relations Between Orthodoxy and Heresy in the Early Church*, London 1954, appears in the bibliography (259) but Walter Bauer's book is omitted. It should be noted in this regard that Turner's book was written with the aim of refuting Bauer's construction.

Ch. 5, 'Opposition Cult 135–80' (161–92), depicts in a sensitive and knowledgeable way the rise of Christian resistance to the Roman state authorities and describes the theological thought of such key second-century figures as Justin, Aristides and Tatian, as well as Polycarp, the representative of an orthodox Christianity (183). Above all Frend details Celsus' criticism of Christianity (177f.).

Ch. 6, entitled 'Acute Hellenization 135–93' (193–228), is orientated on Harnack's description of Gnosticism as acute Hellenization of Christianity and is a competent introduction to the Gnostic currents of the second century.

Ch. 7, which has already been mentioned (229–70), sketches the development of orthodoxy, but without establishing any criteria. The climax is the section on the Apologists (234–44), who are quite rightly described as comprising a movement contemporary with and parallel to Gnosticism and Marcionism. What they share with the two other movements, Frend proposes, is that they are grappling with the formation of a Gentile Christianity in order to work out relations with the old Israel, with Greek philosophy, and with the Roman authorities (ibid). Frend rightly emphasizes that the extent of the apologetic literature attests that there was a market for this kind of campaigning for Christian faith in the second century. (Among the Apologists he includes Quadratus of Athens, Aristides, the Letter to Diognetus [from around 150], Justin, Melito, Athenagoras and Hegesippus.) Although the chapter is entitled 'The Emergence of Orthodoxy', as I have said, it devotes only a few paragraphs to the emergence of orthodoxy, e.g. 250f., where the New Testament canon is discussed. Here Frend remarks: 'In any event, the canon of Scripture took its place with episcopacy, the Rule of Faith, and the liturgy to provide the basis for a disciplined and unified church' (251). In conclusion, Frend formulates the thesis that between 145 and 170 such a change took place that in his own estimation the church represented 'a third race' (257).

With admirable aims and formidable erudition, Frend has surveyed all the sources at our disposal from the first two centuries and presented them impressively. However, I miss two things: 1. there is no treatment of heretical anti-Pauline Jewish Christianity, which must be seen as continuous with opposition to Paul in the period before 70 CE. (At least there is no discussion of these possibilities.) 2. Frend's treatment is too static. He avoids the uneasiness about Paul in the second century, perhaps because Paul was in the hands of the Marcionites and the Gnostics. Indeed, Frend evades the challenge of Walter Bauer, and to my mind is often superficial, simply reproducing texts rather than going deeper and describing, say, the underlying causes of the expansion of Christianity, factors which Harnack worked hard to bring out. But it has to be granted that this weakness may at the same time be a strength of this massive work, since Frend does not leave out any texts. And he is doubtless right in his view that the solution to the riddle of the emergence and expansion of Judaism is identical to that in the case of Christianity.

It is a merit of *The History of Early Christianity* by Niels Hyldahl (ET 1997, Danish original 1993) that he has also emphasized this. Hyldahl wants to identify the historical links between the early history of Christianity and that of Judaism. To carry this out successfully, he thinks it important to take account of the nature and centrality of the Temple in the time of Jesus (45). And he vehemently disputes the view 'that the history of the earliest Christianity was dominated by a conflict between two incompatible wings, i.e. "Judaists" and "Paulinists". In fact the history of earliest Christianity was dominated by a far more serious conflict: the conflict between Judaism and Christianity. As often happens in historical research and other areas, most people seem to have lost the ability to see the wood for the trees!' (184).

The book consists of four chapters: 1. 'Early Judaism' (1–58), 2. 'Jesus' (59–132), 3. 'The Apostolic Era' (133–242), 4. 'The Post-Apostolic Age' (243–300). So here we have a history of early Christianity which not only begins with Judaism in the second century CE but also, unlike the works discussed previously, explicitly includes Jesus in the history of early Christianity.

> Ch. 1 begins from a correct insight: 'In order to understand the origins and history of early Christianity it is necessary first to study the history of the Jewish people in the period between approx. 200 BC to approx. AD 100' (4). In the summary of Ch. 1 Hyldahl argues that there were probably no synagogue buildings in Palestine before the end of the second century BCE and moreover that the Diaspora synagogue buildings that we now know of (the Aphrodisas inscription from the year 200 CE does not in his view reflect a synagogue) must be dated to a much later period than usual.[67] 'This means that as institutions, the Synagogue and the Church developed in parallel with each other and that the Church did not "take over" an existing established institution' (58). Hyldahl's main thesis is that Judaism grew out of the Seleucid and Maccabean periods of Jewish history. 'The Maccabaean revolt saved the Jewish people and the Jewish religion from certain extinction. If we look at the situation from a historical point of view, it also saved Christianity, which emerged from Judaism (cf. Jn. 4.22) and would otherwise have perished with it. And how else should we look at the situation if not from a historical point of view?' (58).[68]
>
> In the next chapter, on Jesus (59ff.), an important thesis for the author is that the Zealot movement is a consistent development of fundamental ideas and principles from the earlier Maccabaean period (67). When Bultmann and his school neglected the question of the historical Jesus, the fact of Jesus' Jewishness became a triviality which had no relevance either for theology or for the church (73). What counted was not *what* happened

but *that* it happened. 'In principle, this was what the gnostics, including Marcion, had done in the days of the early Church' (73).

In the section on John the Baptist (86–101), Hyldahl states that both the fact of Jesus' baptism by John and the authentic saying of John in the Q version (Matt. 3.8/Luke 3.8) show that the Jewish religion was to some degree regarded as insufficient. 'It is therefore logical to assume that Gentiles also had access to John's baptism although there is no evidence that others than Jews were baptized by John' (89). According to Hyldahl, Matt.11.16–19/Luke 7.31–5 may not be exploited as a contrast between the ascetic John and the life-affirming Jesus. 'John was hardly an ascetic in the sense that he saw asceticism as an object in itself – it is more likely that his asceticism was a reaction against the luxury of the royal family (Matt. 11.7–8/Luke 7.24–5). The notion of Jesus as an epicure who though of nothing but himself is simply absurd (101).' According to Jesus, the baptism of John was a divine action behind which God himself stood (89). Moreover John was a priestly messiah (90–94).

In connection with the christological question (101–8), Hyldahl is sceptical that christology arose only after 'Easter', and on the basis of the historicity of the cleansing of the temple thinks that he can make three statements: (a) Jesus was the messiah; (b) Jesus claimed this openly; and (c) his cleansing of the temple was a criticism of the temple and the cult corresponding to the baptism of John (118). Hyldahl passionately emphasizes that the entry of Jesus into Jerusalem (which he regards as historical) was a clearly messianic act and that everyone was aware of its significance (cf. Zech. 9.9–10). Hyldahl concludes his chapter on the christological question with the exclamation: 'Indeed he was the Son of God, the Lord, the Lord's Anointed, Messiah (Jn. 1.41; 4.25), Christ and Israel's king!' (119). This exclamation is remarkable in a work with a historical orientation. Nowhere else does Hyldahl adopt this preaching style.

The next section on the resurrection of Jesus (119–31) is a cautious introduction to the sources of the New Testament, but gives a completely unsatisfactory explanation of Mark 16.1–8 in that it not only regards the discovery of the empty tomb by women as historical but also postulates – contrary to the text of Mark – that the women reported the event (127f.).

Ch. 3 discusses the apostolic age (133–241). It begins with remarks on the chronology of Paul (134–52) in which Hyldahl supports the 'new' chronology,[69] which is especially associated with the names of John Knox, Gerd Lüdemann and Hyldahl himself.[70] The starting point of this new chronology is that before taking account of the data in Acts, a preliminary chronology of Paul must be established on the basis of his letters. The important consequence of this approach for a history of primitive Christianity is that from now on the Pauline mission in Macedonia and Achaea has to be put before the Jerusalem conference (Gal. 2).[71]

After that, under the heading 'Disciples and Apostles' (152–66), Hyldahl turns to the difficult question of the relationship between the authorities in the Christianity of the earliest period. He suggests that James the brother of the Lord was the leading figure in the primitive community from an early time. He writes: 'After the death of Jesus, James was the oldest representative of his family and the obvious candidate to assume what had previously been Jesus' kingship. This is the more evident as the disciples themselves had been entrusted with royal power: Lk. 22.28–30; Matt. 19.28, and the Christians were to be kings and priests and judges: 1 Cor. 6.3; 1 Pet. 2.1–10. Even the apostles had to defer to Jesus' brother James' (165f.). But this ingenious combination directly contradicts the evidence that Peter was granted the first appearance (1 Cor. 15.5) and evidently was superseded by James only at a secondary stage.

In the accounts of Hellenists and Hebrews that follow (166–76), Hyldahl argues strenuously that Acts 6 can no longer be used as evidence for a conflict between Hebrews and Hellenists in Jerusalem. '(A)ll discussions concerning a conflict between two wings in the earliest Christianity must cease once and for all' (175).[72] Rather, the conflict which is described in Acts 6 is a purely Jewish matter (176). In the next chapter, 'The Judaists' (177–97), Hyldahl follows the Scandinavian tradition, according to which there were never anti-Pauline Jewish Christians.[73] In the following section (197–205) about the Jerusalem conference (which Hyldahl dates to 53) and the incident in Antioch, Hyldahl explains once again that James insisted on separating Jewish from Gentile Christians, in order to avoid the threat of Jewish persecution (204). The next section ('The situation in Corinth', 206–31) develops Hyldahl's view of the Corinthian crisis and defines the dispute between Apollos and Paul as a dispute between 'philosophical sociology and anthropology' and the Pauline 'democratic' concept of a Christian community (231). By contrast, the subsequent remarks on 'Paul in Jerusalem' (231–41) attack the interpretation of Paul's adoption of the Nazirate during his last visit to Jerusalem as hypocrisy (234). The question then is whether the account of this in Acts 21 is accurate at all. The fourth and last chapter discusses the post-apostolic period (243–300). Here first of all the significance of the synod of Jamnia is sketched out (243–52) and the Johannine literature is discussed (253–61). After this Hyldahl outlines the relationship between the Roman state and the Christians (262–74). He repeatedly emphasizes that only the Jewish Christians were affected by the persecution, and not the Gentile Christians. A sub-section on 1 Clement, the Pastorals and the letters of Ignatius of Antioch follows (274–86).

Then, turning to Marcion (286–94), Hyldahl discloses the real aim of his reconstruction of early Christian origins. Through his consideration and reconstruction of history he seeks to make clear not the close relation of Christianity to Judaism but the way in which the former is completely rooted in the latter:

Christianity wanted to be true Judaism, the church wanted to be the true Israel (cf. Phil. 3.3). The rejection of the humiliated and generally despised Jewish people, which is so strongly reflected in theology and history alike, made it possible for the Church to proclaim itself the new Israel – not 'new' in the qualitative and eschatological sense of the word as we know from the Old Testament, Paul's letters and the Revelation of John (i.e. Jer. 31.31; 2 Cor. 5.17; Rev. 21.1), but 'new' in a quantitative sense: a 'different' or 'alienated' religion that rejects and denounces its own past. Whenever this happens – as for example in Marcion and his teaching of an unknown god who is not Abraham's, Isaac's and Jacob's God, but a new, strange god whom nobody knows – the Jewish people are deprived of their place in the history of Christianity, and theology no longer deserves to be called by its name (294).

A section on Hegesippus' *Hypomnemata*, the fragments of Papias, and the beginnings of patristic literature (294–300) rounds off the work.

This work is certainly not a real history in the sense of a narrative. Nevertheless, useful new analyses and perceptive observations on the origin of primitive Christianity and its roots in Judaism are to be found scattered throughout. Its usefulness is heightened by the fact that the most important literature on the relevant area is cited at the beginning of each section and occasionally very helpful commentaries on this literature are given. In all areas the book is aware of contemporary scholarship and will therefore also prove to be an important tool for research into early Christianity.

My criticism, in so far as it has not already been made of individual aspects, begins where Hyldahl, loyal to wide areas of the Scandinavian tradition, plays down the significance of anti-Pauline Jewish Christianity. Moreover I would criticize his minimizing of the conflicts over Stephen and, last but not least, the confessional tone that permeates his book. The remark on Marcion quoted above is simply ludicrous on all counts. If it were true, Adolf Harnack and Rudolf Bultmann would not deserve to be called theologians. But none of that can change the fact that Hyldahl, a master of New Testament and patristic research, has added to our discipline a groundbreaking work which will long retain its currency. His method of beginning the history of primitive Christianity with the Maccabean period is an original way of expressing the special character of the relations between early 'Christians' and Jews.

Under the title *Von Jerusalem nach Rom* ('From Jerusalem to Rome'), Michel Clévenot sets out to reconstruct a history of

Christianity in the first century through the lives of individual believers. According to the blurb 'the official history is reflected in the fate of "nameless people"', so that the reader at the same time also experiences a new kind of historiography. Or to use Clévenot's words: 'Instead of offering a conjectural account of the life of "Jesus in his time" I have tried to make his figure stand out from the everyday existence of those who attempted to direct their lives by his' (10).

In a total of 30 'sequences' Clévenot spells out the first century. For example, the fourteenth sequence runs: 'A new Jewish brotherhood in Jerusalem in the years 35–40. *We cannot keep silent about what we have seen and heard*' (82–7). The heading to the twentieth sequence is: 'Uproar among the devotional trade in "Our Lady of Ephesus" in April 57. *Which way could prove to be viable?*' (114–18). The thirtieth and last sequence bears the title 'The letter of Clement of Rome from 96. *How well-ordered!*' (171–4).

There can be no question that Clévenot's approach affords a lively account of the first Christian century and Christians of the first century. Beyond doubt the contemporary Greek and Roman sources which are often quoted at length contribute to this. All in all, however, I cannot see the book as more than semi-learned *belles lettres*, since the source-critical foundation on which Clévenot builds often will not bear the weight. Here are some of the historical defects of this account:

One general weakness is the uncritical use of Acts; indeed, Clévenot merely paraphrases (82–7) the first chapters. Some passages are simply rewritten (86: Ananias and Sapphira [Acts 5]) or individual accounts (from Acts 15) of James the leader of the primitive community are tacitly supplemented by sources of a later date. Note for example 82: 'Their leader James, surnamed "the Just", is truly an ascetic: he drinks no wine, allows his beard to grow, spends his life in the temple, and as a result of much kneeling when praying, his knees already have calluses like those of a camel. He enjoys great respect among the Pharisees.' This description of James as a life-long Nazarite comes from the testimony of Hegesippus in the second half of the second century.[74] None of this inspires much trust.

The eighteenth sequence, which bears the title 'Paul in Athens in the year 51' (106–8), reflects a similarly uncritical use of Acts. Here everything in Acts 17 is accepted as it stands and is supplemented with testimonies from contemporary philosophy ('philosophical idealism'). Clévenot then adds his own view of the gospel, with the following words: 'Now to follow the way of discipleship of Jesus truly does not mean joining the limited elite of those who toil ... How can the mere mention of the craftsman from Galilee and his dealing with the Jewish priests over prostitutes or taxation for the emperor make an impression on these privileged people? What can it mean that the life in him was so strong that one can say that he conquered death? ...' (108).

This is not historiography but a rather flimsy backdating of the author's own view of Christian faith at the expense of historical accuracy. And all this is forced into the chapter on 'Paul in Athens, in the year 51'.

Of course, given Clévenot's specific view of Christian faith there has to be criticism of the Pax Romana (72), and accordingly the last sequence is devoted to 1 Clement. Its author is summarily described as bishop of Rome (173), although at that time there was not yet a monarchical episcopate in Rome, and the question of authorship is hardly to be decided on the basis of 1 Clement itself.

I could point out many further details to indicate that Clévenot has an almost biblicist understanding of the New Testament and that therefore the book cannot be regarded as an accurate or even probable reconstruction of early Christian origins. Nevertheless, the value of its belletristic approach should be pointed out: it paints a vivid background for an understanding of early Christianity, even if contrary to Clévenot's view this has nothing to do with the real course of events.

Michael Goulder's short book *A Tale of Two Missions* (1994 – the US edition published the same year is entitled *St Paul versus St Peter*), which is a popular summary of a planned larger work,[75] explains in an original way why today one can still defend Ferdinand Christian Baur's hypothesis of two missions – of Paul and Peter. He again proposes a unitary solution to all the problems created by the New Testament and patristic texts relating to primitive Christianity (cf. 194), and has given further foundation to the proposals made in this book in a series of articles which are listed in Appendix II (194–6).

Goulder rightly indicates that the early Christian theory of the 'virginity' of the primitive church which still governed the world-view of Cardinal Newman is inaccurate. 'From as far back as we can trace it (to the 40s) there never was a single, united church. There were (in fact from the 30s) two missions: one run from Jerusalem, with Peter and the sons of Zebedee in charge, and later James, Jesus' brother, and other members of his family; the other, run by Paul, from various centres' (ix). Both currents were agreed in their conviction of the importance of Jesus, but in practice they agreed on nothing else. Among other things this affected the validity of the Bible, the question of whether the kingdom of God had already come or not, the sphere of sexual ethics, speaking with tongues along with visions and healings, and last but not least the divinity of Jesus and the resurrection of the dead.

It should be noted that Goulder's account rejects the Q hypothesis as well as hypothetical entities like pre-Pauline hymns, Proto-Thomas theories, etc. In other words, he works on the basis of the existing sources and relates these to his two-mission theory.[76]

What is new in his reconstruction is the thesis that the old Jerusalem christology is accurately reproduced in Irenaeus' report on the Ebionites at the end of the second century. He calls their view 'possession christology', which means that Christ descended on the man Jesus at baptism and left him again at the moment of death.

> In his report on the christology of the Ebionites, Irenaeus points out that it agrees with the christology of Cerinthus. Cerinthus' report on the relationship between Jesus and Christ points out: 'But finally Christ left Jesus and then Jesus suffered and rose again, whereas Christ was untouched by the suffering, as he was a spiritual being' (Irenaeus, *Haer.* I, 26 1).
>
> Since Goulder considers Irenaeus' report accurate (110, etc.), he understands the emphasis on the bodily nature of the resurrection both in Paul and in the Gospels as a secondary product of the Pauline school or party, whereas from the beginning Peter and his followers had advocated a spiritual understanding of the resurrection. This fits the evidence that the earliest experience of the resurrection was of a visionary nature. And since the story of the empty tomb was developed only by the author of the Gospel of Mark, himself a Paulinist, one sees in the silence of the women that the story had not been known previously in his community.
>
> A further interesting detail and its consequences should be mentioned here: the cursing of Jesus presupposed by 1 Cor. 12.3 is said to go back to followers of Peter, who in this way expressed their adherence to the spiritual Christ, whereas for them Jesus was a simple human being (127). Thus Goulder is in a position to follow Baur in deriving the Christ party from followers of Peter. In this connection he again puts forward William Wrede's theory of an 'un-messianic' life of Jesus on the basis of an overall view of the Gospel of Mark, although – this despite the overwhelming present-day consensus – the pre-Marcan tradition already presupposes a 'messianic' life of Jesus.[77] For Goulder, Mark is a Paulinist who is attacking

the claims of the Jerusalem community, for there since 40 James has replaced Peter as leader.

The last chapter, Ch. 25 ('The Noise of Battle', 181–9), puts the whole series of developments in a historical framework of around 140 years (from 48, the date of the apostolic council, to 190, the formation of the Pauline[!] church).

In Goulder's account, many texts appear in a completely new light. The evaluation already offered may be supplemented by one further point: Goulder perplexingly attributes to Peter the teachings in Corinth previously claimed by scholars for Gnosticism (thus for example the non-physical resurrection [169]), whereas in more recent scholarship they are usually understood as further developments of the doctrine of Paul which are to be assigned to the impact of the Pauline preaching on Gentile Christians.[78] Although what Goulder proposes is not impossible, we have to ask whether such a spiritual view of resurrection was at all possible in Jerusalem in 30.[79]

At the same time the reconstruction is burdened with some untenable verdicts on authenticity. Thus 2 Thessalonians is said to be Pauline (84),[80] along with Colossians and Ephesians (114). The Didache is said to be the brief instruction of a disciple of Paul from the year 150 on how a church is to be administered (79). Here the generous assigning of texts to different trajectories takes its revenge, since any kind of literary reference to Paul in the Didache is quite out of the question.[81] So we must wait for the big book by Goulder before giving a final verdict on the value of his overall view.

In 1992 James Tunstead Burtchaell produced a very learned work with the title *From Synagogue to Church*, in which he emphasizes the notable degree of continuity between Judaism and Christianity (191). It is a remarkable testimony to his knowledge of nineteenth-century German theology.[82] To begin with, a general comment: more than half the book is devoted to an account of the history of research (200 out of 357 pages); perhaps that should have been noted in the subtitle. This ambitious work is a kind of constitutional history of the church in the first two centuries, and with its sociological undertones it really belongs in the era of Harnack and Sohm.

Burtchaell is concerned with a question raised a long time ago: were the earliest Christians under the supervision of ordained pastors or under the influence of inspired laity? Who was responsible: bishops, elders, and deacons or apostles, prophets, and teachers? Instead of tracing the church offices backwards, Burtchaell investigates the Jewish communities and finds examples of Christians simply continuing the offices of the synagogues. Thus he claims that from the beginning such officials stood at the head of the Christian communities, but they did not have the most authority. They were at the head of the community but they did not lead it, and they were inclined to follow charismatic lay persons.

> After a history of research from the Reformation (1–60), through the nineteenth century (61–100), the early twentieth century (101–35) and the last 50 years (136–79), and a delineation of the results of research entitled 'A search for a new hypothesis' (180–200), Burtchaell discusses the 'Jewish community organization in the later Second Temple period' (201–27) and 'The officers of the synagogue' (228–71). He cautiously investigates the literary and historical sources on synagogues and their leaders, rejecting the thesis which is occasionally presented that women were in charge of synagogues (245 n. 98).
>
> After examining the New Testament and the Apostolic Fathers, under the heading 'Community organization in the early Christian settlement' (272–338), Burtchaell describes the offices of the church: elders, prophets and teachers, community leaders, deacons, priests, widows and women of prominence. He attributes a great influence to the latter, but does not give them specific offices (328f.).

The Conclusion (339–57) once again sums up Burtchaell's thesis: 'The synagogue was the point of reference for the church ... the daughter was moving with a mind of her own.'[83] But I see the value of this book mainly in its broad survey of the history of research, one which is compelling in its thoroughness and will remain important for all future works on the constitution of synagogue and church. Given its generality, the positive thesis can hardly be refuted, but it does not receive sufficient specific support to sustain it.

Ernst Bammel's book *Jesu Nachfolger* ('Jesus' Successors', 1988)[84] sets out to apply to the investigation of primitive Christianity the fact that in all spheres of life in antiquity there were orders of succession. First of all he points out the different patterns in the environment of Jesus (9–23) and in a balanced way describes their influence on primitive Christianity. The next sections are: 'Jesus and the Legal Traditions of his Time' (24–30), 'James as "Successor" to Jesus (in the New Testament, Jewish Christianity and the Great Church)' (31–51), 'Peter, the "Representative" of Christ' (52–60), 'Traditions of Succession in the Johannine Community and in Other Spheres' (61–6), 'The Paraclete' (67–8), 'Historical Evaluation (the Successor in Christianity, in Manichaeism and in Islam)' (69–73) and finally, 'The "Testament" of Jesus (Luke 22.27ff.)' (74–83).

The chapter on 'James as "Successor" to Jesus' is the most successful. It stands out for its exhaustive use of the Pseudo-Clementines and the Nag Hammadi writings, and decisively demonstrates the significance of the kinship principle in the earliest community.[85] However, Bammel explicitly excludes Jesus from such influences. In reverent memory of my deceased colleague, I offer the following quotation:

> There was hardly a head of the disciples, a representative, etc. He himself detached himself from the ties of custom. The distancing from things, even the persons of this world, is significant. The eschatological tension glows through his time. Did he share it, how can it have been something lasting for him? ... What Jesus gives is inherent in his person. The Fourth Gospel sums it up like this: streams of living water flow from me (7.38). It is inconceivable that another from his circle could have said this of himself. What he does is the work imposed on him ... He performs a work which cannot be detached from his person and thus is incomparable. Thus constancy throughout the change of generations, the continuity of members, can find no precedent in him. And after all it is precisely the need for this which had a decisive influence on the history of primitive Christianity (30).

In 1992 Christian Grappe wrote *D'un Temple à l'autre. Pierre et l'Église primitive de Jérusalem* ('From One Temple to the Other: Peter and the Primitive Church of Jerusalem'), the first major monograph on Peter since Oscar Cullmann's classic study.[86] He set out to investigate the role of Peter within the sociological development of the primitive Jerusalem community. In a wide-ranging book entitled *Images de Pierre aux deux premiers siècles* ('Images of Peter in the First Two Centuries', 1995), Grappe investigates Peter's influence within early Christianity, which made him Paul's partner and counterpart. The content is as follows:

> An introduction (11–34) is followed by nine chapters with the following headings: I. From the disciple to the one who continues his master's work (35–48); II. From the mournful witness of the passion to the martyr (49–82); III. From the repentant sinner to the person open to repentance (83–110); IV. From the fisher of men to the pastor (111–126); V. From the spokesman of the Twelve to the writer (127–150); VI. From the recipient of revelations to the guarantor of a tradition (151–87); VII. From the confessor of an imperfect faith to the opponent of heresy (209–26); VIII. From the foundation to the founder of communities (227–74); IX. From the first disciple to the obligatory point of reference (275–90). All the themes are pursued through the first two centuries and offer an impressive overall picture of Peter which supplements Grappe's 1992 work.

Back to Grappe's 1992 study. After a preface orientated on the questions of sociological method ('The Contribution of Sociology to the Study of the Birth of a Religion', 15–32), the first part is devoted to the topic of 'The Primitive Church of Jerusalem in a Socio-historical Perspective' (33–138). This is followed by a second part headed 'The Place and Authority of Peter within the Primitive Church of Jerusalem' (139–308).

> Grappe proposes that in contrast to the primitive community, which was an exclusive brotherhood programmatically separating itself from the rest of Israel, Jesus did not found a special community, but with his prophetic charisma turned to Israel as a whole. The pre-Easter community of disciples represented a circle which in principle was open to all Israel. In his analysis of the Pentecost narrative, Grappe presupposes that the historical Pentecost corresponded to the festival of the renewal of the covenant in Qumran (183f.). At that time, he claims, the primitive community lived in an allegedly Essene quarter on the south-west hill of Jerusalem, the present-day Mount Zion, right next to the members of the Qumran community (61–6).
>
> Here Grappe is referring to the theses of Bargil Pixner,[87] who writes the following: 'The famous church of the apostles, which is said to mark the place where the apostles prayed after returning from the Mount of Olives,

where Christ was taken up into heaven (Acts 1.1–13), can still be found on the south-west hill of the old city of Jerusalem, which today is called Mount Zion' (287). These theses have been developed further by Rainer Riesner in a major article, 'Das Jerusalemer Essenerviertel und die Urgemeinde. Josephus, Bellum Judaicum V, 145; 11Q Miqdasch 6, 13–16; Apg 1–6 und die Archäologie', *ANRW* II, 26.2, 1995, 1775–992. This work of Riesner's, too, is marked by the assumption of the historical credibility of the first chapters of Acts. Thus for example he regards the casting of lots and the office of bishop in Acts 1.15–26 as historically accurate (1875f.), as also the primitive Christian sharing of possessions (1876–80), because of the parallels in the Qumran texts. Until the official reports of the investigations have been published, the theses of Pixner, Riesner and also Grappe must be regarded as fragile. For in all probability the first chapters of Acts do not derive from eye-witnesses, but according to the consensus of critical scholarship are markedly legendary.

Grappe sees Matt. 16.17–19, the saying about the rock, as an indication that the primitive community in Jerusalem understood itself to be God's temple of the end time; this self-understanding corresponded to that of the Qumran community. This, he argues, is the basis for its self-designation as church, and with this saying Peter legitimated himself as its leader (112–14). Decisive changes occurred during the subsequent history of the primitive Jerusalem community. First, the influence of Jewish movements radically loyal to the law became increasingly strong. Secondly, Peter underwent a dramatic change which bestowed on him the prophetic charisma of Jesus. This change, Grappe contends, is illustrated by the vision in Acts 10.9–16, the narration of which is historically reliable. Luke has wrongly dated it too early. It belongs in the context of the Apostolic Council and Peter's visit to Antioch (cf. 276–9).

Grappe's work is rich in analyses which prompt further reflection. But since he cannot offer any new primary source on Peter, much must remain conjectural, and the remarks about the place where the primitive community lived are simply rash. But on two points Grappe is certainly right: (a) in time there was a conservative trend in the primitive community which is connected with the name of James, the brother of the Lord (cf. also Bammel, above p. 56); (b) Peter gradually became open to freer tendencies. However, I would put this development earlier than Grappe does, all the more so since James was already the chief of the three pillars at the time of the apostolic council.

On the basis of a new treatment of the problem of the Hellenists, Craig C. Hill, in *Hellenists and Hebrews* (1992), sets out to give a new account of the history of the primitive community in Jerusalem between 30 and 70 CE.

> The book consists of an introduction (1–4) and five chapters: '1. Background' (5–18), '2. Acts 8.1–4: The Persecution of the Hellenists' (19–40), '3. Stephen and the Hellenists' (41–101), '4. Galatians 2 and Acts 15: The Relationship between the Churches of Jerusalem and Antioch' (103–47), '5. Further Evidence' (149–97).

Hill treads well-known paths in his polemic against Ferdinand Christian Baur, but he has no real understanding of Baur's work.[88] He constantly asserts that the opposition of Hellenists and Hebrews in Jerusalem is too hastily assumed today (184), and emphasizes that the Hebrews, like the Hellenists, were persecuted by the Jewish authorities (Acts 3–5; 12) (36–7). He does not take into account the fact that the historical value of Acts 1–5 is small. He further fails to explain why in the early period it was exclusively the Hellenist Stephen who became the victim of lynch justice.[89] Hill's criticism of the thesis that hostility to Paul in Corinth has an origin in Jerusalem was evidently worked into the text only at a later stage (see 158 n. 35). In this connection his remark that there are no bases for external opponents of Paul in the context of 1 Cor. 9 is inaccurate as far as 1 Cor. 9.12 is concerned. It is not generally recognized, as Hill claims (158 n. 35), that the opposition to Paul at the time of 1 Corinthians is of internal origin.

Thus the real defect of the book is its inadequate analyses. One example is Hill's treatment of Acts 21 (179–83), which amounts to no more than a discussion of the secondary literature and a paraphrase of the text. Thus one sets this book down in bewilderment and waits for a deeper analysis of the problem of the Hellenists in Acts.[90]

3

A Survey and Critique of Recent
Studies in the Social History
of Primitive Christianity

Since the 1970s the social history of early Christianity has also undergone a tremendous boom in Germany. 'In the second half of the 1960s the diverse shadings already present in the formation of the concept – social-historical, sociological or materialistic interpretation of the Bible, exegesis of liberation – point to a new kind of approach to the texts of early Christianity. The idealistic prison in which the texts seem to have been confined down through the centuries, the nightmare of a tradition which has been a burden on the heads of generations, all this seems to have been done away with by such a new reading of the texts ...'[91] The account of research by Thomas Schmeller, *Brechungen* ('Refractions. Primitive Christian Itinerant Charismatics in the Prism of Sociologically Orientated Exegesis', 1989) rightly says: 'There is no question about it: sociology is in fashion, at least among New Testament scholars. Anyone who has anything to say says it, if at all possible, in the jargon of the sociologist. The number of publications on the theory and practical application of sociological analysis in the widest sense, which has been growing since around 1970, is now legion' (9). This statement is illustrated by a bibliography in which more than 100 titles come from the period between 1971 and 1988.[92]

In the first part the short book discusses 'Sociologically Orientated Exegesis of the New Testament' (9–49) and in the second 'The Ethic of the Jesus Movement' (50–116). The first part is divided into four sections:

61

'1. Concerns and types of exegesis with a sociological orientation' (12–15), '2. History of research' (16–23); 3. 'The spectrum of sociological exegesis' (46–9). The second part contains three sections: '5. The discussion of Theissen's theses' (50–60), 6. 'Individual problems' (61–113) and finally '7. Results' (114–16).

The whole report is objective throughout and one would want generally to trust this informative account. However, occasionally weaknesses are clear. When in the account of the development of the sociological approach (16ff.) Schmeller remarks that in antiquity and the Middle Ages the exegesis of the New Testament took place only within the framework of the church tradition, given the examples of Celsus[93] and Porphyry[94] he is certainly mistaken. The further assumption that the historical turning point of exegesis was 'as is well known (between 1770 and 1790) prepared for by J. G. Semler and J. D. Michaelis and taken for the first time by D. F. Strauss and F. C. Baur (between 1833 and 1842)' is simply wrong. For where in these general remarks is there a reference to the work of H. S. Reimarus or the English Deists? For general information I refer the reader to the book by Stefan Alkier discussed on pp. 1ff. above. It is also erroneous to say that 'up to the end of the nineteenth century New Testament exegesis is largely limited to the investigation of theological and literary problems' (17). That is not true of A. von Harnack or T. Keim. And F. Overbeck should also be mentioned at this point, and, of course, F. Nietzsche. But it is right to note that between 1930 and 1970 questions of social history no longer played a role in exegesis (20).

On the problems of exegesis with a sociological orientation (45ff.) Schmeller cunningly observes that the whole trend is still in an experimental stage: 'Here so far the sequence seems to me to be that first the sociological model is discovered, and then the New Testament problem to be explained by it. It will certainly be necessary to reverse this procedure ...' (46). On the further objection that all results of this sociologically orientated trend so far could just as well have been achieved without sociological technical terms and methods, Schmeller rightly asks: 'Why *were* they not produced by historical criticism at all? Is it not the case that sociological interest which compels working with sociological technical terms and methods has heuristic value?' (48).

In his critical discussion of Theissen's work,[95] Schmeller rightly emphasizes that Theissen's thesis of preventive censorship is untenable. According to Theissen preventive censorship excludes from the oral tradition that which is not experienced. From a sociological perspective this statement is by no means certain and the texts in the New Testament also clearly tell against it. Here 'the radical demands of Jesus after Easter[96] were certainly also understood in a non-verbal, metaphorical sense ... which makes it improbable that they were handed down only by itinerant charismatics and allows us to imagine that they were piously preserved in local communities' (66). Throughout primitive Christianity Schmeller sees in the history of developments a connection between the itinerant charismatics behind the Q document, Matthew and the Didache – in contrast to the Hellenists of Acts and Paul, whom he claims to be distinctive and clearly different types (116).

In 1995, six years after his account of research, Thomas Schmeller produced his own social-historical investigation, *Hierarchie und Egalität* ('Hierarchy and Equality. A Sociological Investigation of Pauline Communities and Graeco-Roman Associations'). It covers the social history of Pauline communities and Graeco-Roman associations. After a survey of the history of research from the time of Heinrici to the present day (11–18), he gives an admirable account of the social strata in the Roman empire (19–53). (Here the texts and translations of four select association inscriptions printed as an appendix [96–115] should be noted; they are particularly suitable for advanced courses in the background of primitive Christianity.) Schmeller sums up the result of this section with the words: 'Associations were not simply gatherings at which the social hierarchy was set aside. Rather, they achieved a relaxation of social pressure by reproducing hierarchy but combining it with a certain equality' (53).

The references in the letters of Paul to differentiations of status, offices in the community and the status of individual members of the community (within the community and in society as a whole) produce the following picture: the baptismal tradition of Gal. 3.28 in fact corresponded to social reality. 'This high degree of integration in Pauline communities cannot be adequately grasped with Theissen's concept of the "love patriarchalism" which it is legitimate to use for the post-Pauline period. Rather, its ethos is stamped by a group identity in solidarity' (95).

Schmeller has made an important contribution which offers a vivid introduction to a topic of social history and is admirably suited for teaching.

The Americans John E. Stambaugh and David L. Balch have written a notable study on *The Social World of the First Christians* (1986). Their approach is from social history. They are concerned to use recognized data as a basis for consolidating the result of modern sociological research into the social environment of the New Testament.

> After Ch. 1 ('Historical Background', 13–36), Ch. 2 is concerned with 'Mobility and Mission' (37–62). Ch. 3 ('The Ancient Economy', 63–81) describes the economic activities of the ancient world, and Ch. 4 ('Society in Palestine', 82–106) reconstructs the Palestinian world of the Jesus movement. Its subject is the urbanization of Galilee, a process which produced tensions among the rural Jewish farmers. It discusses the question of the social context of the preaching of Jesus and his controversies with the Pharisees. Ch. 5 ('City Life', 107–37) turns to the Greek and Roman cities of the empire in which the first generations of Christians lived. It offers a survey of the environment, the population and the spheres of social interaction: work, play, family, groups and religious culture. Ch. 6 ('Christianity in the Cities of the Roman Empire', 138–67) brings together the different factors of the social environment of the New Testament and compares the organization of the early Christian communities with corresponding phenomena in the pagan world. This is followed by a survey of the specific urban centres which are important for the New Testament: 'Syria: Antioch' (145–9), 'Asia Minor: Ephesus and Other Cities' (149–54), 'Macedonia: Philippi and Thessalonica' (155–57), 'Achaia: Corinth' (157–60), 'Rome' (160–65), 'Egypt: Alexandria' (165–67).
>
> Bibliographies for further study of the problems discussed and indexes of New Testament passages and an index of names and place conclude the work.

This American joint work is exclusively orientated on the phenomena which it describes and has no reflections on method. For example there is no discussion of the theoretical problems of a social history. Rather, it is simply presupposed that social references were important for the Christian communities of the early centuries; the question is what the societies in which the early Christian movement gained a footing looked like, and what characteristics of those societies can help us to understand the rise of that movement. The great strength of this book lies in its vivid narrative style and the way in which cameos or mosaics are brought together. To this degree it makes rewarding reading not just for specialists but also for all those who want to find a way in. Even if occasional details need to be corrected,[97] we can learn from this book how special attention to social factors deepens the historical perspective.

Ekkehard W. Stegemann and Wolfgang Stegemann provided a comprehensive social history of primitive Christianity in 1995, which was published in English translation in 1999 under the misleading title *The Jesus Movement: A Social History of Its First Century*. The introduction (1–4) describes the aim: the book is meant to be neither a political history nor a history of events but 'an overview of the economic and social living conditions of the groups and communities in the New Testament who are either connected with the historical Jesus or confess the risen Christ' (1). With this I already have problems, because the historical Jesus is not to be found in the New Testament, but is a modern abstraction.[98] The book consists of four main parts, which can also be read separately (cf. xix).

> Part One, which contains a considerable amount of information and has been written on the basis of the recognized standard works, discusses the 'Economy and Society of the Mediterranean World in the First Century' (5–95). It is subdivided into three sections: 1. 'The Type of Ancient Mediterranean Societies' (7–14), 2. 'The Economic Situation of Ancient Mediterranean Societies' (15–52), and 3. 'Stratification and Social Situation in the Ancient Mediterranean Societies' (53–95).
>
> Part Two discusses the 'Land of Israel, the Social History of Judaism, and the Followers of Jesus' (97–247).
>
> The first section of Part Two (= 4) is devoted to the 'Economic Situation in the Land of Israel' (104–25); the next section (= 5) discusses 'Social Development in the Land of Israel' (126–36), and the following one (= 6) covers 'Religious Pluralism in the Land of Israel in the Hellenistic-Roman Period' (137–86).

The authors consider the formation of groups, basic tendencies and characteristic movements, religious institutions like temple, synagogue, and house, and basic religious currents in the Hellenistic-Roman period (purity and asceticism as

behaviour that drew boundaries, apocalyptic as a phenomenon of dissidence, the sociology of the circles behind apocalyptic), and finally discuss the formation of groups in the
Hellenistic-Roman period, with the Essenes, Pharisees and
Sadducees viewed as deviant phenomena (149ff.). Their view
is that deviancy theories are so fruitful for descriptions of the
formation of groups in Judaism in the Hellenistic and Roman
periods because they allow us to understand these as reactions
to the crisis and at the same time to explain the different
forms that they took (151). However, it is only later (244f.)
that deviancy is defined, so that for a little less than 100 pages
the reader is relatively helpless when reading the remarks.
Nor can I see how historical phenomena would be better
explained or understood at a single point by the acceptance
of the term 'deviancy'.

The next section of Part Two (= 7) describes 'Jesus' Followers
in the Land of Israel in New Testament Times' (187–220).[99]
The authors include among the followers of Jesus the Jesus
movement proper, the primitive community in Jerusalem
which came into being after the death of Jesus, and the messianic communities of the period after 70 (Matthew and John).
But one must express serious doubts whether the Gospels of
both Matthew and John come from Palestine (cf. the relevant
textbooks).

> The authors adopt a 'charismatic interpretive concept' in their socio-
> logical analysis of the Jesus movement (193ff.). 'Thus for charismatic
> movements the violent death of the genuine bearer of charisma is in no
> way a catastrophe; rather, it can be the initial spark, as it were, for the
> development and reshaping of the charisma' (195, in italics in the book).
>
> However, it should be noted that the historical circumstances of the
> death of a charismatic are understood differently by scholars within the
> framework of the charismatic concept of interpretation, so that at this
> point we may in principle ask about the historical plausibility of such
> sociological concepts.
>
> For example, starting from the concept of charisma, Michael N.
> Ebertz[100] sees the death of Jesus and the later foundation of a church as a
> counter-charismatic process which was initially bound up with the collapse
> of the charismatic legitimation faith in Jesus (257). Helmut Mödritzer
> (1994), to whose contribution I shall be returning on pp. 70ff. below,
> thinks it impossible 'to speak of counter-charismatic processes which then
> necessarily led to the death of Jesus ... Only because the charisma of Jesus

had not yet come to an end at the end of his life, but on the contrary many disciples continued to follow him and he endured his martyrdom consistently, could Jesus' charisma in the last resort also survive his death' (167).

So I dispute the Stegemanns' view that the origin of Christianity can in some way be made more plausible by their concept of charisma supported by sociology than by the historical-critical method, orientated on phenomena. In any case the authors have difficulty in giving a sensitive account of historical processes; this is strange in a social history of primitive Christianity. Reference should be made in this connection to the section 'Continuity and Transformation of the Charisma after the Death of Jesus' (213f.), which gives a relatively abstract account of the explosive process in the community after the death of Jesus. The authors write:

> We see the crucial continuity and at the same time the beginning of the transformation of charisma in the ecstatic, visionary experiences immediately after the death of Jesus among the followers of Jesus, especially in the close circle of Jesus' disciples and followers. According to the earliest tradition, the Resurrected One appeared to Simon Peter (Cephas) and the circle of twelve as a whole, then to a larger circle of more than five hundred followers, as well as James, the brother of Jesus, and all the apostles (1 Cor. 15.5–7) (213).

(The authors skip the important piece of historical information that the appearance to the more than five hundred happened 'at once'.)

The chapter titled 'Jesus' Followers in the Land of Israel in New Testament Times' (187–220) ends with the following sentences: 'Thus in our opinion it was the charismatic dynamic that separated the Jesus movement more and more clearly from Judaism in Palestine. It is obvious that in the period of the first Jewish Revolt, this meant a special danger. We believe, therefore, that it is entirely conceivable that at the beginning of the rebellion as Eusebius reports (*Hist. Eccl.* 3.11.1) the church took flight from Jerusalem to Pella beyond the Jordan and thus into the Roman-protected realm of Hellenistic cities' (220).

However, at this precise point the question is not what is possible or conceivable, but what is probable. And in general, the probability of an historical verdict leads to new sociological insights. In reading the Stegemanns' book one occasionally gets the impression that it works deductively instead of inductively. It would be better if reconstructions and the discovery of the meaning of a text came first, and not general knowledge about the society of the time and particular sociological theories from which this or that determination follows.

The next section of Part Two (= 8) discusses 'Messianic Communities in the Land of Israel after 70 C.E.' (221–47). After dealing with the integration and reshaping of Judaism after 70 (221–3), the authors turn to the New Testament sources, here the Gospel of Matthew (223–6) and the Gospel of John (226f.). Both Gospels are said to have been written in the land of Israel, an assertion which of course provokes counter-arguments (cf. below, Chapter 6).

The next sub-section discusses 'Conflicts between Messianic Communities and the Remnant of Judaism in the Land of Israel after 70 C.E.: Basic Considerations' (231–47). Here the different exclusions and penalties, persecutions to the point of killing, are thoroughly and explicitly described. At the end there are sociological interpretations which seek to deepen the historical result. The authors' conclusion is that 'the dynamic process of the exclusion of Christ-confessing Jews as a deviant group is also still recognizable in the texts. The application of the "forty (lashes) minus one" is to be interpreted as the punishment of deviants. The verbal slanders mentioned are examples of the public labelling of a deviant group' (246). There is no need for lofty sociological terminology to say this.

Part Three is devoted to the 'Social History of Christ-Confessing Communities in the Cities of the Roman Empire' (249–358). The authors mention four sociological criteria for distinguishing sociologically between Christ-confessing communities and followers of Jesus:

'First, the Christ-confessing communities are composed of Jews *and* non-Jews ... Second, Jews and non-Jews in these communities programmatically realized an *unrestricted* – though in part controversial – social interaction. Third, the Christ-confessing communities existed as minority groups in the context of the *pagan majority society* of their urban locations. And fourth, *alongside and outside* the Diaspora synagogues, they were the representatives of Judaism outside the land of Israel' (251).

Part Three is divided as follows: A first section (= 9) describes the 'Concept and Basic Characteristics of Christ-Confessing Communities' or fundamental characteristics of the Christ-confessing communities (262–87); a second (= 10) again analyses the 'Social Composition of Christ-confessing Communities' (288–316); and a third (= 11) discusses 'External Conflicts of Believers in Christ with the Gentiles and Jews in the Diaspora' (317–58).

Part Four deals with the 'Social Roles and Social Situation of Women in the Mediterranean World and in Early Christianity' (359–407). The individual chapters deal with the following themes: 'Gender-specific Spheres and the Social Stratification of Women in Mediterranean Societies' (363–77); 'Women among the Followers of Jesus in the Land of Israel' (378–88); 'Women in Urban Christ Communities' (389–407). All this is again written with great knowledge and circumspection, so that the result is beyond doubt an instructive survey. The most important results are these: that women were among the followers of Jesus can hardly be doubted historically; their prominent role at the end of Jesus' life is an indication of charismatic experiences of women as followers of Jesus; the women who followed Jesus, like the men, probably belonged to the lower levels of the society of the time; and their behaviour in public made them seem like women of a doubtful profession.

Presumably Mary Magdalene was single, since she 'is not characterized as the virginal daughter of her father' (385). The authors find no indication in the Synoptic tradition 'that the women of the Jesus movement consciously set themselves against the precepts of Judaism related specifically to women' (386). In a summary on the Pauline communities, the Stegemanns conjecture 'that basically women had a share in most of the charismatic gifts of the Christ-confessing communities, whether in the fulfillment of missionary functions, in the performance of tasks in certain areas of competence in the local communities, or in active participation in the assemblies of the *ekklesia*. In Corinth women also shared in many forms of self-expression in the assembly itself. This indifference to gender with regard to the spiritual leadership of the communities apparently resulted from the charismatic equality of Christ-confessing men and women, which found its social expression in baptism. So the charismatic element was egalitarian' (397).

The Stegemanns argue that 1 Cor. 14.33b–36 is not to be deleted. 'Most reasonable, in our view, is the attempt to explain that Paul is addressing different roles of women in Chapters 11 and 14. That is, the presumed opposition between 1 Corinthians 11 and 14 dissolves if one notes that in the Christ-confirming *ekklesia* there were two social experiences that were also judged differently outside the community: on the one hand, acts of worship (praying, prophesying, and the like), on the other, consultation and teaching dialogues (*didache*, 1 Cor. 14:6, 26)' (399). The result is: 'We support the thesis here that in Paul's opinion (married) women have no right to speak in the *teaching dialogues* or consultations of the *ekklesia* but are to be silent and ask their husbands at home. Their participation in acts of worship of the community assembly, by contrast, is not discussed here; rather it is presupposed on the basis of 1 Corinthians 11' (400). But this thesis about the form of the text and the breaks around 1 Cor. 14.33–6 is hardly correct: v. 33b begins abruptly, whereas v. 37, which refers back to vv. 29–32, takes up a train of thought which has been interrupted.

The Stegemanns offer a wealth of material which can illustrate the social depth dimension of New Testament texts. Their enterprise deserves unqualified recognition and gratitude. But one often gets the impression that a quite specific sociological theory is being artificially applied to the texts. In addition I miss something in the book which the authors may not have aimed at but which in my view must nevertheless be present in a work which contains the word 'history' in the title: namely, the question of the historical facts and more precise analyses of primitive Christian texts. To give another striking example, I have singled out the remarks on the Lord's supper, where the authors write: 'The celebration of the Lord's supper (1 Cor. 11:20), the breaking of the bread, probably also goes back to the earliest followers of Jesus. It must be seen in the context of the fact that the Jesus movement gathered in homes ...' (217). This statement, which is simply thrown out, conceals the history-of-religions problem which lies in the sacramental consumption of the blood and body of Jesus.

That brings me to another book from the sphere of the sociology of primitive Christianity to which reference has already been made. This is the Heidelberg dissertation by Helmut Mödritzer, *Stigma und Charisma im Neuen Testament und seiner Umwelt* ('Stigma and Charisma in the New Testament and Its Environment'), which appeared in a revised form in 1994.

Starting from the terms stigma and charisma, which he defines sociologically, Mödritzer presents an outline of the sociology of primitive Christianity which exhibits all the advantages and disadvantages of such an approach. He begins in Chapter I ('Stigma, Stigmatization, Self-Stigmatization, Conceptual Definitions', 7–36) with a definition of the two central terms. For Mödritzer, stigma means 'an experience of marginalization and impotence which threatens identity in respect of social influence, and charisma (means) the capacity to establish new values and exercise social influence (free from institutional recognition)' (7). Here he consoles himself that 'the central concept of this work occurs in the New Testament itself and does not first have to be transported artificially into the New Testament texts' (10), since in Gal. 6.17 Paul himself writes that he bears the wounds of Jesus in his body. But perhaps one might be allowed to point out that the wounds that Paul means do not necessarily correspond to the significance of stigma in more recent sociology. The same is true for charisma, which also appears in the New Testament (cf. esp. 1 Cor. 12.4, etc.) but has a quite different meaning today.

Mödritzer distinguishes four forms of self-stigmatization. The first is provocation: 'provocateurs generally challenge social ideas, whether of morality, work or behaviour' (24). Secondly, the other side of provocation is asceticism, which also represents a form of self-stigmatization (ibid.). Thirdly, there is a kind of exhibitionism in which the individual element clearly stands in the foreground; Mödritzer defines this as a deficient form of self-stigmatization. A fourth and last type of self-stigmatization is represented by ecstasy. It involves the adoption of primarily culpative stigmata, which are so harshly sanctioned that they can prove fatal; martyrs are regarded as the prime example of this (25). Here Mödritzer prefers to use the term 'forensic self-stigmatization' and moreover always sees his third and fourth types of self-stigmatization together, under the 'common denominator of forensic self-stigmatization' (26).

Equipped with these tools, in Ch. 2 Mödritzer sketches out 'Forms of Self-Stigmatization in John the Baptist' (37–94); in Ch. 3, 'Forms of Self-Stigmatization in Jesus of Nazareth' (95–167); in Ch. 4, 'Forms of Self-Stigmatization in Paul' (148–244); and finally 'Forms of Self-Stigmatization in Ignatius of Antioch' (245–64). It is not surprising that he rediscovers the three (or four) forms of self-stigmatization mentioned in the several figures he investigates. I shall simply take up his thesis on Jesus.

Unlike John the Baptist, who lived on the periphery of society, Jesus of Nazareth practises 'self-stigmatization ... in the centre of society. Forms of ascetic self-stigmatization (absence of family, possessions and home, a renunciation of protection and self-defence) do not serve him (as they do the Baptist) as accusation or penance but are attempts to win over his hearers to his cause ... The martyrdom of Jesus represents an act of forensic self-stigmatization. It is not so important here whether Jesus foresaw or forecast his death (he certainly risked it), as that his death corresponded to a behavioural tendency which stamped his whole life – a self-stigmatizing feature which after Easter became the basis of an interpretation of the cross as *self-surrender and an atoning death*' (266f.).

One would have liked to learn more – historically! – than Mödritzer offers about the change from the life and cross of Jesus to Easter. All he says is: 'If a deliberate way of dealing with guilt and its intended removal seems to be probable in the life of Jesus ... there is much to be said for the assumption that even more after his death people began to interpret him in these categories: if as a result of his crucifixion Jesus had been annihilated physically, but not the sphere of action in which he worked, in this way at the least with the Easter appearances his death could be understood in an atoning and therefore *de-stigmatizing way*' (234).

In other words: what Jesus advocated was advocated even after his death, or, to use Willi Marxsen's words, the cause of Jesus went on. Not only is no sociological jargon needed for this, but Mödritzer does not consider how the Easter appearances could have and did come about. I miss a pattern of questioning which takes causality into account. It seems to me that with Mödritzer's method one can read almost anything into the text if one makes the concepts wide enough. Thus for example he understands the idea of pre-existence and incarnation contained in the Pauline text Phil. 2.6–11 as 'defective self-stigmatization' (cf. 267). But this is humbling oneself to the point of being human, which can hardly be self-stigmatization unless one presses the term – which Mödrizer does in abundance.

It is the merit of Mödritzer's work that he sharpens our perception of the common features of the four persons from the early period of Christianity mentioned. But this ploy hardly has any great historical value, for, as he himself recognizes, the relevant characteristics also apply to figures from the environment of early Christianity and to persons in Jewish texts. The comparison between Mödritzer's article and that of Ebertz discussed earlier on p. 66 above shows that different sociological patterns of explanation lead to completely different historical assessments. Besides, this kind of application of sociological insights and categories is hardly a contribution to the clarification of primitive Christianity.[101]

Wayne A. Meeks from Yale University produced his book *The First Urban Christians* in 1983.[102] (The German translation has a postscript by Gerd Theissen [382–7].) In the introduction (1–8) Meeks deals with the question of why a social description of early Christianity is needed. He rightly complains about the air of unreality that pervades most current works on the New Testament. He wants to know how people really became Christians in the first century and what it meant at that time to be a Christian (cf. 2). One can infer Meeks' historical interest from this question and it arouses high expectations for his book. Methodologically Meeks assumes the position of a moderate functionalist:

> That is, the sort of questions to be asked about the early Christian movement are those about how it worked. The

comprehensive question concerning the texts that are our primary sources is not merely what each one says, but what it does (7).

However, Meeks deliberately limits himself to the Pauline mission field.

Chapter 1 discusses the 'Urban Environment of Pauline Christianity' (9–50). Here it is striking that Meeks naively describes the sphere of Antioch on the Orontes as Pauline Christianity (10). It is no coincidence that this is precisely the point at which most recent works on the relationship between Antiochene Christianity and that of Paul begin; we shall be returning to them later (see pp. 116ff. below). Meeks simplifies the problem of the relationship between Antioch and Paul by dismissing chronological questions briefly with no exegetical sensitivity (cf. e.g. 199 n. 8).

The topic of Chapter 2 is 'The Social Level of Pauline Christians' (51–73).

Here, according to Georg Schöllgen's[103] critical examination of Chs 1 and 2, Meeks' main finding is that the social structure of the Pauline communities essentially reflects that of the surrounding urban society, and the leading figures both in the mission and also in the local communities have in common the fact that they belong to social risers. Schöllgen makes a number of objections, the most important of which may be mentioned here: Meeks is wrong in his tacit assumption 'that all Pauline communities display precisely or even approximately the same social stratification' (74). Moreover he does not succeed in demonstrating that the great majority of the Pauline communities consisted of small craftsmen and traders (76f.). 1 Thess. 4.11f. does not show that the great majority of the communities consisted of independent craftsmen, for almost all urban professions involved crafts. Nor can 1 Cor. 16.1–4 support this thesis. Finally, even an approximate definition of the social structure of the home cities as a point of reference for the Pauline communities has yet to be made, 'and the lack of adequate source material does not allow us to expect usable results for the future either' (77). Schöllgen concludes his criticism with these remarks: 'As often, the adoption of modern sociological theories – however plausible they may seem in themselves – comes to grief in the study of antiquity on the difference in the nature of the material at our disposal, which ultimately determines the methods and modes of procedure' (80).

Ch. 3 discusses 'The Formation of the Ekklesia' (74–110). Meeks investigates 'Models from the Environment' (75–84), the 'Fellowship and its Boundaries' (84–107) and 'A Worldwide People' (107–10) without investigating the historical roots of the Pauline concept of the church. Thus the classic article by Karl Holl [104] is not taken into consideration and the important issue of the collection for the Jerusalem community is taken up almost as an afterthought (110). Here we have only the terse remark that in the last years of his career Paul exerted himself considerably for the collection among the saints in Jerusalem, and that 'At the meeting in Jerusalem between the Antioch representatives and the Jerusalem "pillars", Paul and Barnabas had undertaken a formal obligation "to remember the poor" (Gal. 2:10), and Paul evidently regarded that obligation as incumbent not only on the Antiochene Christians but also on the later converts of Asia Minor and Greece' (110).

We can see from these remarks the neglect of the historical dimension of this agreement over the collection. It is potentially misleading to say that in the last years of his career Paul exerted himself considerably for the collection, since for him everything depended on the collection as the symbol of unity between Jews and Christians; indeed a concern for the collection runs through all the Pauline letters like a scarlet thread (apart from 1 Thessalonians, Philippians and Philemon). It is also incorrect to say that apart from 24.17 (?) Acts never speaks of the collection (thus 230 n. 176), for there is already explicit mention of a collection in Acts 11.29, and the relation in the history of the tradition between the collection mentioned here and the collection mentioned in the letters of Paul would need to be clarified.[105]

Meeks rightly infers that the collection was not accepted by the Jerusalem group (110).[106] But here his careless treatment of the influence of the Jerusalem community on the Pauline communities takes its revenge. Both issues are brushed aside very superficially (81, 132), with the derogatory remark that 'the ghost of Baur has been raised again recently' in the works of various scholars (223 n. 41). Indeed Meeks discovers no influence from the great figures of Jerusalem on the Pauline communities: 'The original apostles of Jerusalem thus seem to have had little or no direct authority so far as the Pauline churches were concerned' (132).

I would like to formulate my criticism at this point as follows: Meeks shows very fine parallels to the Pauline understanding of the church in the environment but neglects to root the understanding of the church in the history of the theology of primitive Christianity. As Theissen writes in the postscript to the German edition: Meeks' book 'is research into Paul in which Paul no longer stands alone at the centre' (386). I think that that is something of a disadvantage.

These remarks bring me to Ch. 4, 'Governance' (111–39). This begins with a description of the conflicts in the Pauline communities (111ff.). Here too the sociologically orientated analysis is a very superficial way of dealing with historical problems, particularly when it is said almost in passing that a council of elders met in Jerusalem under the presidency of the twelve apostles (112). Meeks goes on: 'Such an organization, unmentioned by Paul, may in fact have existed, but it is also possible that the Acts picture is of a later style of organization, which it projects onto the past' (ibid). Thus something is said and immediately retracted. The interested reader gets no precise information about the historical facts in the early period of the primitive community in Jerusalem.

Chapter 5 'Ritual' (140–63) is the most valuable section of the book. Meeks deals with the question what rituals do (142), and from this starting point he goes through the rituals of initiation (baptism), the ritual of solidarity (the Lord's Supper) and other unknown and controversial rituals. All this gives a lively impression of the forces at work in the Pauline communities. Here too, however, as is clear from a look at the treatment of the Lord's supper (157ff.), the genetic question is neglected and social history is practised at the expense of the history of religion.

Chapter 6 discusses 'Patterns of Belief and Patterns of Life' (164–92). Meeks is interested in 'the social force of what the typical member of the Pauline churches believed' (164). Subsections are: 'One God, One Lord, One Body'(165ff.), 'Apocalyptic and the Management of Innovation' (171ff.), 'The Crucified Messiah' (180ff.), 'Evil and Its Reversal' (183ff.) and 'Correlations' (190ff.).

All in all, Meeks' book contains many interesting observations on the social depth-dimension of the Pauline communities. But social history proceeds at the expense of history, and neglects to set Pauline Christianity as Paul understands it in the history of the theology of the first century. Here it cannot be unimportant that Paul describes his own mission directly and without reservations as starting from Jerusalem (Rom. 15.19), and develops his own understanding of the church as opposed to that of the Jerusalem community, and promotes his own apostolate not only as a breakaway rival of the Jerusalem apostolate but also in relation to it (cf. Gal.1–2). Here Meeks does not allow the texts to speak, as is unfortunately the case with many authors who focus on social history. In short, general reflections on social structure are made at the expense of individual analysis.

The study by Eckhard Plümacher on *Identitätsverlust und Identitätsgewinn* ('Loss and Gain of Identity') – 'identity' is never defined – is, like that of Meeks, an investigation of Pauline Christianity as an urban phenomenon.

After an introduction ('Christianity as an Urban Religion', 7–9), in the first chapter Plümacher turns to the 'Identity Crisis of Subdecurion Groups' (10–25). At many places 'the participation by broad groups of the subdecurion population in their poleis was their sole source of identity and status. However, the times of this participation were irrevocably past' (24).

As is already clear from the title, Ch. 2 ('The Ethics of Popular Philosophy as a Way Out of the Crisis', 26–30) shows the possibility of a spiritual emigration from the polis by means of ethics. 'There was a firm expectation that those who had lost status and identity in the polis or who had not achieved it at all would be inclined now ... to satisfy the need for identity and status from other than political sources' (30).

Ch. 3 ('Christianity and the Subdecurion Crisis', 31–48) demonstrates that no Christian source directly responds to the phenomena of this identity crisis (35). However, 'Christian authors clothed the statements which expressed their homeland and identity in a language which derives from the very context in which many unsuccessfully fought for their integration' (38). Thus Hebrews and Ephesians use a conceptuality (stranger, fatherland, resident, city, commonwealth, fellow-citizen, community, etc.) which had a technical significance in the political world of the Greek cities (cf. 38); cf. especially Hermas, *Sim.* I 6, a passage which Plümacher evaluates as 'a link to relevant experiences in the subdecurion population' (44).

Ch. 4 ('The Role of Christian Ethics', 49–53) indicates how for Christians, in keeping with the overcoming of the crisis by popular philosophy, an ethical programme proved to be a way out. Thus Origen could see an essential goal of the Christian mission in converting people to the four Platonic cardinal virtues, 'the possession of which had earlier made the citizen of the virtuous city of popular philosophy' (52).

After Ch. 5 ('The Identity Crisis of the Urban Elites', 54–60), under the title 'Ways out of the Crisis' (61–9), Ch. 6 discusses the question of possible ways out: rising into the imperial aristocracy of the knights or even senators (61), literary flight into the transfigured past (62), or inner emigration from the polis based on the argument that in any case activity for the state does not correspond to the ideas of the wise (cf. Seneca, *de otio*) (64–5).

Ch. 7 ('Christianity and the Subdecurion Identity Crisis', 70–80) gives three reasons that led members of the urban elites to Christianity (74–80): (a) the refusal of Christians to engage in public affairs, which was worth imitating; (b) an elitist ethic; (c) an ecclesiastical and heavenly career structure (Tertullian, *idol.* 18,9), which was not dissimilar to that of the polis.

Last, Ch. 8, 'Christian References to the Decurional Identity Crisis' (81–93), shows that Christianity sought to offer a way out of the identity crisis of the urban elites. According to Clement of Alexandria (*Strom.* IV, 172, 2f.), the church is an unwalled city not ruled by tyrants. The city of heaven and the polis-ekklesia share the fact that they are based on God's will.

Plümacher's book, to which sufficient attention has yet to be paid, offers important insights into the reciprocal relationship between the Christian church and Roman aristocracy at the time of the rise of early Christianity. It illuminates the motives for becoming a Christian and thus explains the spread of early Christianity. All in all, the book is an important contribution to the political and social history of primitive Christianity. The renewed emphasis on the ethic of the early Christians as a factor in attracting new converts which must not be underestimated seems to me to be important.

As the subtitle ('A Socio-historical Study of Institutionalization in the Pauline and Deutero-Pauline Writings') indicates, Margaret Y. MacDonald's book *The Pauline Churches* (1988) is concerned with institutionalization in the seven Pauline letters accepted as authentic and in a further section with Colossians, Ephesians and the Pastoral Epistles.[107] In an introduction (2–30), MacDonald explains her project and sets out to demonstrate why she uses the social sciences, demarcating them from previous historical-critical methods which she claims to have been exclusively concerned to depict a history of ideas. She argues that it is not the case 'that the straightforward action of ideas determined shapes' (6). Rather, '(w)ith the aid of sociological analysis the process of institutionalization is traced from its earliest stages' (9). She concludes with the thesis: 'The study has investigated the transformation of the early church from its loosely organized, charismatic beginnings to its more tightly-structured nature in the second century' (235). Now such a result or such an acceptance of the development of the church from loosely organized charismatic beginnings to the more closely structured churches in the second century is not a new insight, and hardly needs a sociological analysis. And the following remarks on the Deutero-Paulines have hardly been substantiated by sociological analysis:

For his (Paul's) associates who wrote Colossians and Ephesians, the goal was not so much to legitimate the formation of a sect as to ensure its continued existence – to

stabilize community life in the absence of the Apostle ...
The social situation underlying the Pastoral Epistles is
marked by a strong desire to protect the community against
false teachers. Deviation has become a problem in community life (235f.).

Of course the historical-critical approach one-sidedly criticized by MacDonald also has a social dimension, and must not
be vilified as being obligated to a mere history of ideas. Furthermore, in her remarks one misses the insight that the
Pastorals were 'published' as a corpus of letters. She does not
go into the question of the relationship between the corpus of
the Pastorals and Marcion's antitheses, an issue which needs
clarification.[108] And she defames Walter Bauer's approach as
being associated with the history of ideas (225ff.), as if the
Göttingen scholar always looked out for the idea behind a
development. She remarks again almost in an exhausting way:
'(W)e have discovered that the division between groups is not
made purely on the basis of doctrinal positions but on the
basis of a complexity of social factors' (229).

Here reference should also be made to a continuation of
MacDonald's work (*Early Christian Women and Pagan Opinion*,
1996). She begins where Elisabeth Schüssler Fiorenza left off
chronologically in her work *In Memory of Her* (New York and
London 1983), at the beginning of the second century, and
analyses developments to its end. She defines her task in the
introduction (1–47). Here the methodological reflections
make up around 20 per cent of the whole work. The preface
states:

> In conducting this study I was frequently required to ven-
> ture outside my own field of Early Christian Studies to
> consider the work of anthropologists of Mediterranean
> societies and the work of scholars in the area of women and
> religion. Given the interdisciplinary nature of my study, I set
> out deliberately to write a book which I hope will interest
> specialists, but will also engage more general readers (xi).

It would take us too far afield to report here on the methodological reflections, which among other things are

concerned with the categories of 'honour and shame' (David
Gilmore), 'private and public', and with the theory of 'illegi-
timate power'. Rather, it is important to investigate how far
the book offers new insights into details of primitive Christianity and how far the development of early Christianity is
described as being unusual.

> In Part One ('Pagan reaction to early Christian women in the second
> century CE', 49–126), MacDonald discusses Pliny, Fronto, Apuleius, Lucian
> of Samosata, Galen and Celsus to offer the following conclusion:
> 'Throughout this discussion of how women figured in the pagan critique
> of early Christianity I have examined the relationship between image and
> reality: the interplay between the world of historical events and the social
> construction of the reality including impression, rumour, and stereotype.
> When analysing public opinion of early Christianity, it is evident that
> image and reality both are operative, and they may never fully be separated
> despite the most conscientious attempts at scholarly dissection' (120).
>   Part Two deals with 'Celibacy, women, and early church responses to
> public opinion' (127–82), and Part Three with 'Marriage, women, and
> early church responses to public opinion' (183–248). A 'General conclu-
> sion' (249–58) ends the book. In it MacDonald reiterates her overall
> perspective: 'My main goal in writing this book has been to illustrate that
> the history of early Christian women includes the public reaction to their
> lives. I have shown that an understanding of how women figured in public
> opinion about the church furthers our knowledge of early Christian
> women' (249). Hence 'scholars investigating non-Christian reactions to
> the birth of Christianity should no longer ignore the presence of early
> Christian women' (258).

All this is narrated and reconstructed in an extremely lame
way and falls short of increasing our historical insight into
the second century. The relevant parts in Lietzmann's *History
of the Early Church* and Harnack's *Mission and Expansion of
Christianity*, neither of which appears in the Bibliography
(259–71), offer more. However, what I gratefully learn from
MacDonald is the task of examining closely the particular
location of the different sources.

In *Kommunikation und Gemeindeaufbau* ('Communication
and Community Building. A Study of the Origin, Life and
Growth of Pauline Communities in the Communications
Structures of Antiquity', 1991), Reinhold Reck, starting
from the current phenomena of dissolution in present-day
established churches (1f.) and the crisis in the tradition of

Christian faith (322), investigates the original situation of the church (2). His study does not set out to prove or demolish any specific thesis. 'Its efforts are directed more towards reading the letters of Paul with the aid of the tools of modern communication sciences against the background of the structure of communication in antiquity and with respect to the origin, life and growth of the communities' (318).

> After 'I. Introduction' (1–5), in 'II. Communication and Communication Science' (6–61), Reck adds a short historical survey with an introduction to 'Approaches and Models of Present-day Communication Research' (10–29), on the 'Concept of Communication' (30–49) and on a further 'Differentiation of Communicative Factors' (49–67).
> 'III. Structure of Communication in Antiquity' (68–157) discusses languages, travel, the nature of news, the free associations, communication between the social strata, and three concepts of world-wide communication. Special topics like journeys, in-group language, banks, elementary teaching, letters of commendation and mass communication are discussed knowledgeably.
> The main part of the study is 'IV. Communication in Pauline Communities' (158–317). First of all Reck describes the 'problems of using the sources' (158–61) and points out what it means that the gospel embodies the 'initiative force of primitive Christian communication' (162–4). This applies because the gospel itself is 'essentially communicative', since it is only 'real gospel as preached' and has 'the basic structure of message' (162). Then follows a description of processes of communication 'in the origin' (165–98) and 'in the life of the communities' (199–317).

All in all, despite its aim of relating to the present day, this is an extremely careful work on questions of communication in the Pauline communities within the communication structures of antiquity. The work is attractive for its great knowledge and is one of the indispensable studies on the social history of primitive Christianity.

The dissertation by Marlis Gielen, *Tradition und Theologie neutestamentlicher Haustafelethik* ('Tradition and Theology in the Ethic of the New Testament Household Codes', 1990), offers little new in individual exegetical insights and follows current opinion on such basic issues as the authorship of Colossians, Ephesians and 1 Peter (namely that they are deutero-Pauline or Petrine, cf. 6–23). But it carefully elucidates the exegetical discussion and in a section on the sociological background to the New Testament household codes (68–103) excels in offering an extremely careful stocktaking of research with a sociological orientation.

Moreover the excursus on the *patria potestas* (146–57) and the section on the ruler cult (421–6) are of high quality. The book ends with a section on 'Opportunities and Limits of the Ethic of the New Testament Household Codes as a Model for a Christian Controversy with Social Norms Today' (557–69). When Gielen writes that 'on the Christian side it must be argued that the manifold tasks in family, society and state are to be performed communally and *functionally with equal rights,* but *introducing different characteristics as man and woman*' (568), one wonders whether this result could not have been arrived at without being preceded by 567 pages of text.

4

A Survey and Critique of
Recent Studies in Primitive
Christianity from the Perspective
of Feminist Theology

In the last two decades feminist theology has experienced an unsuspected boom, although in Germany it has not yet taken root in the academic world. The situation in the USA is different,[109] and it is from there that the most important contribution so far to a feminist-theological reconstruction of Christian origins derives.

Elisabeth Schüssler Fiorenza, who trained in Würzburg under Rudolf Schnackenburg, has later taught in the USA, first at the University of Notre Dame and since 1983 at Harvard University. Her book *In Memory of Her: A Feminist Theological Reconstruction of Christian Origins*, which appeared in 1983,[110] has become internationally recognized as a pioneer work in the feminist reconstruction of early Christianity.

Reference should first be made to Schüssler Fiorenza's main interest and her strongly emphasized theological claim. To be fair, I shall quote her at length in her own words. On the purpose of her analyses she writes:

'The explorations of this book have two goals: they attempt to reconstruct early Christian history as women's history in order not only to restore women's stories to early Christian history but also to reclaim this history as the history of women and men. I do this not only as a feminist historian but also as a feminist theologian. The Bible is not just a his-

83

torical collection of writings, but also Holy Scripture, gospel, for Christians today' (xivf./ ^{2}xlivf.).

Feminist theory also emphasizes 'that all texts are products of an androcentric patriarchal culture and history' (xv/^{2}xlv). 'The attempt to "write women back into early Christian history" should not only restore early Christian history to women but also lead to a richer and more accurate perception of early Christian beginnings' (xvi/^{2}xlvi). 'Historical "objectivity" (sic!) can only be approached by reflecting critically on and naming one's theoretical presuppositions and political allegiances' (xvii/^{2}xlvii).

How can early Christian origins be reconstructed in such a way that they are understood as 'women's history'? Her answer is: '(A) feminist reconstruction of early Christian beginnings seeks to recover the Christian heritage of women because ... "our heritage is our power"' (^{2}xx/1). 'Historical biblical studies, like historical studies in general, are a selective view of the past whose scope and meaning is limited not only by the extant sources and materials but also by the interests and perspectives of the present' (xxii/^{2}lii).

What relation does Schüssler Fiorenza's above claim to be able to approach historical objectivity have to this? In the section on 'Models of Biblical Interpretation' (4–6) it becomes clear how Schüssler Fiorenza relates to the traditional approaches in historical criticism: she distances herself from both the dogmatic and the positivist historical approaches which, she argues, still predominate in historical-critical research. She writes: 'Although this scholarly detachment is historically understandable it is theoretically impossible' (5). Well roared, lioness! And all that is asserted *ex cathedra*, before we have been offered a line of exegesis.

Instead of this, Schüssler Fiorenza proposes that she will use the model of liberation theology. 'The various forms of liberation theology have challenged the so-called objectivity and value-neutrality of academic theology. The basic insight of all liberation theologies, including feminist theology, is the recognition that all theology, willingly or not, is by definition always engaged for or against the oppressed' (6). In my view that simply means saying farewell to the truth; here I am aware that Schüssler Fiorenza rejects the understanding of scholarship on which my judgement is based, that which aims at offering objective interpretations of the text and being a 'presuppositionless' historical reconstruction (5).[111]

It would be fruitless to pursue Schüssler Fiorenza's theoretical reflections further. For constant harping on problems of method can easily lead away from specific texts. Moreover, the impression might too easily arise that those who understand nothing of the subject-matter talk instead about method. Instead of this, in what follows I shall concentrate on comparing Schüssler Fiorenza's textual analyses and reconstructions with what the texts contain according to our present state of knowledge, and at the same time sketch out the contribution of these analyses to research into primitive Christianity. By contrast, the remarks which she keeps scattering about on feminist theory, the concept of revelation, androcentric language and so on belong in other reports and are to be noted here only where they are significant for strict historical reconstruction.

The section 'Androcentric Selection of Historical Traditions' (48–53) is promising. Here we have the certainly correct statement: 'Many of the traditions and information about the activity of women in early Christianity are probably irretrievable because the androcentric selection or redaction process saw these as either unimportant or as threatening' (49). But in this section Schüssler Fiorenza also abruptly states that all the Gospels know 'that Mary Magdalene was the first resurrection witness' (50). Here Schüssler Fiorenza has tacitly claimed the Gospel of Mark in favour of her thesis of the androcentric selection of historical traditions. But in Mark a woman is truly not the first witness of the resurrection, but together with two other women is a hearer of the preaching of the resurrection of Jesus (cf. Mark 16.6). It does not help to say that in the pre-Markan story of Mark 16.1–6, 8a the early Christian confession 'Jesus of Nazareth, the crucified one, was raised' was revealed first of all in an appearance to the Galilean women disciples of Jesus (139); for a confession can hardly be revealed in an appearance.

After the section on 'Patriarchal Canonization and Function' (53–6), which because of the patriarchal context of the process of canonization (cf. the Pastorals) requires a hermeneutics of suspicion, and the chapter 'Towards a Feminist Model of Historical Reconstruction' (68–95), in Part II ('In

Memory of Her: Women's History as the History of the Discipleship of Equals' [97–241], following a long introduction on to the question of method, Schüssler Fiorenza finally undertakes a kind of reconstruction of early Christian origins. But there are yet more remarks on method at the beginning (99–104). Schüssler Fiorenza asks, 1. whether two clearly different forms of the early Christian movement can be sketched out; 2. how the historical-critical method can be used in such a way that we get beyond the texts of the Gospels to the historical reality of Jesus and his movement; and 3. how the origins of the early Christian movement are to be reconstructed in such a way that 'we recover the story of Christian women as the story of *Jewish* women since our sources make a recovery of our Jewish feminist roots difficult' (99).

Chapter 4 describes 'The Jesus Movement as Renewal Movement within Judaism' (105–59). According to Schüssler Fiorenza, the 'earliest gospel strata assert again and again that Jesus claimed the *basileia* for *three* distinct groups of people: (1) the destitute poor; (2) the sick and the crippled; and (3) tax collectors, sinners and prostitutes' (122). However, it does not become clear how Schüssler Fiorenza understands Jesus' concept of the kingdom of God; sometimes (120f.) it is apparently symbolic; at other times she simply quotes Luke 17.21 (cf. 119).

Moreover one is struck by the ideologically based argumentation according to which we now suddenly discover that women were tax collectors, Sadducees and Pharisees (see the examples in the German translation, 155, 165, etc.) ...[112]

Schüssler Fiorenza discovers in the Jesus movement of Palestine the 'equality from below' that is expressed in some parts of the present-day women's movement, and cites Luke 7.35 (Q) as support (132). She writes: 'The earliest Palestinian theological remembrance and interpretations of Jesus' life and death understand him as Sophia's messenger and later as Sophia herself. The earliest Christian theology is sophialogy. It was possible to understand Jesus' ministry and death in terms of God-Sophia, because Jesus probably understood himself as the prophet and child of Sophia' (134).

But all three wisdom logia are secondary in the history of the Q tradition and accordingly cannot be used for the original Jesus tradition: The first wisdom text, Matt. 11.19e/Luke 7.35, is a secondary insertion. It is not an independent logion or even a proverb but an expansion that presupposes Luke 7.31–34 (or Matt. 11.16–19c). It has nothing to do with the generation which rejects Jesus; here the Q community is contrasting itself as 'children of wisdom' with the generation of Israel which rejects Jesus. The second wisdom text, Luke 11.49–51, is also a secondary insertion. The third wisdom text, Luke 13.34f., is similarly a later insertion and the conclusion of the previous section in Q.

For all those seeking historical information and plausible historical reconstruction in Schüssler Fiorenza's feminist-theological reconstruction of Christian origins, reading is a torment. With arbitrary exegesis she attempts to show that the early Christian movement opened up positions of leadership for women and therefore could be called egalitarian.

No wonder, then, that Schüssler Fiorenza also places women among the immediate followers of Jesus; the group of twelve is simply passed over. The Jesus movement, which by general agreement consisted of itinerant charismatic males, now includes women. The reason given is this: 'To claim that such a radical a-familial ethos is asked only of the male wandering charismatics but not of the local sympathizers is a serious misreading of the texts' (146). Where are the texts attesting women who followed Jesus (on Mark 15.40 see pp. 91f. below)?

The conclusion of Chapter 4 is that: 'Only when we place the Jesus stories about women into the overall story of Jesus and his movement in Palestine are we able to recognize their subversive character' (152).

Ch. 5 bears the title 'The Early Christian Missionary Movement: *Equality in the Power of the Spirit*' (160–204). Scattered through the chapter there are again theses that serve to re-evaluate the role of the woman in early Christianity: Phoebe (Rom. 16.1–2) was not a deaconess commissioned for women's work but a minister of the whole church of Cenchreae (170). That does not emerge from the wording. Three women, namely Lydia and her companions (cf. Acts 16.15), are said to have been founders and leaders of the church of Philippi, with whom 'Paul had entered into a "communal partnership" (*societas*)' (178). This thesis is derived solely from Acts. Finally Prisca – by means of an uncertain historical judgement – becomes the teacher of Apollos (179). This is probably inferred from the order of the names Prisca and Aquila in Acts 18.26. Now because of this evidence, which can also be found in Acts 18.18; Rom. 16.3; 2 Tim.4.19 (the names are the other way round in Acts 18.2; I Cor. 16.19), one may conclude that Priscilla was more active in the community than her husband. But it does not follow from this that she was also Apollos' teacher, for the remark to this effect rests on the redactional shaping of the scene Acts 18.24–19.7 with which Luke seeks to integrate Apollos into Christianity, understood in Lucan terms (thus the consensus of present-day research into Acts).

Ch. 6 is headed 'Neither Male and Female. *Galatians* 3:28 – *Alternative Vision and Pauline Modification*' (205–41). Schüssler Fiorenza rightly regards the text as a pre-Pauline baptismal declaration. The text is 'best understood as a communal Christian self-definition rather than a statement about the baptized individual' (213).

There follows a notable defence of the authenticity of 1 Cor. 14.33–6 (230–3). Schüssler Fiorenza assumes that Paul can accept the spiritual participation of virginal, holy women (cf. 1 Cor. 7.1,34) in community worship but that in 14.34f. he is arguing against married women taking an active part in worship (231). Then follows an admirable section on 'Patriarchal Images and Metaphors' (233–5).

Part III, 'Tracing the Struggles: Patriarchy and Ministry' (245–342), concludes the book. It consist of Ch. 7 ('Christian Mission and the Patriarchal Order of the Household' [251–84]) and Ch. 8 ('The Patriarchal Household of God and the Ekklesia of Women' [285–342]), which I shall pass over here.

There follows an epilogue ('*Toward a Feminist Biblical Spirituality: The Ekklesia of Women*' [343–51]), which, as is already evident from the title, develops an application of the insights of the book.

I am not quite clear how far Schüssler Fiorenza's book is a reconstruction of Christian origins or beginnings. Rather, it may better be seen as a search for the role of women in the jungle of primitive Christianity – a search which is bursting with ideological features. Many textual analyses are very far-fetched; those mentioned in the report could easily be supplemented.[113] Moreover the content of the book is difficult to understand, since time and again there are long and meandering excursions into feminist theories and theology. The theological zeal behind this book is at least as absolutist as the patriarchalist exegesis of primitive Christianity and modernity which Schüssler Fiorenza attacks. It is hardly much use in moving forward constructive research into primitive Christianity. Therefore it provides only a few suggestions worth noting, and I shall be returning to these later.[114]

Luise Schottroff, a pupil of Herbert Braun,[115] produced a feminist social history of early Christianity in 1994 under the title *Lydia's Impatient Sisters*.

As in the case of Schüssler Fiorenza I shall first consider the theological principles. Here are some key comments: 'For me, the most important school of justice I know is the biblical tradition' (xv). At another point she says: 'I have experienced truly profound blessedness in women's and peace liturgies, when the word of the Bible has begun to speak even before we have to interpret it. It has given us the blessing of experiencing our community and of discerning clear goals precisely because the injustice has been named. The word of God has transformed people frozen with fear into energetic, attentive and impatient sisters and brothers' (xv-xvi).

The scholarly ideal of biblical study is dismissed with the following sentences: 'The implicit or explicit claim of Western biblical scholarship to being objective, neutral, and scientific requires unambiguous rebuttal' (57). So in reading Schottroff one gets the same impression as one does on reading Schüssler Fiorenza: goodbye and good riddance to scholarship. For really there are no longer any scholarly truths. However, I shall not discuss this epistemological question here. In the following report I want to measure Schottroff by her own claim, test her results in the light of the critical consensus on the history of primitive Christianity, and examine whether her analyses result in a fertile development of the knowledge available.

First of all, though, in fairness, I should quote from a recent review: 'Luise Schottroff's book represents a milestone on the course of German-speaking feminist-liberation theological social history which in the uncompromising definition of its standpoint and polemic will above all appeal to those women and men who feel an obligation to the paradigm of liberation theology.'[116]

Schottroff's book consists of four main parts: I. Feminist Social History: Historical Method and Hermeneutics (1–65); II. The Everyday Life of Women (67–118); III. The Critique of Patriarchy and the Power to Become a New Being (119–73); IV. Liberating Praxis of Women and Men (175–223).

Now Parts II-IV consist essentially of textual exegesis followed by hermeneutical reflections along the lines of feminist theology. In other words, here we do not have history in the proper sense but reflections of a theological nature based on texts from the Bible. Especially at this point Schottroff's focus on the 'word of God' becomes visible. All her exegeses of specific texts contain valuable observations which point us further, but they are hardly usable for the history of primitive Christianity in the narrower sense. Here criticism of the patriarchate is one exception; like that of Schüssler Fiorenza, in individual cases it offers new insights into early Christianity and rightly puts its finger on the fact that the role of women in early Christianity has long been obscured by scholarship. Moreover the two scholars are agreed (a) that there were women followers of Jesus and (b) that women were the first witnesses to the resurrection of Jesus.[117] I shall not go into this further in my report on Schottroff but return to it in my overall assessment.

Particularly important in Part I is Schottroff's fundamental criticism of leading concepts that have influenced research so far into primitive Christianity. The concept of Gentile Christianity which has dominated the historiography of primitive Christianity over the centuries (30) contains not only an *androcentric* but also a *Eurocentric* prejudice: 'The notion of "Gentile Christianity free from the law" is *androcentric* because the central issue is said to be the circumcision of men ... (T)he notion of Gentile Christianity is *Eurocentric* ... the idea of a European church is introduced into the book of Acts ...' (13).

Schottroff therefore prefers to speak of messianic communities in the Jewish Diaspora. Until far into the second century she sees Christianity as one messianic movement alongside others within Judaism, since in her view a 'church of the nations free of the law is an anti-Judaistic, Eurocentric construction that is hostile to women. Such a construct is foreign to the New Testament' (14).

There is also much that is right in this aggressive statement: (a) In fact the term Europe, if it appears in works at all,[118] should be used circumspectly, since it does not occur in the ancient texts. (b) The term 'freedom from the law' has its problems, as the Gentile Christians adopted the Jewish law in a reduced way and no longer understood the problem of the law in the Pauline sense. But what expression should take its place? (c) At the same time, for the sake of the texts the term 'Gentile Christianity' must be retained.[119] For from the beginning of the second century most Christians were born Gentiles or had grown up in a Gentile Christian family. Such a church could no longer define itself as a messianic group. And this insight overturns her entire construction of messianic communities far into the second century. The 'messianic' community of the Ebionites, which regarded itself as the successor of the Jerusalem church, was declared heretical by the Gentile Christian great church (cf. Irenaeus, *Haer.* I, 26 2).

Schottroff's analyses of the patriarchate in connection with Cicero's *De republica*, e.g. I 54; I 64; III 37, and *De officiis*, e.g. I 54, II 73 (22–9), are particularly valuable and more profound than those of Schüssler Fiorenza. But learned excursuses on ancient legal and social history, and reflections on the development of new concepts in research into primitive Christianity are only one side of Schottroff's remarks. She also reflects on a political fight (cf.18, etc.), but that is not relevant to this discussion.

Given its approach, this book is not a feminist social history of early Christianity but more a collection of sermons, orientated on conflict, on the oppression of the poor and women in the first and twentieth centuries with many learned excursuses on the religious and social history of antiquity.

I shall now take stock and assess the actual historical yield of the feminist works by E. Schüssler Fiorenza and L. Schottroff on the history of primitive Christianity – and only on this topic.

(a) The involvement of women in the Jesus event. There is only one text which speaks directly of women as part of Jesus' following, Mark 15.40. The parallels to this, Matt. 27.55f. and Luke 23.49, along with Luke 8.2, are revisions of the Markan original and are not additional information about the Jesus movement itself. In other words, the textual basis for the main thesis of the two scholars is extremely narrow.

On Mark 15.40f.: the mode of expression of Mark 15.41 recalls the image of women serving Jesus at table. In keeping with Mark 1.13, 31, Mark 15.41 must therefore be understood to refer to actions involving personal care and atttention.[120]

(b) Women as the first witnesses of the resurrection. Schüssler Fiorenza and Schottroff vehemently defend this thesis;[121] in fact they both depend on its consequences for the assessment of the role of women in the Jesus movement, since if the statement were affirmed, women would certainly have had an important role in the activity of Jesus. But on this point, too, the texts speak another language. Paul knows no women as witnesses of the resurrection, and from the point of view of the history of tradition John 20 is a very late text, and the vision on the way in Matt. 28.9f. likewise has only a secondary character. The tradition of the empty tomb and that of the appearances were originally separate and coalesced only in the subsequent history of the tradition. Only in the course of this convergence did traditions about appearances to women come into being. They are thus clearly of later date and therefore cannot be used for the thesis that the first testimony to the resurrection came from women.[122]

At this point it seems to me that further analyses of the role of the woman in ancient Judaism and Hellenism in the first century are urgently necessary, since only on this basis can we expect results which take us further in reconstructing the role of women with Jesus and in primitive Christianity. This lack must be stated explicitly, as the existing works have still not produced a consensus.[123] Thus for example the 1990 monograph by Léonie J. Archer, *Her Price is Beyond Rubies. The Jewish Woman in Graeco-Roman Palestine* (a revised and expanded version of her 1983 University of London dissertation), is inadequate. It simply collects all the evidence on the status of women from the Mishnah and the Talmuds, the extra-canonical Jewish writings, the Qumran writings, the writings of Josephus, Philo and Eusebius, and the Muraba'at documents (291–300). The result is a collection similar to that which had already been made by Paul Billerbeck in his Commentary on the New Testament from the Talmud and Midrash.

Ch. 1 (17–122) discusses a girl's early years up to her twelfth birthday; Ch. 2 (123–206) marriage, Ch. 3 (207–50) a woman's married life, and Ch. 4

(251–90) death. In this book we hear nothing of the beginnings of a possible equal status of the woman in the first century, because even the abundant Talmudic sources are read with the eyes of a Ben Sira or the author of the Testaments of the Twelve Patriarchs. Things must not have been as gloomy as Joachim Jeremias still thought, [124] but how far were there really 'equal rights' for women in first-century Palestine? Is for example the book of Judith representative? Such matters still need research, and more emphasis on local history may well be necessary.

5

A Survey and Critique of Recent Studies in the Environment of Primitive Christianity

The textbook by Everett Ferguson, *Backgrounds of Early Christianity* (1987, [2]1993; page nos are given for both editions), is attractive. It is learned, easy to understand, and is skilfully arranged for use in teaching. Chapter 1 deals with the political history (1–36/[2]5–44), Chapter 2 with society and culture (36–110/[2]45–136), Chapter 3 with Hellenistic-Roman religions (111–253/[2]137–298), Chapter 4 with Hellenistic-Roman philosophies (254–314/[2]299–371), Chapter 5 with Judaism (315–463/[2]373–546) and Chapter 6 with 'Christianity in the Ancient World' (464–96/[2]547–583).

Ferguson is a pupil of A. D. Nock, whose influence permeates the book. The aim of the book is an analytical and systematic introduction to the Roman, Greek and Jewish political, social, literary and religious world, a necessary basis for a historical understanding of the New Testament and the early church. Granted, it is addressed mainly to beginners who have little or no knowledge of the classical and Hellenistic period and post-biblical Judaism, but it is far more than a primer. Even advanced readers will learn from this book, especially when they see from the work that Ferguson has himself visited, explored and – as the countless photographs indicate – photographed the places that he describes. The standpoint is moderately conservative and in some respects recalls Frend's work (see above, p. 43). Ferguson also resembles Frend in his deficient understanding of Walter Bauer's thesis. For example he accuses Bauer of understanding orthodoxy in narrow institutional terms and of having 'minimized the evidence of "orthodoxy" in the apostolic fathers of the early second century' (489/^{2}575), but he does grant that the North American followers of Bauer, Robinson and Koester, have 'performed a useful service in reminding us of the considerable diversity of early Christianity and that the early history of the church was not a straight line development doctrinally or organizationally' (490/^{2}575). Accordingly, a concern with the problems raised by Bauer is not the strongest aspect of Ferguson's book.[125] But on the whole it is reliable, and indexes of subjects (497–510/^{2}585–605) and references (511–15/^{2}606–11) make it easy to use. The bibliographies enable one to read further and are current with the latest scholarship (the second edition of 1993 adds the most important literature published after the first edition), as are the remarks on the topics of the book mentioned above.

Hans-Josef Klauck has described *The Religious Context of Earliest Christianity* (2000) in order, as the subtitle indicates, to provide *A Guide to Graeco-Roman Religions*. The table of contents (vii-xi) gives a survey of the book (I. Daily Life and Liminal Experiences: Civic and Domestic Religion; II. The Fascination of the Mysterious: The Mystery Cults; III. Popular Belief: A Panorama – Astrology, Soothsaying; Miracles, Magic; IV. Divinized Human Beings: The Cult of Rulers and Emperors; V. In Search of Happiness: Philosophy and Religion; VI. In Search of the Divine Origin: The Gnostic Transformation) so that a detailed report is unnecessary. Klauck's 'account concentrates on the Graeco-Roman sphere; it does not deal with Judaism with which Christianity has a quite different (because much closer) relationship' (xiii). Yet I would hasten to ask: Does not ancient Judaism represent a specific aspect of the Graeco-Roman world? The selection of specific areas 'is guided to a certain extent by external considerations: in the light of the New Testament, with a view to a better understanding of its texts' (10).

This New Testament perspective is expressed, for example, in the cross- references to the New Testament (9f., 53, 80, 85, 104, 127, 151f., 167f., etc.; see also the 'Index of selected biblical texts', 505). The whole work can be regarded as a significant contribution to the knowledge of religions in the environment of primitive Christianity. It is completely up-to-date with current research.[126] Klauck is also to be praised for offering a chapter of more than 70 pages on ancient Gnosticism (429–503) that has become a Cinderella of New Testament research. This essay is current with the most recent state of research, and offers a useful non-technical introduction to the Nag Hammadi texts discovered in 1945 (443–8, with a survey of the extant writings, 446f.). Klauck had earlier announced this major chapter in the following words:

> There may be disagreement about whether this belongs together with these other topics; but gnosis turns up with regularity in exegesis as a somewhat nebulous matter, and it has at some periods been an essential determinant of the debate about the history of religions. Thus the intended readers of this book ought certainly to be interested in knowing whether or not a gnosis existed before and outside Christianity (11).

In this connection I would like to stress that, contrary to Klauck, the figure of Simon Magus from Acts 8 should be regarded as an indication of a Gnosticism that was at least contemporaneous with the first Christians. Klauck, however, feels certain that '(t)he Church fathers and the gnostics themselves searched in the New Testament for a possible head of the school of the gnostic movement, identified Simon Magus as their candidate and attributed this significance to him' (450). But later only Simonians referred to Simon Magus as the head of their school (cf. the 'Great Proclamation' in Hippolytus, *Ref.* VI, 9–18), while other Gnostics did not. Moreover, it is likely that the author of Acts has inserted a reference to the consort of Simon Magus, Ennoia or Epinoia, in the expression *epinoia tes kardias*, Acts 8.22. *Epinoia* is a hapax legomenon in the New Testament and a technical term for the feminine *syzygos* in Simonian gnosis as we know it from the second-century sources. The use of *epinoia* at this point in Acts finds an explanation in the assumption that Luke is referring ironically to Simon's female *syzygos,* the embodiment of Simon's confusion and the root of his heresy.[127] In the story in Acts, Luke disparages the *epinoia* as material aspiration. Simon wants to buy the Holy Spirit in order to be able to go into the business of dispensing the Spirit for profit and this aspiration is attributed by Peter to Simon's *epinoia tes kardias.*

In distinction to Klauck's view that the oldest literary evidence for the gnosticism of the Simonians is from Irenaeus (*Haer.* I, 23) (449f.), it must be stressed that Justin Martyr already presupposes gnostic teachings of 'Simon' a generation earlier.[128] In his *I Apology* (26.3), written around 155 CE, Justin mentions the following tenets of Simon's followers: 1. Simon is the first god, and 2. Helen who travelled around with Simon and had previously dwelt in a brothel is the first thought (*prote ennoia*) generated by Simon. The whole Simonian myth of creation, fall and redemption seems to be contained in what Justin is relating. For the first thought of the first god had in all likelihood generated the universe, and, having been degraded, had to be rescued by the highest god. Indeed, such a myth meets the definition of gnosticism agreed upon by the Messina Conference.[129] It contains the idea of the divine consubstantiality of the spark in man that is in need of being reawakened and reintegrated, i.e., consubstantiality between the *salvandum* (*ennoia/epinoia*) and the *salvator* (Simon). The periphery of the divine, the *epinoia,* enters into a crisis and can be saved only through an intervention by the god Simon.

The Simonian myth briefly reported by Justin is certainly earlier. For in the 'Exegesis of the Soul' (NHC II, 6)[130] there is a similar myth of the fallen soul. Here the soul assumes the role of Helen and shares her fate. Thus the text depicts the way of the fallen soul, which has forsaken her true bridegroom and in the world is exposed to prostitution. After the soul has recognized her unfortunate situation and repents of her actions, the heavenly bridegroom comes to her and takes to himself the soul which has now been adorned and purified. This union of bridegroom and bride represents the redemption of the soul: 'And so this marriage is made perfect according to the will of the Father ... *This is* the resurrection from the dead. *This is* the salvation from captivity. *This is* the ascent to heaven. *This is* the way up to the Father' (134.5–17).[131] In other words, precisely at this decisive point further reflections are necessary on the history of the tradition and chronology which – briefly put – in all likelihood make the Simonian religion a candidate for a full-blown gnosticism in the first century CE.[132]

> In 1987 Klaus Berger and Carsten Colpe produced a history-of-religions textbook on the New Testament, which later appeared in English as *Hellenistic Commentary to the New Testament.* 'The selection of texts contained in this book has been made from the point of view of the history of religions understood rather narrowly, with the emphasis on the *religious* dimension of this phrase. The texts are thus presented in the order of the New Testament writings' (7/18).[133]

By way of introduction, Part A remarks on the theological significance of work on the history of religion: 'History-of-religions comparison is not the whole of exegesis, but it is a necessary, indispensable part, for such comparison lifts the biblical text out of its isolation and relates it to non-canonical texts from its environment' (11/19). The history-of-religions comparison does not set out apologetically to demonstrate the absoluteness and uniqueness of Christianity (cf.12/20). Moreover the authors point out that history-of-religions comparison 'is not guided by the intention of destroying the "historicity" of reported events; that is not at all possible, since exegesis can prove nothing either positive or negative about whether an event reported in the Bible happened as it is described. In reality, the task and purpose of this comparison is not destructive, but historical, since it seeks to apprehend the location of a statement within the stream of history' (13/21).

Here at the same time, however, we must be critical and ask whether the historical question must not be a legitimate element of exegesis, at least since modern times, all the more so since Luke himself insists on the historical reliability of his narrative (cf. Luke 1.1–4). Of course the exegete has to deny the historicity of the virgin birth etc., as well as that of most sayings and actions that were ascribed to Jesus after his death.[134]

> In their selection the editors distinguish between group A, categories which comprise contrast and differentiation (in which they include metamorphosis, adoption with the contrary tendency, intentional contrast, implicit antithesis, etc.), and group B, categories which emphasize similarity (these include reference, convergence, witnesses for a common basis, borrowing, imitation, etc.) (18–26/23–32). Presumably no normal reader will understand this difficult definition of the selection of the material, which goes into great detail; it seems to me to be a hobby of the German authors, who elsewhere as well show a predilection for over-subtle differentiations. In other words, in a textbook on the New Testament which is intended for a wider range of readers – the German original appeared within the Das Neue Testament Deutsch series – these categories will produce misunderstanding; moreover, it could easily be demonstrated in detail that they are superfluous. One could have wished for briefer and more comprehensible explanations. And while the editors are right to have dropped the long overworked category of literary dependence, and with it talk of influence, it is a different matter to introduce these 25 different concepts and only then begin with the text.

The translated parallels, which are offered throughout the New Testament, are usually accompanied by brief but learned commentaries, and references to further literature. Sometimes mutually exclusive views of Berger and Colpe are mentioned (see, e.g., 190f./492 on the question of an interpolation in 1 Thess. 2.15). The whole is intended as a contribution to a better understanding of the New Testament.

> I am disappointed at the extremely scant attention paid to the texts from the epoch-making discovery at Nag Hammadi, particularly since Colpe took part in their interpretation and made sound contributions to the *Jahrbuch für Antike und Christentum* (1972–82). Only a handful of passages refer to the Nag Hammadi documents, and not always is it indicated that the reference is indeed to a Nag Hammadi texts. For example, at Gal. 3.28 a parallel to the Tripartite Tractate (NHC 1) is cited (277f./471). Heb. 7.1–28 prompts a reference to 'Melchizedek' (NHC IX 1) (303f./519f.). However, the Apocalypse of Adam (NHC V, 5), which is referred to in connection with Rev.12.1–18 (324/572), is not indicated as a Nag Hammadi writing at all. It is cited only as the 'Coptic Apocalypse of Adam'. Nor can one be indifferent to the failure to note parallels to New Testament texts like 2 Tim. 2.18 ('the resurrection has already taken place'). Here the Letter to Rheginos (NHC I, 4) should certainly have been cited.

The 1995 English translation of Berger and Colpe's work by M. Eugene Boring increases the number of parallels by about a third and provides a very useful index.

A comparison of the numbers of the parallels in the first German edition with the English translation appears on 590–3, a bibliography on 594–601, an index of ancient authors on 602–13, a subject index on 613–19 and an index of biblical references on 620–33. Here some Nag Hammadi texts appear on 609–10, along with other writings under the heading 'New Testament Apocrypha and Other Early Christian Literature'. In 658, based on Berger and Colpe, we find in connection with Rev. 12.1–18, 'Coptic Apocalypse of Adam 78–79 (second century AD)'. However, the English translation has the abbreviation NHL in brackets, which indicates that the standard translation of the Nag Hammadi texts edited by J. M. Robinson has been used.

It is a pity that the Nag Hammadi Library, first translated by American scholars, has not been taken into greater account in the American edition of Berger and Colpe's book. Evidently even in the country of the origin of the first complete modern translation of the Nag Hammadi texts, specialists in New Testament and patristics work in separate compartments. It would have been simple to consult Craig A. Adams, Robert L. Webb and Richard A. Wiebe, *Nag Hammadi Texts and the Bible. A Synopsis and Index*, NTTS 18, 1993, to note the corresponding allusions to the Nag Hammadi texts there and to add the most important ones to the revision of Berger/ Colpe. I regard as a particularly blatant omission the failure to note 'The Trimorphic Protennoia' (NHC XIII, 1), which offers new comparative material for the origin of the prologue of John.

So the overall verdict on the *Hellenistic Commentary to the New Testament* cannot be an exclusively positive one.

Alan E. Bernstein's *The Formation of Hell* (1993) may be read as a contribution to our understanding of the environment of the New Testament and early Christianity. Its subtitle is 'Death and Retribution in the Ancient and Early Christian Worlds'. For centuries the idea of hell, identified with separation from God and torment by fire, worms and darkness, was a central image in Western culture. In this work Bernstein investigates how and why this belief in hell arose.

In Part I (19–130) Bernstein discusses the underworld as pictured by the peoples of Greece and Rome. In this chapter the section on the spirits of the dead (93–106) is particularly striking; it is developed sensitively, and perhaps is of greater significance for the New Testament than is generally recognized. Part II deals with life after death in ancient Judaism (131–202);

here we find discussions of the spirits of the dead (133–53), the separation of the dead (154–77) and eternal punishment (178–202). Part III deals with hell in the New Testament (203–66), and Part IV with tensions in early Christianity (267–334).

As Bernstein himself says in the preface (x), he has investigated every existing text from the periods mentioned dealing with the question of the fate of the dead. His method is to sketch the content of the texts and to compare them with the text discussed previously. Thus, for example, in connection with early Christianity he shows how the punishments after death have become harsher because inner sanctions were more necessary. So between 1 Thessalonians and Revelation the church used hell as means of retribution for both internal deviants or external opponents. These statements, which are explicitly labelled as hypotheses (210), are untenable in this form. For 1 Thessalonians already speaks explicitly of judgement (1.10), and this is also to be included in the scenario of 1 Thess. 4.13–17. As these hypothetical reflections (cf. also 201ff. on the eternal judgement in Judaism) are constantly interspersed but not central to the formation of a theory, they can be left aside. Still, all in all, Bernstein has produced an impressive work. Because of its abundant indexes (343–92) it is also a good tool for illuminating the history-of-religions background of the New Testament and understanding the New Testament documents better.

Prophecy and Inspired Speech in Early Christianity and its Hellenistic Environment (1995), by Christopher Forbes, is related to the present subject only to the degree that it makes a contribution to understanding primitive Christianity in the light of the history of religions. Forbes examines the thesis that the Corinthians advocated an inspired way of speaking deriving from pre-Christian times, with which Paul was in conflict. This thesis is defended in current scholarship generally on the basis of 1 Cor. 12–14 and parallels in the history of religion. Forbes regards this view as incorrect, and to refute it investigates the Hellenistic parallels generally adduced along with the corresponding passages from the New Testament.

Several problems must be noted, however. 1. Few if any modern commentators advance the thesis of the direct adoption of speaking with tongues from the pre-Christian period in Corinth, as Forbes claims. Rather, he has constructed for his own benefit an enemy which he can then attack – and all the more furiously because of his inaccurate description. 2. Forbes does not take into account the basic literature on the nature of prophecy, from Heinrici's commentaries on the Corinthian letters, through Johannes Weiss's great commentary in the Meyer Commentary series, to Hermann Gunkel's pioneering 1888 work on the Spirit and its continuation by Heinrich Weinel in 1899. Dieter Georgi's work on Paul's opponents in 2 Corinthians also has detailed remarks on prophets in the New Testament environment and certainly should have been taken into account.[135] 3. Forbes overlooks the fact that Paul clearly urges the Thessalonians to speak in tongues ('do not quench the Spirit', 1 Thess. 4.19), and thus also the Corinthians (1 Thessalonians was composed during the preaching at Corinth by which Paul founded the community), so that in the light of these insights the whole problem of speaking with tongues should be investigated once again.[136] Forbes engages in rash exegesis when for example he asserts that 'in other tongues' (Acts 2.4) is older than 'speaking in tongues' (1 Cor.14). After all, he knows from the redaction-critical investigation of Luke-Acts that by adding 'other' in Acts 2.4 Luke interprets speaking in tongues as speaking in foreign languages. Therefore it is incomprehensible that he can conflate 1 Cor. 14 and Acts 2.

For these reasons, despite its diligence (particularly in its account of Hellenistic inspiration and enthusiastic religion, chs 5–7) I cannot regard this work as one which advances the study of primitive Christian religion.

By contrast, the first volume of collected articles by Hans Dieter Betz, which was published in 1990 under the title *Hellenismus und Urchristentum* ('Hellenism and Primitive Christianity'), is enjoyable and always instructive. Betz sees early Christianity as one of many religious groups in Hellenism, and each of the articles is devoted to one of these individual groups.

Their coverage extends from 'Lucian of Samosata and Christianity' (10–21) and 'Creation and Redemption in the Hermetic Fragment Kore Kosmou' (22–51) to the topic of 'Magic and Mystery in the Greek Magical Papyri' (209–29) and 'The Problem of the Resurrection of Jesus in the Light of the Greek Magical Papyri' (230–61, previously unpublished). An introduction written for this volume (1–9) defines the original context of these articles on the environment of primitive Christianity, which are now once again accessible. Some of the articles have additions which list the new literature on the topic concerned. Finally, here is a quotation which deserves unqualified assent:

> Every theologian today must be clear ... that the understanding of primitive Christianity and its classical work, the New Testament, is dependent on a knowledge of the history of religion in antiquity in the broader sense. Scholarly understanding always touches on the comparison of phenomena and problems. Moreover the New Testament must first of all be seen in the framework of the political and social, cultural and religious world of antiquity. Without this presupposition, the writings of the New Testament would be inconceivable. Only if this reintegration into the ancient world has taken place can there be a pertinent further interpretation of the texts (9).

Several major works with a history-of-religions orientation have recently been published on the christology of primitive Christianity. I begin with the Munich Habilitationsschrift of Hermann von Lips, *Weisheitliche Traditionen im Neuen Testament* ('Wisdom Traditions in the New Testament').

The work is in two parts. Part 1 discusses 'Understanding, Themes and Traditions of Wisdom in the Old Testament and Early Judaism' (11–192), and Part 2, which is even longer, is entitled 'Wisdom Traditions in the New Testament' (193–452).

In the first part, Lips essentially reports the consensus of scholars on the Old Testament and Judaism. It surprised me that the action-outcome connection is not regarded as specific to wisdom but 'is rather simply presupposed as common sense in Israel as in antiquity generally' (96). But we may leave that aside. What is notable is Lips's attempt to make a precise division between the hypostatization and the personification of wisdom, and between a poetic and linguistic identification of wisdom as a human characteristic and an identification focusing on the mythical aspect of wisdom as a property of God (153–66). Lips deals only peripherally with the idea of the development of wisdom into gnosis, a topic which has occasionally been addressed in recent research, and rejects it (cf. 114–17). It is here that my criticism of the mammoth text would begin: the body of the text amounts to 470 pages, much of which is printed in very small type, but it fails to analyse any texts from the New Testament environment (cf. also the index of references, 499ff.).

> Surely a Nag Hammadi text like 'The Gospel of Thomas' (NHC II, 2) is worth noting, as are wisdom writings like 'The Teachings of Silvanus' (NHC VII, 4) (note the hidden reference to it on 115 n. 340), 'The Trimorphic Protennoia' (NHC XIII, 1), 'Bronte' (NHC VI, 2), etc. It seems to me that the very business of studying the New Testament exclusively against the background of the Old Testament and early Judaism is based on a mistaken presupposition. In addition Lips investigates the New Testament on a canonical basis, instead of relating it to primitive Christianity. Moreover it is quite amazing that in the discussion of 1 Cor. 1–2 (318–49), while works on the Gnostic background to 1 Cor. 1–2 are mentioned in the bibliography, at no point is a single Gnostic text cited which contains the antithesis Paul declares between the spiritual and psychical person (cf. simply 'The Hypostasis of the Archons' [NHC II, 4]).[137]

The book makes a divided impression. New Testament examples are carefully discussed and weighed once again, though the substance of the results seldom goes beyond what has been said previously, and granted, comprehensive notice is taken of the secondary literature. But the work as a whole does not open up any new perspectives. So beyond doubt it remains a helpful reference book to what has been said by scholars about the wisdom texts in the New Testament, the Old Testament, and early Judaism; but all in all it is not much more than a collection of existing material, and incomplete at that, because of the absence of Gnostic material.

The Heidelberg dissertation by Manuel Vogel, *Das Heil des Bundes* ('The Salvation of the Covenant', 1996), undertakes an overall description of post-biblical covenant theology on the basis of Jewish and Christian literature up to the beginning of the second century. Its aim is to provide an evaluation of the phenomenon of 'post-biblical covenant theology' in the history of theology (cf. 351).

Part I discusses the topic of 'Covenant as a Sociological Category' (33–106), Part II 'The History of Israel and the Election of the People of God' (107–62), Part III 'Salvation as Fellowship with God' (164–222), and Part IV 'Covenant as the Basic Concept of Jewish Identity' (223–359). The categories 'soteriology', 'history', 'salvation as fellowship' and 'identity' which underlie the four main parts here serve to define different perspectives on one and the same subject.

Vogel's presupposition is that early Jewish and primitive Christian forms of literature are to be understood as a unity. The reason he gives is that 'in respect of the reception of the concept of the covenant in Christian texts, the movement from Judaism to Christianity as a transition to another system of religion shows itself to be a fiction' (30).

Since occurrences of the term 'covenant' are infrequent in the New Testament, however, Vogel hardly does justice to the phenomenon of primitive Christianity. (In many cases, moreover, the term 'covenant' appears only in quotations.) And historically one cannot understand the imminent separation of Judaism and Christianity in this way.

Mary E. Mills, in *Human Agents of Cosmic Power in Hellenistic Judaism and the Synoptic Tradition*, 1990, discusses the period from the second century BCE to the second century CE in connection with the traditions of miracle workers, exorcists and wise men, as these also appear in Hellenistic Judaism and the Synoptic tradition. These traditions are read against the background of a cosmic myth. As the foreword indicates, the study 'is an investigation into the history of ideas, tracing the variety of belief concerning cosmic structures and the value given to prominent human figures, rather than a purely form-based survey of the relevant texts' (7). Mills investigates the background of Hellenistic culture with special reference to the understanding of magic and myth in antiquity.

The greater part of the study is concerned with particular texts from the literary traditions on Moses (37–48), Solomon (49–61), Enoch (63–77), Tobit (79–92) and Jesus according to Mark (93–108). Mills writes that her interest in the sphere of magic and religion was aroused by Harnack's *Mission and Expansion of Christianity* (7). However, the purpose of her work has not really become clear to me. It is full of odd things, as for example when in Ch. 7 ('Jesus according to Mark', 93–108, see esp.153 n. 2) and in the bibliography (158–78) she seems to believe that Wrede wrote his book on the messianic secret in 1971, or when Emil Schürer (who is merely mentioned once, along with Geza Vermes, 178) is not quoted in the work.

Mills has also overlooked such important literature as M. Black's commentary on 1 Enoch and that of H. W. Holländer and M. de Jonge on the

Testaments of the Twelve Patriarchs (both appeared in 1985). The 1896 edition of the text of 'The Sword of Moses' (M. Gaster) has been superseded by Peter Schäfer's 1981 'Synopsis of the Hekhalot Literature'. Acts 8 does not say that Simon Magus had 'that power of God which is called Great' (118), but that he *is* the power of God. In connection with Moses as an agent of a cosmic power, reference should be made to Moses' throne vision in 'Ezekiel the Tragedian' (68–82), which is not even mentioned.

Pieter W. van der Horst, *Essays on the Jewish World of Early Christianity*, 1990, is extremely important for the New Testament environment because of its treatment of Judaism. The book contains fourteen of Horst's essays from between 1978 and 1990, all of which are devoted to 'less known aspects of Judaism in the Hellenistic and Roman periods (*c.* 300 BCE to 500 CE)' (9).

Special attention is paid to the writing Pseudo-Phocylides (19–62), which shows important parallels to the paraenetic portions of the New Testament and has received increased attention in the last decade. One important article is on the Testament of Job ('The Role of Women in the Testament of Job' [94–110]); it investigates the role of women in the Diaspora. Horst argues that TestJob 46–53 is evidence that Jewish women in the Diaspora had many of the same rights as men. Other articles deal with Hellenistic Jewish literature (including the historians and ethicists). To my mind the high point is the first translation into a modern language of the earliest Shiur-Qomah manuscript (British Library ms. 10675), which probably comes from the tenth century ('The Measurement of the Body. A Chapter in the History of Ancient Jewish Mysticism', 123–35). The SQ texts are contained in 34 manuscripts from different times and in different places. All in all they represent seven recensions, all of which go back to a lost original text. The author rightly sees parallels in the description of the body of God in the Elkasaite writing from the beginning of the second century (124). Although the names of the members of God are completely absent from the Book of Elkesai, the parallels are nevertheless extremely interesting.[138] Still Horst decides on the early post-Talmudic period as the date of the composition of this writing.

These reprinted articles by Horst are admirably suited to bringing out hidden Jewish parallels to primitive Christianity. His contributions are all the more welcome because he brings to light mystical, magical and half-lost Jewish sources.

Larry W. Hurtado's book *One God, One Lord* (1988) deals knowledgeably with early Christian piety and ancient Jewish monotheism. Hurtado derives the idea of Christ's divinity from Jewish sources, and shows that early Christians made use of Jewish concepts of an angelic helper in order to express the dignity of Jesus. In opposition to Philo and other Jewish contemporaries who also knew divine mediator figures, he argues that the early Christians worshipped or prayed to their mediator figure. This explains the ultimate break with Judaism. In other words, for Hurtado the source of the conflict between the primitive Christians and the non-Christian Jews was not the divinity of Jesus but the question whether one might pray to him. Early Christian piety is to be designated binitarian (114). It is notably different from the broad Jewish monotheistic tradition.

Even if Hurtado may have underestimated angel piety in Judaism,[139] his book has the advantage of having offered a clear reason for the separation of Jews and Christians, and one which is worth discussing,

The collection of articles by the Jewish scholar Daniel R. Schwartz, *Studies in the Jewish Background of Christianity*, 1992, is an important contribution. It makes available in English translation eleven articles published in Hebrew between 1980 and 1989 and five previously unpublished works. All the articles have been revised and brought up to date by references to more recent literature. They are prefaced by a previously unpublished lecture, 'Introduction: On the Jewish Background of Christianity' (1–26), which is of interest for research into primitive Christianity, and which deserves particular attention in the present context. From the outset Schwartz emphasizes that any investigation into a religion has its limits. There may be data of religious importance that the historian must leave untouched. (Yet this seems to be unwarranted in cases of divine intervention that are associated with *historical* claims, see below, pp. 176f.) Christianity is established on such a datum, the resurrection of Jesus. Without it the movement would never have begun, but it is not accessible to historical verification. The correctness of religious perceptions needs no proof, as numerous martyrs attest (2f.). Schwartz continues:

In other words, the historian of the Jewish background of Christianity can hope to explain only how the Jewish world in which Christianity arose allowed for or encouraged that to occur. He cannot attempt to explain the most significant specific events which, according to Christian belief, set the new religion on its way, and he cannot, given the sources, hope to say anything very specific about Jesus (3).

According to Schwartz, both Hellenistic Diaspora Judaism and the Qumran community (which was likewise influenced by Hellenism) helped prepare the way for Christianity by their spiritualization of the Torah. He argues that Paul was a Hellenistic Jew (3f.) and John the Baptist heir to the spiritualized Torah rigorism of Qumran (cf. 24). Both in fact detached themselves from the people, the land, the temple and thus from the law in their persons. For his followers Jesus bridged the inner conflict between spiritualizing and relativizing the law on the one hand and a perfectionist demand for obedience on the other (24f.). Before his call, Paul's human weakness brought him grief over the demand for obedience to the Torah (25f.) – a remarkable return to a psychological interpretation of the conversion of Paul which one thought had been superseded.

> The other individual studies cannot be evaluated here. They contain important contributions on the Pharisees (44–80), Christian research into the Zealots (128–46), and on Josephus and questions of the chronology of Judaea (155–282: e.g. the accession to office of Felix: 49, Festus: 56; accordingly Paul must have stood before Felix in 54 [Acts 24.27]). All the contributions make a highly specialized contribution to the environment of primitive Christianity and stand out for the thorough way in which they grapple with the history of research.

The collection of articles by Peder Borgen, *Early Christianity and Hellenistic Judaism,* 1996, arose out of an interest to understand better the relationship between early Christianity and Judaism and the interaction between the two and the wider Graeco-Roman world. Nevertheless, the title of the volume is somewhat misleading, since Hellenistic Judaism does not play a central role in all the contributions.

An introduction sums up the individual contributions and makes the overall perspectives clear. Borgen explicitly abandons the distinction between Palestinian and Hellenistic Judaism and instead prefers to speak of a complexity of Judaism inside and outside Palestine (cf. 2). In my view it would be better to differentiate between 'Hellenistic Judaism' (outside Palestine) and 'Hellenized Judaism' (in Palestine). Otherwise the real differences are too easily blurred and everything becomes too sketchy.

> The characteristics of such a broad-brush way of working emerge in the previously unpublished article 'Autobiographical Ascent Reports: Philo and John the Seer' (309–20); Borgen thinks that Philo went into heaven (*Spec leg* 3, 1–3) just as the seer John did (Rev. 1.1, etc.). But the visionary and auditory experiences of John in a difficult political situation have a different character from the world of experience of an Alexandrian scholar, all the more so since Philo's hovering in heavenly regions is to be seen more as a metaphor for devoted self-immersion, and Philo does not in fact speak of an ascent into heaven. The other article, 'Militant and Peaceful Proselytism and Christian Mission' (45–69), adopts a similar broad-brush approach to the material. Thus in collecting evidence for mission in the Jewish and/or Christian perspective, Borgen indiscriminately uses literary fictions (Judith, Esther), accounts of coercive actions (Josephus) and eschatological fantasies of rule (Philo, Paul).
>
> In the introductory article on the participation of Jews and Christians in pagan cults (15–43) Borgen enriches the discussion of the incident at Antioch with the suggestion that the emissaries of James merely insisted that Gentile Christians and Jewish Christians eat at different tables in the same room (cf. 28). But would that explain Paul's sharp reaction?
>
> The various articles on the Gospel of John (103–229) can be skipped over; here, in a critical discussion of F. Neirynck, Borgen attempts to demonstrate the independence of the Gospel of John from the Synoptics.

All in all, this collection of articles by Borgen leaves one with mixed feelings. It contains interesting ideas, but on close inspection they often produce an improbable picture.

In 1995 Peder Borgen edited a collection of articles on *The New Testament and Hellenistic Judaism* (1995) with Soren Giversen. It stems from a conference at the theological faculty of the University of Aarhus in 1992. In the introduction (9–13) Borgen sums up the content of the fourteen contributions. However, apart from the fact that the authors compare New Testament writings with Hellenistic Judaism, no inner

logic is evident. I shall single out the most important contributions, which are in English unless otherwise indicated.

S. Giversen deals with the letter of Barnabas ('The Covenant – theirs or
ours?', 14–18); L. Hartman ('Guiding the Knowing of your Hearts', 19–36)
traces the content of 2 Tim. 3.16 through Jewish texts. Nikolaus Walter's
contribution in German on 'Hellenistic Diaspora Jews at the Cradle of
Primitive Christianity' (37–58)[140] is attractive for its programmatic breadth
and its important observations; it emphasizes that the term 'Hellenistic
Judaism' should always be used for the Judaism of Alexandria.[141] He again
rightly emphasizes that 'an intensive and active Hellenistic schooling was
available to Alexandrian Jews not first in the time of Philo but already 200
years earlier' (44). As a representative of Jewish Hellenism, Philo 'is by no
means isolated; rather he has a long pre-history of efforts at Hellenistic
education in the Judaism of Alexandria' (46).

On Jerusalem Walter well observes: 'So if in general we can also speak of
a "Hellenized" Judaism in Jerusalem, for me the designation "Hellenistic
Judaism" means more than being merely passively subjected to the
influences generally effective at the time. At any rate, at the time of primitive Christianity (and of course already at the time of Jesus) there were
synagogues in Jerusalem, in which at least Greek was spoken as the most
common language, but where even more of real Hellenization could be
traced' (46f.).

Later (48f.) Walter puts forward the absurd thesis that the preachers
active against Paul in Galatia were Jews who did not believe in Christ, 'who
accused Paul of stopping half-way (and here already were betraying the
foundations of Judaism), whereas now by demanding that the Pauline
mission should observe the Torah they wanted to guide it into the stream
of making proselytes'.[142] But why then does Paul narrate the history of his
relation to the primitive community if these were non-Christians or, to put
it more cautiously, if these Jews did not belong to the Christian community?

Marinus de Jonge ('The So-called Pseudepigrapha of the Old Testament
and Early Christianity', 59–71) helpfully brings together the Old Testament pseudepigrapha known in early Christianity (Life of the Prophets,
Ascension of Isaiah, V Ezra, Testaments of the Twelve Patriarchs, etc.). In
his view a study of these documents results in an increasingly differ-
entiated view of the relations between Jews and Christians in the second
and third centuries (71). In a learned article 'The Son of David: Solomon
and Jesus' (72–87), James H. Charlesworth not only argues for the historicity of the narrative in Mark 10.46–52 but also seeks to explain the real
content of the term son of David with which Bartimaeus addresses Jesus.
As son of David, Jesus, like Solomon, had amazing powers of healing. It
should be noted that Solomon is indeed son of David. Charlesworth even
thinks that the place where Jesus is invoked as son of David can be attested
historically: it is of course Jericho. In an article on 'Apotheosis and

Resurrection' (88–100), Adele Yarbro Collins repeats her well-known theory that according to Mark 16.1–8 Jesus was transported from the tomb to heaven.[143] Aaye Pilgaard ('The Hellenistic *Theios Aner* – a Model for Early Christian Christology', 101–22) examines whether the Hellenistic *theios aner* conception was a model for early Christian christology. Without further qualification, the use of the Hellenistic conception of the divine man as a model for early christology – so Pilgaard – only causes confusion. I would want to recall that Ludwig Bieler, who introduced the term 'divine man' into the discussion in 1936, emphatically designated it an 'ideal type'.[144]

Of the other seven contributions I shall mention only that by Niels Hyldahl ('Paul and Hellenistic Judaism in Corinth', 204–16). He says that there was tension between Paul and Apollos and that the opponents behind 1 Cor. 1–4 were the adherents of Apollos. In the light of 1 Cor. 16.12 that is improbable, and also because in 1 Cor. 4.6, the characteristics common to Paul and Apollos are emphasized. Moreover, Hyldahl understands Apollos as a Hellenistic philosopher of Alexandria, who stimulated Paul to think philosophically.

All in all, this composite volume sheds light on some aspects of the relationship between the New Testament and Hellenistic Judaism, though the quality of the contributions is uneven.

Under the title *Der Gesalbte* ('The Anointed'), 1991, the extremely learned Erlangen Habilitationsschrift by Martin Karrer (482 pages) investigates the foundations for the title Christ in the Old Testament, early Judaism and the New Testament, and in every case brings in the development up to the time of the early church.

An extensive introduction (11–92) with a survey of the history of research (12–47) and a preliminary linguistic investigation of the history of 'Christ' as a title and name (48–92) is followed by a 'foundation' (93–405). This is about the background in reality (95–213: surveys of the anointing to be king and priest as well as the function of anointing in the cult); the 'conceptual framework of the Jewish legacy' (214–376) and the 'challenge posed by Graeco-Roman ideas from anointing to immortality and deification' (377–405). Ch. 3, headed 'Yield' (406–13), rounds off the work. A bibliography (414–52) and index (453–82) increase the usefulness of the book.

The presupposition of Karrer's study is that Jesus was not called 'the anointed' by either his disciples or his opponents (406). Mark 8.27–30 was written 'in the Jewish Hellenistic

community of the peripheral sphere of Palestine' (358), and
Mark 12.35–7a represents a later reflection directed against
the scribal presupposition that the Christ must be David's son
(285). But the title 'Christ' from Mark 14.61 is also said not to
take us back behind the later tradition of the trial of Jesus
(348). Remarkably, Karrer takes a positive view of this negative
result. It is not a weakening but rather a strengthening of the
concept of the anointed: 'For in this way he interprets not
only Jesus' activity in itself but his activity and his dignity after
the resurrection, bringing in the passion. *Christos apethanen*,
"It was the anointed one who died", the brief formula that
came into being as a direct response to the death of Jesus,
contains the core of the New Testament understanding of the
anointed. It expresses the anointed in his personal uniqueness' (406).

But: 1. 'Christ' is subject, as is clearly evident from the
positioning of Christ in 1 Cor. 15.3 at the beginning; 2. in
early Christianity the 'resurrection' is given essential priority
over the death. In other words, the dignity of Jesus as the
Christ who could die for sins was possible only after the
statement of his resurrection. And here Karrer's study leaves
all the questions open.

In 1992, in connection with the first Princeton symposium on
Judaism and Christian Origins, James H. Charlesworth edited
The Messiah. Developments in Earliest Judaism and Christianity. In
the introduction ('From Messianology to Christology: Problems and Prospects, 3–35), he rightly refers to the enormous
increase in the number of new documents which are regarded
as pseudepigrapha and to the progress in Qumran research.
He also emphasizes that the view often advocated in Christian
research – that in the time of Jesus the majority of Jews were
expecting the Messiah – is based on an error (6). However, his
suggestion that William Wrede did not know Ethiopian Enoch
and IV Ezra (34) is sheer nonsense and can be explained only
by his ignorance of the history-of-religions school. Nevertheless, Charlesworth has edited a handsome volume for
which specialists from Europe and North America have written important contributions.

After the editor's introduction, Part 2 is about 'Messianic Ideas and the Hebrew Scriptures', with reports by J. J. M. Roberts ('The Old Testament's Contribution to Messianic Expectations', 39–51); J.-G. Heintz ('Royal Traits and Messianic Figures: A Thematic and Iconographical Approach [Mesopotamian Elements]', 52–66); and P. D. Hanson ('Messiah and Messianic Figures in Proto-Apocalypticism', 67–75).

Part 3, with eight contributions in all, deals with 'Messianology in Early Judaism and Early Rabbinics' (77–58); Part 4 is devoted to '"Messianism" in Social Contexts and in Philo' (259–361); Part 5 discusses the topic '"The Messiah" and Jesus of Nazareth' (363–422); and Part 6 '"The Messiah", "The Christ", and the New Testament' (423–568).

The high point of the volume is the article by Martin Hengel ('Christological Titles in Early Christianity' [425–48]), written on the basis of extensive preliminary work. Hengel argues that christological thought between 50 and 100 CE displays far more common structures than New Testament research has sometimes claimed. 'The unfolding of New Testament christology, however strange it may appear to us today, was certainly not idle speculation or a haphazard mythological "wild growth". We find rather an amazing inner consistency from the oldest Christian confession to the Prologue of the Fourth Gospel' (447).

Hengel's remarks on the postulation of an essential unity of Diaspora Judaism and Palestinian Judaism are rejected by H. Anderson ('The Jewish Antecedents of the Christology in Hebrews', 512–35: 514). 'Hellenistic Jews of the Diaspora like Philo or the author of Fourth Maccabees or the author of Hebrews, were not quite the same as their Palestinian contemporaries. The intricate intermingling of Greek philosophy and Jewish religious thought we find in their works would scarcely have been possible in Palestine' (516).

It would take me too far afield to describe the individual contributions in more detail.[145] It must suffice to say that this collection is another milestone in research into early christology.[146]

6

A Survey and Critique of Recent Studies in Primitive Christianity in the Different Centres of the Roman Empire

Since the end of the 1970s research has evidenced a renewed interest in the local history and development of the churches in the main centres of the Roman empire. I begin with Antioch and Rome because here we have communities which were not founded by Paul and therefore are pre-Pauline churches in the true sense. I then turn to churches from the Pauline sphere of influence: Philippi, Thessalonica and Ephesus. Corinth is not the focus of specific attention at this point as the local history of this community still needs comprehensive treatment.[147] Nor is the community of Alexandria discussed, because it cannot be recognized until the second century.[148] I do not think it necessary to describe the situation of the Jerusalem community according to recent research, as I have discussed this at length elsewhere.[149] However, at this point I want to add that the authenticity of the letter of James,[150] which has recently been argued for from certain sides, would call for a reassessment of the Jerusalem community and its leader, James. I still regard the letter of James as inauthentic and see the historical James as an opponent of Paul.[151] I draw these conclusions from the information in the authentic letters of Paul and a critical reading of the Acts of the Apostles.[152] However, criticism of the Acts of the Apostles should not be exaggerated either. If it is, the result is what can be read in Burton L. Mack's most recent book: '(T)he emergence of a Christian congregation in Jerusalem in the immediate wake of the traditional gospel story of Jesus needs to be deleted from the traditional imagination of Christian origins. There is absolutely no evidence for it.'[153] Evidently Mack does not note that Paul himself presupposes the existence of a Christian community in Jerusalem in the earliest period (see Gal. 1.17–18).

1. Antioch

These attempts began with the plans of American scholars to write a social history of Antioch on the Orontes, including the Jewish and Christian communities.[154]

In this connection mention should be made of the joint work by Raymond E. Brown and John P. Meier, *Antioch and Rome*, published in 1983, in which Brown took responsibility for the part on Rome (87–216) and Meier for that on Antioch (11–86). They bring together in an unpretentious way the sources that apply to each of them. Challenging other approaches, Meier convincingly locates the Gospel of Matthew in Antioch (15–27). Starting from Gal. 2 and Acts 11–15, he reconstructs the earliest Christianity in Antioch from 40 to 70 and then, starting from the Gospel of Matthew, that of the second Christian generation (45–72); the next section (73–84) depicts the history of the church of Antioch after 100 CE on the basis of the letters of Ignatius. In relation to this it should be emphasized that Meier dispenses with any explicit methodology of social history; as was customary in the time of Harnack, he merely locates the texts carefully, relates them to one another, and investigates them from specific aspects (questions of ministry, events, conflicts, etc.). In this enterprise it is important first of all to make clear which texts belong to Antioch (for the part on Rome see pp. 120f. below).

Whereas apart from Meier's sketch there have been no recent monograph treatments of the Christian church of Antioch in the subsequent period,[155] two works on individual aspects of the history and theology of the community of

Antioch should be described next. Their authors are Anton Dauer and Eckhard Rau.

According to its subtitle, Anton Dauer's monograph *Paulus und die christliche Gemeinde im syrischen Antiochia* ('Paul and the Christian Community in Syrian Antioch') is a 'critical study of modern research with some remarks which take it further'. That is a precise description of the content. The ratio of texts to notes (1–128/129–275) shows how much effort Dauer has given to documentation. A comprehensive bibliography (278–99) increases the usefulness of the book.

Dauer's contribution combines redaction-critical with historical interests. He too is concerned, supposing the traditional chronology to be correct, to fill in the apostle's remarkable silence about the long period of his stay in and around Antioch as a collaborator in the mission there. His thesis is that the unfortunate outcome of the incident at Antioch (Gal. 2.11ff.) had a traumatic effect on Paul. Even on his later visit to Antioch, reported by Acts 18.22, the dispute had not still been settled, as the terse language indicates.[156]

> It is not said that he greeted the community or that it gave him a joyful welcome, that he reported on a successful mission (thus 14.27) and worked in the community (thus 15.35). Nor is anything said about his taking leave of the community when he set off for his third missionary journey, as for example 13.3 or 15.40 mention. All that could indicate that during this stay in Antioch the tense situation was far from being resolved (75).

With the thesis of a trauma, Dauer has abandoned his redaction-critical principles and engages in unrestrained psychological exegesis. At the outset, the real point in time of this journey to both Antioch and Jerusalem should have been discovered. We must rule out a visit in the middle of the travels to bring in the collection. (The same objection must be made against dating the Antioch incident at the point of Acts 18.22 proposed by Schwemer [cf. n. 155].)

Fortunately, the thesis of a trauma affecting Paul – which is unfortunate because it can neither be verified or falsified – is not the focal point of Dauer's book. Far more important is the section on 'Antioch – a place where Paul is taught the Christian faith: traditions in the letters of Paul before or alongside the Pauline traditions' (77–120). For here Dauer clearly separates what by consensus is the pre- and post-Pauline textual material from the primary source of the letters of Paul; this illuminates well the theological tradition with which Paul finds himself in conversation.

According to his subtitle, Eckhard Rau, *Von Jesus zu Paulus* ('From Jesus to Paul', 1994), discusses the 'development and reception of Antiochene theology in primitive Christianity'.

> Rau's starting point is that 'in the metropolis of the Roman province of Syria a step was taken by some of the Hellenists who had been driven out of Jerusalem, the success of which laid the foundation for the rise of a large community (Acts 11.19–21). And here Paul worked in the circle of prophets and teachers (Acts 13.1) for the majority of the period covered by Gal. 1.21–2.14 – and that was far longer than the few years which he devoted to the independent mission in Greece and Asia Minor after he had left Antioch!' (7).
>
> The source-critical basis for Rau is the thesis already put forward by Harnack that Acts 6.8–8.4a (par. 11.9a); 11.19b–21 represents a pre-Lukan context, a claim that again raises the question of the Antiochene source (13). Here we are said to have an aetiology of the Antiochene mission to the Gentiles (74f.). The conflict between the Hellenists in Jerusalem[157] and their accusers was not over the Law but the Temple. Stephen, whose speech in Acts 7 Rau evidently regards as authentic, is said to have continued Jesus' criticism of the Temple (cf. Luke 13.34f.).

I cannot see that Paul persecuted the Hellenists because of their criticism of the Temple (by way of comparison see Gal. 1.13–14). Rau's other thesis, that the abandonment of circumcision in the Antiochene community represented a position within Judaism which was faithful to the Law (83), is equally difficult to follow. So I cannot see anything in the book which carries us forward, apart from the valuable survey of the background to the criticism of the Temple (46–63): (a) Zeno and Hellenism; (b) Cicero's *Xerxes* and the Heraclites of Cynicism; (c) Flavius Josephus and (d) Philo of Alexandria.

Nicholas H. Taylor's *Paul, Antioch and Jerusalem* derives from a 1990 Durham dissertation written under James D. G. Dunn. Taylor sets out to investigate Paul's relation with the communities in Antioch and Jerusalem with special reference to sociological insights. In advance he emphasizes the importance of the Antiochene community for Paul's relationship to the Jerusalem church (9).

> The introduction (13–59) presents the state of research, the method, the terms 'relationship' and 'authority', the sources, and a discussion of chronological questions. Part I discusses 'Paul's Conversion and the Beginnings of his Christian Career' (61–86) and the relevant sources (Gal. 1; Acts 9); Part II is devoted to 'Paul's Work in and from Antioch' (87–144); and the topic of Part III is 'Paul's Independent Mission' (145–217).
>
> Taylor faces the problem that according to the current view Paul's independent mission comes only in the later part of his life. Instead of criticizing this thesis, he sets out to collect plausible reasons for the long 'preparation'. For example, he extends the period of Paul's conversion. Note his remarks on Paul's connection with the Damascus community: 'Joining the Damascus church completed Paul's conversion-initiation process, in the latter part of which Ananias appears to have played a significant role. Paul's social integration in Damascus provided him with a new dyadic identity and brought about a reduction in his post-conversion dissonance' (84).
>
> Contrary to the report in Gal. 2.1–10, Paul here is said to have taken part in the conference in Jerusalem as a delegate from Antioch. The tie to the community of Antioch which gave him his identity was broken only after the incident in Antioch (Gal. 2.11ff.) and led to the independent mission attested by the extant Pauline letters. However, Paul's break with the community in Antioch was only provisional. In the apostle's visit to Antioch, which is reported only in Acts 18.22, Paul again reconciled himself with the community, but without giving up his newly acquired independence.
>
> Objection: Acts 18.22 cannot be directly brought in to assert a visit to Antioch. Here (cf. 45, 47), Taylor refers only to various studies from the secondary literature instead of investigating the text himself. He believes that during the stay in Antioch reflected in Acts 18.22 Paul himself heard of the apostolic decree for the first time (147). His now relaxed attitude to Antioch and Jerusalem is expressed in 1 Corinthians (183–94), in Romans (194–7), and in the collection in the Pauline communities (197–204). Here Taylor emphasizes that the collection Paul organized in his last years was not identical with the collection agreed on at the conference (198). Yet Paul explicitly says the opposite, just as he emphasizes in Gal. 2.1–2a that he travelled independently to Jerusalem for the conference (and not as a delegate of the Antiochenes). In fact he writes that he immediately and without delay took steps to bring in the collection (cf. Gal. 2.10).

Taylor hardly analyses texts anywhere, but for the most part reports on other scholarly positions and then weighs the arguments of others. Moreover, while the introduction (28–44) announces that the historical-critical interpretation will be supplemented by sociological insights, these appear only in brief notes and footnotes with cumbersome terminology and only assert rather than prove. For example, Taylor's house of cards includes the thesis already mentioned on p. 74 above that Paul took part in the Jerusalem conference as a delegate from Antioch; the early date of Galatians, which is said to have been written shortly after the incident at Antioch (45f., 155f.); and the assumption of a visit to Antioch between Paul's second and third journeys to Jerusalem (Paul would then have undertaken the long journey to Macedonia and Achaea twice between the second and third visit to Jerusalem). The attempt to fill out the long 'period of preparation' for Paul's independence cannot therefore be considered successful. Either the details of the years remain unknown, since there are no primary sources, or we reconstruct a new chronology of Paul that is superior to the old. All in all, too many analyses of the text remain unsatisfactory, where they appear at all (219 on the collection, 226 on 'Paul and the Church in Jerusalem').

2. Rome

Reference has already been made to the relevant section in the book by Brown and Meier in which R. E. Brown surveys the sources which come from Rome and describes their content (87–216). Here 2 Peter is regarded as a document which, using the name of Peter, seeks to adopt a middle position between the extreme stance of the followers of Paul and that of the followers of James. But such tendency criticism is hardly sufficient to advance the phenomenon of 'Roman Christianity'. This task was tackled for the first time in the research of the last 30 years, almost with a hammer blow, by the Bern dissertation of Peter Lampe, *Die stadrömischen Christen in den ersten beiden Jahrhunderten* ('The Urban Roman Christians in the First Two Centuries. Investigations in Social History') 1987, [2]1989. See further Karl P. Donfried and Peter

Richardson (eds), *Judaism and Christianity in First-Century Rome*, Grand Rapids and Cambridge 1998.

> Lampe's interest is 'to investigate the urban Roman Christians in the first two centuries in their everyday life, the social reality in which they lived. To seek out these people in their "situation" and take them seriously is first of all an end *in itself* – regardless of the question how this situation relates to their theology, to the statements of their faith … Regardless, too, of the correlations in which factors of social history are contained, the question should be asked: where – if at all – reciprocal relations between situation and theology can be discovered' (xif.).
>
> Lampe's work is in six parts: I. Introduction. The beginnings of urban Roman Christianity up to the detachment from the bond with the synagogue (1–9); 2. Topography (10–52); III. First diachronic section. Reports on urban Roman Christianity generally (53–123); IV. Second diachronic section: prosopographic investigations (124–300); V. Parties in urban Roman Christianity (301-45); VI. Concluding observation (346–9). There are four appendices (I. Disciples of Marcion; II. Justin – elements of education; III. Tatian – elements of education; IV. Parties in urban Roman Judaism).

Lampe's book has been worked out with tremendous diligence and is attractive for the way in which it takes account of every possible literary, epigraphic and local historical source for Rome from the first three centuries. No one before Lampe has ever produced such a model prosopography of the Christian communities of Rome.

So far Lampe has been criticized above all for his thesis that the Christianity of Rome reflects 'the social stratification of more or less all of society' (first edition, 113).[158] Lampe slightly changed this sentence in the second edition,[159] without being able to disguise the fact that the extant sources make it impossible to define precisely what specific strata belonged to the community. Nevertheless, my initial remark stands, namely that Lampe has presented an indispensable treasure trove for the history of the Roman community in the first two centuries, one which is attractive for its completeness and arouses wonderment at its acumen, even if at several points the reader is of another opinion. Two examples will suffice.

> The first example, which arouses some suspicions about Lampe's methodology, is his discussion of Marcion (203–19). Thus he writes on the social

background of the 'demiurge in Marcion' (203–19): '*The two characteristics of the demiurge mentioned (warlike; unstable/contradictory) are transparent to the experiences of a naukleros during the reign of Trajan.* This horizon of experience may explain why for shaping his picture of the demiurge Marcion takes precisely these two characteristics from the tradition and attaches importance to them ... At the time of Trajan there was an almost permanent state of war' (209). Now both before this and later Lampe relativizes the monocausal derivation of theological statements from situations in social history that can be described (347f.). But it must be noted that at this point Lampe's model would presuppose that Marcion had already developed his view of the evil or just demiurge at the beginning of the second century, which contradicts the consensus on the chronology of Marcion.

The second example is the unsatisfactory treatment of the events surrounding the edict of Claudius (4–9, cf. supplement 442), in which Lampe earnestly claims that the chronology of Acts 18 is to be trusted more than Dio Cassius, 'who edited his chronological information at the earliest at the end of the second century' (8), so that it is a century later (ibid.). Even if the dating on the basis of Acts 18 is fraught with uncertainties, according to Lampe: 'The dating by Dio Cassius is even more so' (ibid.). Yet Lampe totally ignores the redaction characteristics that do not allow us to use Luke's 'chronology' without further ado. My criticism is that Dio Cassius had archival material at his disposal: furthermore, at other places, too, the author of Acts is chronologically wrong – moreover in the strict sense in Acts 18 he does not presuppose any chronology at all – and has probably himself fabricated the 'chronology' in Acts 18 – without any knowledge of sources.

First, Luke strings together episodes in Acts by means of loose chronological indications (for example Acts 6.1: 'in these days', 12.1: 'about that time', 19.23: 'about that time', etc.). We must therefore wonder if Luke is not presenting selected episodes rather than a continuous history. Furthermore, we should note the difference between the space allotted to the first 13 to 14 years of Paul's life as a Christian (a little over four chapters: Acts 11.26–15.41) and that allotted to the last five to seven years after the Jerusalem conference (14 chapters: Acts 16-28).

Secondly, the chronological information offered by Luke is often conditioned by his theological intentions. Luke is concerned to show that Christianity is a politically safe religion; it is ready to be adopted as a world religion. Moreover, Luke thinks in terms of eras of the history of salvation. The last stage begins with the formulation and adoption of the apostolic decree at the Jerusalem conference. The decree, which James enunciates in Acts 15.19–20 (cf. later 15.29; 21.25), consisted of four requirements for Gentile Christians: to abstain from things sacrificed to idols, from blood, from things strangled, and from fornication. These are things which the Jews considered to be the grossest abominations of the pagans. Paul is then free to operate his mission among the Gentiles. For Luke, this decree means that Paul stands in continuity with the primitive church. Placing the Pauline mission *after* the adoption of the decree thus primarily serves dogmatic rather than chronological interests.

Thirdly, another point worth emphasizing under this heading is one that has seldom been noticed. Though Luke several times reports on visits by Paul to a given locality, he presents detailed information about the apostle's activity there only in *one* report, while any other visit is described in rather general terms. In the list that follows I shall give the reports with the detailed information first and after that the reports which are rather general: Thessalonica (Acts 17.1–10; cf. 20.2); Philippi (16.12–40; cf. the two visits in 20.2, 3–6); Corinth (18.1–17; cf. 20.2–3); Ephesus (19.1–20.1; cf. 18.19–21). It is unlikely that Luke had access to local traditions that were related to *one specific visit* only. He seems rather to have gathered various reports stemming from Paul's several visits to a given locality and combined them into a single account.

The Roman biographer Suetonius (early second century CE) writes:

> 'Claudius expelled the Jews from Rome who were exceedingly riotous because of the instigator Chrestus.'[160]

Now, the Roman historian Dio Cassius reports an imperial command regarding the Jews for the year 41.[161] He writes:

> 'As for the Jews, who had again increased so greatly that by reason of their multitude it would have been hard without raising a tumult to bar them from the city, he did not drive them out, but ordered them, while continuing their traditional mode of life, not to hold meetings.'[162]

As for the relationship of these two pieces of information, one must point out that Suetonius' language can be interpreted to mean that only those Jews who rioted were expelled. In this case 'Dio's statement offers no contradiction, since he denies only that there was a general expulsion of the large Jewish population'[163] like the one under Tiberius.[164] It is only if one tries to combine Acts' statement about the expulsion of *all* the Jews from Rome with Suetonius' account that difficulties for the reconstruction of the date of the expulsion arise. But 'all' in Acts 18.2 is clearly one of the many hyperbolic generalizations in Luke-Acts (cf. Luke 2.1; Acts 11.28; 21.30) and cannot help us in chronological matters, nor can the combination of Claudius' edict against the Jews with the tradition of a trial against Paul before Gallio (Acts 18.12).

That is the way Lampe and many New Testament scholars proceed today. Yet they overlook the fact that 49 CE as the date of Claudius' decree against the Jews, which can be found in the work of the church father Orosius (fifth century) as part of an oral tradition from 'Josephus',[165] may have simply been reconstructed on the basis of the account in Acts 18.1–12 by subtracting the 18 months found in Acts 18.11 from the dates of Gallio's term in office, which could be figured out by checking the records in the archives. Hence it is certainly secondary. 'What one can read in many places, namely that the year 49 for the edict of Claudius fits exactly with the relative chronology of Acts, is precisely what could make Orosius' note suspicious.'[166] 41 CE – and not 49 CE – is clearly the most likely date for the edict of Claudius concerning the Jews,[167] the more so since one would have expected Tacitus (whose reports about the first six years of Claudius have been lost) at least to have some reference to such an act.[168] Thus it is regrettable that Lampe shows so little awareness of the real problem of Acts' chronology and of the way in which to arrive at the most likely date of both Claudius' edict against the Jews[169] and the date of Paul's first arrival in Corinth.[170]

A further contribution to the social history of Roman Christianity comes from James S. Jeffers (1991). His book, *Conflict at Rome*, is an attractive attempt to oppose the Christianity of Hermas to that of 1 Clement, often with good reason.

On the relationship between 1 Clement and the book of Hermas, Jeffers remarks: 'The *Shepherd* attempts to create peace within the congregation, since division implies sin. But unlike I Clement (viz. in 51.1–2), it does not borrow from Roman ideology to support its conception of peace. It represents those who have found only grief from relationship with the state' (139). By contrast, the group around Hermas 'represents a resurgence of charismatic authority arising in protest against the ideology of groups like Clement's and attempting to recapture what it considered the golden age of the church: the apostolic era, when charismatic authority predominated ... Hermas ... represents a resurgence of latent charismatic authority' (159).[171]

The merely peripheral attention paid to Marcion (188) and other Gnostics (189) who are also part of Roman Christianity and were working in Rome at the same time as Hermas is inadequate. The question of Justin's relationship to the urban Roman Christian community is not raised. I am not quite clear about the relevance of Chapter 4 ('The House Church of Clement', 63–89), as the archaeological question is not answered. (Conclusion: 'We cannot be certain that the San Clemente complex was once the site of Clement's house church' [87]). Jeffers' book is highly selective, but his remarks are useful.[172]

3. Macedonia

(a) Philippi

Two new monographs on the Christian community in Philippi have appeared at the same time. Lukas Bormann describes in the first chapter of his book *Philippi* ('Philippi. City and Christian Community in the Time of Paul', 1995) ('Introduction', 1–7):

'the task of making interpretative links between the political and religious situation of the Roman colony of Philippi and the first Christian community living there ... In what follows I shall attempt to investigate and establish the possibilities of such reciprocal interaction (viz. between political and cultural factors) by means of a limited local example, the Roman colony of Philippi and its first Christian community' (1).

Ch. 2 discusses 'Philippi in historical perspective' (11–29), Ch. 3 'Philippi in the perspective of the history of religion' (30–67), and Ch. 4 defines the place of 'Philippi in ancient historiography' (68–86), beginning with the *Res Gestae* of Augustus and extending as far as Dio Cassius. The second part of the book begins with Ch. 5 (87–126). Under the title 'Paul and the Community in Philippi' Bormann first of all discusses the usual introductory questions and argues for a literary-critical division of Philippians. There are said to have been three letters to the Philippians: A, 4.10–20 and 4.21–3; B: 1.1–3.1 and 4.2–7; C: 3.2–4.1 and 4.8f.

The heart of the book is Chapter 7 (161–205), entitled 'The Relations between Paul and the Philippian Community as Reflected by Hellenistic-Roman Social Conventions'. Bormann wants to show that Roman patronage or the client relationship offers the appropriate horizon of understanding for the exchanges between Paul and the Philippians. For the Philippians had interpreted the situation of Paul waiting for his trial 'in the framework of the client relationship as a shared emergency which called for solidarity' (212). Paul's trial is 'the classic situation of the collaboration of patron and client. The motivation for a shared appearance is not primarily the result of the personal tie but a result of the common cause with which they were concerned' (213). The key for the relations between Paul and the Philippians (cf.136) is contained in the letter of thanks in 4.10–20, for more precise indications of the object of the exchange between Paul and the Philippians can be inferred from it. In conclusion, Chapter 8 sums up 'the significance of the patron or client relationship for the community in Philippi'.

But without taking account of the whole letter, Phil. 4.10–20 must be far too narrow a basis for such a far-reaching hypothesis. Further, it is questionable whether the first Christians in Philippi were in fact predominantly Romans, for whom the client relationship to the Julian-Claudian house applied. The good Greek names Epaphroditus, Euodia and Syntyche do not fit this.

The second work on the community in Philippi is the Habilitationsschrift by Peter Pilhofer, *Philippi. I. Die erste christliche Gemeinde Europas; II. Katalog der Inschriften von Philippi* ('Philippi. I: The First Christian Community of Europe', 1995). The extensive second volume of some 916 pages ('Philippi II: Catalogue of the Inscriptions of Philippi', 2000) is a collection of all the inscriptions from and around Philippi, as well as inscriptions from other places which mention persons from Philippi. Pilhofer always supplies the text, gives a German translation and after that extensively quotes the comments of the first editors. In addition he adds his own observations. In Volume I he continually references Volume II, thus basing his conclusions on a vast body of collected inscriptions (767 altogether). Concluding this remarkable volume are a bibliography (837–52), indexes (853–903) and a concordance that relates this collection to the first editions of the inscriptions (905–16).

> In Vol. I, after an introduction (1–48) which discusses the literary and archaeological evidence and new literature on the topic, Ch. 1 discusses 'Philippi in the First Century' (49–113). Ch. II is devoted to 'Paul' (114–52). Then follow chapters on 'Luke' (III, 153–205), Polycarp (IV, 206–28) and 'The History of the Christian Community in Philippi' (V, 229–58). An extensive bibliography including various indexes (259–311) rounds off the work, which also contains nine maps.

Pilhofer's main aim is 'to utilize the events in the local history of Philippi for the interpretation of the relevant early Christian texts' (36). Now there can be no doubt that Pilhofer has collected all the conceivable material for Philippi, as Lampe has for Rome. But occasionally doubts remain about the treatment of the New Testament texts. In Chapter II, Pilhofer strangely asserts that the mention of the tribe of Benjamin in Phil. 3.5 is a consequence of Paul's confrontation with the *tribus Voltinia* (124). His arguments run thus: a walk through the city of Philippi at the time of Paul shows 'that at least "official" Philippi at this time was an exclusively Latin city. For Paul, who came from the East, this city was therefore a completely new experience ... (1) On walking through the city, at least in the centre, Paul would find almost exclusively Latin inscriptions. (2) In so far as the names of *cives Romani* appeared on these inscriptions, as a rule they would bear the term VOL (*Voltinia tribu*)' (120f.). In my view this is fallacious, since the mention of descent is quite understandable in the context of the rivalry with opponents (cf. also 2 Cor. 11.22), and moreover there were numerous non-Roman Christians in Philippi, as Pilhofer himself demonstrates (135–9). Equally unconvincing is Pilhofer's suggestion that *politeuma* in Phil. 3.20 must be read against the background of the *politeuma* of the *tribus Voltinia* that each Roman citizen of the Roman colony Philippi has received (122).

Moreover in Chapter III (153–205) Pilhofer seriously imagines Luke to be a Macedonian who had excellent knowledge of Macedonia and especially Philippi. But there is another explanation of the local colouring in Acts 16 cited as an argument – note the similar local colouring in Acts 17 and Acts 19 – and there is no confirmation of Acts 16 from the primary source, Paul's letters. (At this point in his work on Philippi [4–6], Bormann is rightly sceptical.)

In general it is striking that Pilhofer displays considerable self-confidence – both in the critical discussion of other authors (cf. 35–48) and also in interpretations which he claims to be original (cf. 245 on the point of reference of 'beginning of the gospel' in Phil. 4.15[173]). At the same time it has to be pointed out that Pilhofer, with his two volumes on Philippi, has provided future scholarship on Paul's favourite community with an invaluable tool.

(b) Thessalonica

Peter Pilhofer's pupil Christoph vom Brocke has written a book, *Thessaloniki – Stadt des Kassander und Gemeinde des Paulus. Eine frühe christliche Gemeinde in ihrer heidnischer Umwelt* ('Thessalonica – City of Cassander and Paul's Community. An Early Christian Community in its Pagan Environment', 2001), which is organized along the same lines as that of his doctoral supervisor on Philippi. A first chapter deals with 'Thessaloniki in the First Century AD' (12–101) in which all the available data on the architecture, the economy, and the society in Hellenistic and Roman times are presented. A second chapter centres on Paul (103–85) and specifically focuses on 1 Thess. 1.8; 1 Thess. 1.9; 1 Thess. 2.3–6; 2.13; 1 Thess. 2.14b; and 1 Thess. 5.3. In general the author suggests reading the various texts against the background of Roman data: e.g. the slogan 'peace and security' in 1 Thess. 5.3 is directed against the ideology of the Pax Romana (167–85). A third chapter deals with Luke (188–271) by analysing Acts 17.1–10. The historical value of this section, according to the author, is very high, and so is that of v. 10a, the account of the night flight to Beroea (268–71).

Although vom Brocke seems to be too credulous at times with respect to Acts, and although at times he too directly moves from Paul's statements to Roman slogans (see on 1 Thess. 5.3.), he has produced a remarkable work. But one question still remains to be asked: from whom did the author of Acts obtain the material if he was not a companion of Paul?

4. Ephesus and Asia Minor[174]

In 1976 Ulrich B. Müller produced a study of 'Jewish Christianity and Paulinism in Asia Minor at the end of the First and Beginning of the Second Century AD' (thus the subtitle of his book 'The History of Early Christian Theology'). Chapter I is titled 'The Historical Location of the Apocalypse of John' (13–52), Chapter II 'The Historical Location of the Opponents in the Pastorals' (53–77), Chapter III 'Jewish Christian Tradition and Paulinism as Alternatives' (78–94). Generally speaking, the book sets out to investigate the Jewish Christianity 'that would give up the total tie to the Law and thus become capable of influencing the rest of Christianity' (95), and omits those Jewish Christians who were continuously hostile to Paul (84). Here already one may question the value of such a definition in a historical work. Müller's most important contribution is his analysis of the opponents in the Pastorals. Unfortunately the expression 'creep in' (2 Tim. 3.6) has led him to imagine opponents (especially itinerant teachers) who have come into community of the author of the Pastorals from the outside and have caused confusion among the women there (62). Yet an internal origin of the heresy is more probable.

> Thus 1 Tim. 1.1 speaks of those who have suffered shipwreck in the faith, and continues in a deliberately stylized way, based on 1 Cor. 5.5: 'Among them Hymenaeus and Alexander, whom I have delivered to Satan that they may learn not to blaspheme' (1.20). The historical basis is the exclusion from the community of the two persons mentioned. However,

that may not have prevented certain circles from gaining influence, as over the women who are referred to. The author seems to be referring to this when at another point he issues the warning, 'Avoid such godless chatter, for it will lead people into more and more ungodliness, and their talk will eat its way like gangrene' (2 Tim. 1.16), and in connection with this again mentions two people: 'Among them are Hymenaeus and Philetus, who have swerved from the truth' (2 Tim. 2.17f.). But that means that Hymenaeus, Philetus and Alexander are original members of the Pauline group from which the author of Pastorals also comes, but at present are carrying on their own activity outside this association of communities. This similarly happens with a reference to Paul, since they teach that 'the resurrection has already taken place' (2 Tim. 2.18).

Now this thesis is not Pauline in itself, but was put forward by disciples of Paul (Eph. 2.6) and also by numerous second-century Gnostics. At this point it can be understood most plausibly as a slogan of the followers of Paul, if it is noted that it was put forward within the Pauline community and was a contributory cause of the break-up of this community.

If we note, further, that the activity of the opponents in the Pastorals is often described as 'teaching' (1 Tim. 1.3,7; 4.1; 6.3; 2 Tim. 4.3; Titus 1.11), it is plausible to assume that they are to be included among the teachers, to whom in the second century not only the Gnostics Valentinus, Ptolemy and Marcus but e.g. also the Apologists Justin and Tatian belonged. The opponents of the Pastorals were concerned, like e.g. the author of Rheginos (NHC I, 4), to cultivate and develop the legacy of Paul, and have amazing similarities with Ephesians and the opponents of 2 Thessalonians.[175]

In 1991 Paul Trebilco produced an extremely learned work on *Jewish Communities in Asia Minor*. He goes against the current insight that the synagogues there had shut themselves off from their surroundings. Rather, he establishes a lively interaction between Jews and Gentiles for Sardes and Priene (37–57), Acmonia (58–84) and Apamea (85–103). Trebilco's book is a treasure trove for all future works on primitive Christianity in Asia Minor. To give just one example: in the chapter on 'The Prominence of Women in Asia Minor' (104–26) he demonstrates from inscriptions the position of women as leaders, a matter of great significance for the yet unresolved question of the status of women in the early Christian communities (see above, pp. 91–3).

Werner Thiessen has produced *Christen in Ephesus* ('Christians in Ephesus'), a work on local history relating to the community of Ephesus (1995); the sub-title ('The Historical and Theological Situation in the pre-Pauline and Pauline Period and at the Time of the Acts of the Apostles and the Pastorals') precisely defines the scope of his work.

It begins with '1. Methodological Reflections on a Geographically Orientated Account of the History of Early Christianity' (11–27). There follow: '2. Pre-Pauline Christianity in Ephesus' (28–89); '3. Paul in Ephesus' (90–142); '4. Paul's Farewell Discourse to the Ephesians (Acts 20.18b–35)' (143–247); '5. The Community of the Pastoral Letters' (248–341) and '6. The Dispute over the Heritage: Post-Pauline Christianity in Ephesus (Summary)' (342–52).

In sharp dissent from Kümmel's criticism of Koester and Robinson's *Trajectories*, described on pp. xif. above, Thiessen argues that investigations of individual centres must be made if we are to gain an overall picture of primitive Christianity (25). That sounds good, but is by no means what happens in Thiessen's remarks on Ephesus. For he limits himself to texts of the New Testament canon (27), and Acts gets a key place. But the letters of Paul are a primary source, and methodologically one must always start from them. According to Thiessen, Acts 19–20 contain a relatively large amount of historical material (142). At the same time he wants to demonstrate that Acts was composed in Ephesus (226–47). He claims that Apollos was the founder of the community of Ephesus, and that the Pauline mission went on to be successful there. The result of this was that the community of Ephesus saw itself as Pauline and became a centre of Pauline tradition. Thiessen rejects the thesis that the heretics in the Pastorals were Gnostics. Rather, they were Jewish Christians who appealed to Paul (328), but at the same time observed the Law and as Christians still saw their homeland in Judaism (347).

Thiessen does not devote a single word to the patristic tradition on John; the result is a truncated description of the church of Ephesus. I do not believe that for all the diligence that Thiessen shows (the bibliography and index cover more than 50 pages [354–410]), such a work really advances research into Christianity in Ephesus, particularly when the methodological presupposition of the *de facto* equal treatment of the testimony of Acts and the authentic letters of Paul is questionable.

Matthias Günther's 1995 book entitled *Die Frühgeschichte des Christentums in Ephesus* ('The Early History of Christianity in Ephesus') was accepted that same year as a dissertation by the Göttingen theological faculty (supervisor Gerd Lüdemann). It is an 'account of the history of Christianity in Ephesus in the first and second centuries. The presupposition for this is an examination of all relevant sources' (13). That is a praiseworthy undertaking, since, as Günther remarks in the opening sentence, there is no thorough history of the early history of Christianity in Ephesus (1). But one can immediately see from a comparison of the two sentences that he understands history in the sense of a reconstruction of tradition; i.e. in an old-fashioned way the work combines source criticism and tradition history, and examines which sources or traditions are rooted in Ephesus. So far no one has carried that out for Ephesus in the first two centuries, and where it has been taken on as a task, the period to be discussed has been limited to the period of the New Testament canon (cf. the work by W. Thiessen).

Ch. 1 ('Results of Research into the Early History of Christianity in Ephesus' [1–12]) brings together the analyses so far, from F. C. Baur to F. Vouga. As the indication of a problem it is emphasized that in more recent research, in contrast to earlier research, a juxtaposition of Pauline and Johannine Christianity is too readily presupposed. Ch. 2 ('The Aim and Method of the Present Work' [13–16]) sketches out the mode of procedure, which has already been mentioned in my introductory remarks. It is simply a matter of beginning with what is clear and illuminating what is less clear from it. Günther stresses: the sources or individual traditions to be used must be rooted in Ephesus; here he adopts a chronological division, anticipating the results of the individual analyses. Ch. 3 ('Early Christianity in the City of Ephesus' [17–28]) offers a survey of the political and religious history of Ephesus and arrives at the conclusion 'that Ephesian Christianity both as a social and a political entity played quite a small role up to the end of the second century' (28). Ch. 4 ('Ephesian Christianity in the Reign of Claudius [AD 41–54] and the Pauline Mission in Ephesus' [29–75]) turns to the earliest phase of Christianity in Ephesus. Here Günther analyses the well-known Pauline references to Ephesus or Asia and comes to the conclusion that *before* Paul's mission (1 Cor. 16.9) a non-Pauline community existed in Ephesus under the leadership of Apollos (35–8). Ch. 5, 'Ephesian Christianity to the End of the Reign of Domitian (up to 96)' comes next (75–123). The second part of this chapter is the real basis of all that follows. Here Günther reconstructs the second foundation of the Ephesian community by the presbyter John. He carefully goes through the already known texts: Polycrates (85ff.), Papias (96ff.) and 2 and 3 John – whose author he thinks is the presbyter John, here following Georg Strecker. This presbyter John is regarded as a chiliast, on the basis of the frequent use of him by the chiliast Papias; this results in the link to 2 John, whose author calls himself a presbyter and who according to 2 John 7 supposedly expresses the chiliastic expectation of a future coming in the flesh. Ch. 6 (124–60) discusses 'Christianity in Ephesus at the Time of the Reign of Trajan (AD 98–117)'. There is an analysis of the letter to the Ephesian community (Rev. 2.1–7), the traditions about Cerinthus attached to Ephesus, and the letter of Ignatius to the Ephesians. Ch. 7 (161–204) discusses 'Ephesian Christianity to the End of the Reign of Severus (to AD 197)'. In the first subsection Günther analyses Justin's *Dialogue* for traditions rooted in Ephesus. The analysis of *Dialogue* 80–82 (165–70) is a model of analytical work. The argument that *Dial.* 80.4a, 5–81.4 is a text which came into being in Ephesus seems convincing. On pp.184–92 the next section discusses Christianity in Ephesus as reflected by Apollonius's work against Montanism (Eusebius, *Church History* V 18).

This is an independent work which with great perspicacity cuts a path through the undergrowth of the Christian communities in Ephesus in the first two centuries. Granted, it does not offer a history, but instead a carefully worked out framework – almost a chronicle of Christian Ephesus in the first two centuries – which can be regarded as a starting point for all future research. Many of the individual results are new and worth noting, quite apart from the overall thesis of the work. The layout is sensible, the individual steps are easy to follow and the treatment of the sources is superior. Transitions and tables help with the reading of the book, which because of the wealth of sources analysed is often demanding.

The difficulties this work confronts affect all sketches of tradition history. In the present work the question arises whether the material is sufficient to make probable the bold thesis of a second foundation of Christianity in Ephesus by the presbyter John and its further development in such a concrete way down to the end of the second century.

The book *Ephesos, Metropolis of Asia* (1995) edited by Helmut Koester goes back to a 'Symposium on Ephesos' at Harvard

Divinity School. 'Participants were not only archaeologists, but also scholars of the classics, history of religions, New Testament studies, and the history of ancient Christianity' (xvii). Koester rightly continues a little later: 'In the field of New Testament studies, the Holy Land of Israel is but a memory of first beginnings; Asia Minor and Greece quickly became the centers of the new religious movement. Ephesos, the metropolis of Asia, was the center of the early Christian missionary enterprise ... If students of the New Testament wish to benefit from archaeological scholarship, they must become better acquainted with nonliterary material unearthed by others, and they must participate in the process of interpretation' (xviii).

Without any doubt, these are programmatic statements that any history of primitive Christianity should carefully keep in mind. Yet only two papers in the book under discussion deal specifically with the history of primitive Christianity at Ephesus. One of them is Koester's essay 'Ephesos in Early Christian Literature' (119–40), the other is 'The Cult of the Roman Emperors in Ephesos: Temple Wardens, City Titles, and the Interpretation of the Revelation of John' (229–50) by Steven Friesen. Whereas Koester, basing his comments on an exhaustive survey, suggests that from 'its very beginning in the middle of the first century, the Christian community of Ephesus exhibits a remarkable diversity' (139), Friesen wants the Revelation of John to be understood 'in its local setting as part of a clash of religious ideologies, for it represents an assault on fundamental issues of social organization in late first-century Asia' (250).

This collection of essays is also a milestone in research into the history of primitive Christianity at one of the centres of the Roman empire.[176]

As its title indicates, Rick Strelan's *Paul, Artemis and the Jews in Ephesus* (1996) is devoted to one aspect of Paul's activity in Ephesus.

> The book, which goes back to a dissertation at the University of Queensland supervised by Michael Lattke, discusses in its first part (1–125) the pagan cults in Ephesus and in the second part (126–302) Paul's relation to

the cult of Artemis and to the Jews, on the basis of Acts and the letters of Paul. Two appendices follow, (a) on the question what associations the self-designation *ethnōn apostolos* had for Paul (303–6) and (b) on the survival of Jewish thought and Jewish practice in Ephesus (306–9); here Strelan rightly warns against putting the transition from Jewish to Gentile Christianity too early.

The information about the pagan cults in Ephesus, above all the cult of Artemis, is good. The second part, which is of special interest to New Testament scholars, seeks to establish the thesis, contrary to current opinion, that Paul had no great missionary success in the city. Perhaps he gained around 25–40 converts in an overall population of 200,000 (129). The failure is clearly evident from Acts 19.23–40. Part 2, Section 2 (165–273), headed 'Paul among the Jews in Ephesus', seeks to demonstrate that Gentile Christianity did not exist in Ephesus. By contrast, the Pauline gospel proved attractive to Jews (183). The Jewish-Christian character of the community there emerges from the fact that Ephesus did not participate in the collection for Jerusalem (202ff.)

Strelan had two purposes. The first was to investigate the cult of Artemis and to reconstruct Paul's religious environment. Here he can point to the age-old origin of the cult of Artemis in Ephesus and its marked effect in the first two centuries CE. The influence of Paul and other Christians was indeed small. Despite the claim that Paul had great success among the Gentiles in Ephesus, there is little evidence of this. In fact we must concede that only a few Gentiles belonged to the Christian fellowship in Ephesus.

The second aim of the work was to show that for Paul Ephesus was difficult ground, so difficult that he himself claimed little success for Ephesus, and was even in danger of his life. He never speaks of the Ephesians as a model to be imitated by Christians in other cities; indeed, what he says about Ephesus is mostly negative. So far everything seems to be plausible. But Strelan's positive thesis is problematical. He argues that the success that Paul had in Ephesus relates to his success among the Jews, so that we should talk of Pauline Jewish Christianity in Ephesus. That emerges both from the letters of Paul and from Acts (225). Really nothing can be more absurd, for there is no evidence for this lofty thesis, and the ideological intent behind the statements is more than clear.

In this connection reference should also be made to Strelan's thesis that the designation *ethnōn apostolos* does not mean 'apostle of the Gentiles' since the term *ethne* refers instead to the Jews who lived outside Judaea. '(T)hey need no longer look to Jerusalem but they are called to join the community of those in Christ' (306). Perhaps *ethnos* is also a genitive of *origin* ('Paul comes from the gentiles' [303]). Strelan does not go into either Galatians or Rom. 11.13, which contains the decisive evidence against this thesis.

One puts the book down with mixed feelings. It is certainly impressive by virtue of its knowledge of the religious environment of Ephesus, an accomplishment which is noteworthy for a dissertation. But too many objections arise to both content and method – the most fundamental being that Strelan treats Acts and the letters of Paul as sources of equal value (21).

7

A Survey and Critique of Recent Studies of Individual Problems

1988 saw the publication of a prize-winning work by Jozef Verheyden on the emigration of the Jerusalem Christians to Pella: *De vlucht van de Christenen naar Pella* ('The Flight of the Christians to Pella. An Investigation of the Testimony of Eusebius and Epiphanius').[177] It analyses all the explicit and implicit Pella texts in great detail and suggests that Eusebius himself drafted the note about Pella in *Church History* III 5,3 because of his theology of history. The objection to this is that the note about Pella cannot be Eusebius' own creation, because in the report in *Church History* III 11, which is certainly redactional, he does not build on the Pella note and the return of the community to Jerusalem.[178]

Verheyden's redaction-critical resolution of the Pella problem must therefore be regarded as a failure, although he has produced strong reasons against the historicity of the flight to Pella.[179] However, it must once again be stressed how much effort lies behind this work and how carefully Verheyden has worked through the scholarly literature produced so far on the Pella question. This research literature is presented in no less than 1032 sometimes extensive footnotes. To this degree Verheyden's book remains an indispensable tool for future research.

The composite volume *The New Testament in Early Christianity*, edited by Jean-Marie Sevrin (1989), contains extremely interesting contributions from the Thirty-Sixth Colloquium Biblicum Lovaniense in 1986 on the influence and reception of the New Testament writings in the first and second centuries. The articles are not all in English.

Barbara Aland discusses 'The Reception of the New Testament Texts in the First Centuries' (1–38, in German). The first part is devoted to 'textual tradition and textual awareness in the Christian writers of the early period and of their quotations of the New Testament' (5–24); the second part discusses 'the New Testament manuscripts of the early period' (24–38). Aland demonstrates that the Gnostics and especially the Valentinian Ptolemy quote relatively accurately, also 'where the focal point of their exegesis is not affected' (20). Here they reflect 'probably only a general development which can be noted from the middle of the second century onwards in Christian literature and which – had more been preserved – would also be detectable in the quotations of the New Testament in the literature of the mainstream church (ibid.)'. Her extremely interesting conclusion from the precision of the quotations by Ptolemy is:

> Consequences for the early history of Christianity in Egypt possibly arise from this. The papyrus discoveries from an early period in Egypt with their usually good New Testament text need not then suggest a non-Gnostic, orthodox Christianity in Egypt. But these papyri could well have been used by Gnostics (13f.).

The article by Andreas Lindemann, 'The Apostle Paul in the Second Century' (also in German, 39–67), investigates all the allusions and reactions to the letters of Paul and the quotations from them. He repeats his thesis that it was not the reception of Paul by Marcion and the Gnostics that brought about the reception of Paul by the mainstream church, but that there was a significant Pauline tradition independent of Gnosticism and Marcion.[180] Thus in his conclusion he maintains: 'It would certainly be wrong to characterize the second century of the Christian church as a period of the universal reception of Paul ... It is even more mistaken to accuse the theology of the second century and especially the mainstream church of having "'forgotten" Paul' (67).

At the same time, Lindemann (52–60) defends his position against criticism like that of Klaus Koschorke,[181] which has been raised in the meantime. The dispute focuses on the question whether there was a specific affinity to Paul in Gnosticism. At all events, in sketching out his results (67) Lindemann at least concedes that the orthodox acceptance of the legacy of Paul is later than the Gnostics.

In an extremely significant contribution, Frans Neirynck ('The Apocryphal Gospels and the Gospel of Mark', 123–75) investigates the recent attempts made by American scholars (John Dominic Crossan, Helmut Koester, etc.) to discover sources of the Gospel of Mark in the apocryphal Gospel literature (Gospel of Thomas, Gospel of Peter, Egerton Papyrus, Secret Gospel of Mark). In a welcome way Neirynck sets the relevant 'sources' side by side with Matthew, Mark and Luke, so that readers can form their own judgements. At the end there is an appendix on the Gospel of Peter (171–5). Here Neirynck prints the existing Greek text and marks the redactional additions claimed by Crossan, the removal of which from the extant text produces Crossan's sinister 'Cross Gospel'.

Some other articles in this volume can be mentioned only briefly. In a detailed investigation of the Synoptic tradition in the Didache, Christopher M. Tuckett (197–230) comes to the conclusion that the Didache presupposes the finished Gospels of Matthew and Luke (230). B. Dehandschutter ('Polycarp's Epistle to the Philippians: An Early Example of "Reception"', 275–92) argues for the unity and the originality of Polycarp's letter to the Philippians,[182] and in a profound article Jan Helderman deals with 'Melchisedek's Influence. A Traditio-Historical Investigation of a Macro-Complex in NHC IX, 1, 1–27,10 (Melchisedek)' (335–62, in German). He investigates all references to Melchizedek from 11Q Melch to the Nag Hammadi tractate from Codex IX (though this latter text is seriously damaged). Important intermediate stages are said to be Hebrews and the Testaments of the Twelve Patriarchs. However, Helderman does not go beyond stating specific motifs (cf. 357), and in an excursus on 'The Melchizedekians and Egypt' (359–62) he energetically argues that these (Theodotus the Moneychanger and Theodotus the Tanner) are to be seen in a genetic relationship with the Nag Hammadi writing from Codex IX.

Graydon F. Snyder, *Ante Pacem* (1985), discusses the archaeological facts of church life before Constantine. This very
clearly arranged volume deals in Chapter I with history and
methodology and in Chapter II with early Christian symbols
like the lamp, the anchor, the vase, the dove, the boat, etc.
Chapter III treats pictorial representations like frescoes,
mosaics and sarcophagi; Chapter IV discusses pictorial interpretations (Jonah, Noah and Daniel); Chapter V early
Christian buildings (the church in Dura Europos, etc.);
Chapter VI inscriptions and graffiti; and Chapter VII papyrus
documents. Chapter VIII draws conclusions for christology,
ecclesiology, worship, the question of rural and urban
Christianity, the state, and language. We discover from the
volume that over many years Snyder has himself seen each
document and each individual building that he presents.[183]
Details of the important literature are given at the beginning
of each chapter and the illustrations are excellent. However,
it is sobering to note that there is not a single extant Christian
document or symbol or image from the end of the second
century. In this connection I would refer to Frend's work (see
above, pp. 45ff.).

The work of Hans Conzelmann's old age, *Gentiles – Jews –
Christians: Polemics and Apologetics in the Greco-Roman Era*, discusses controversies in the literature of the Hellenistic-Roman
period. It arises completely from the original sources and
is the masterpiece of an exegete with a solid classical education. The work has almost the character of a handbook and
contains an analysis of the 'Evaluation of Judaism in Greco-
Roman Literature' (45–133), the 'Debate of Hellenistic
Judaism with the Hellenistic-Roman World' (135–233), and
'Christians and Jews from the Beginnings of Christianity to
the Time of Origen' (235–342). Here it should always be
noted that Conzelmann regards his book as a theological
work. In the introduction he remarks: 'This book has not
been written out of that fascination with antiquity as such that
is presumably enjoying a boom ... Precisely as a strictly historical work derived directly from the primary sources, my
book is directed to the present' (1).

What Conzelmann has in mind becomes clear in the last page of his book. He writes: 'The early issue between Jews and Christians is the issue of faith. This issue cannot be avoided psychologically – by being polite to each other – nor can it be avoided by having one side or the other reduce the article of faith (in the present situation this is a temptation only on the Christian side)' (342). Shortly after that Conzelmann continues by quoting article VII (2) of the Augsburg Confession of 1530 in order to determine the essential nature of the church. The text runs: 'The church is a holy congregation in which the Gospel is purely taught and the sacraments are rightly administered.' The translator, M. Eugene Boring, has not only attributed this to Calvin (it was, of course, written for the most part by Melanchthon) but has also mistranslated *evangelium pure docetur* by 'the pure gospel is taught'. Similar blatant ignorance of Latin by a North American (Harvard) scholar is noted by Pilhofer, *Philippi*, I, 38-41. In many cases Latin is no longer required in ThD or PhD programmes of New Testament or Early Christianity in the United States.

One wonders whether and why these confessional statements have any place in the book, since they have no relevance at all for historical study (cf. my similar question with respect to Schmithals above, pp. 11f.). Fortunately Conzelmann's confessional statements are only a frame for the contents; the latter are an analytical masterpiece and have not yet received the attention that they deserve.[184]

> It is laudable that in the English edition of this book the translator has added the following material to the German edition: his own preface (ix-xii), which sketches out the political background to Conzelmann's book; as well as lectures by Dietz Lange ('In memoriam Hans Conzelmann' [xiii-xviii]) and Eduard Lohse ('Theology and Exegesis. In Memory of Hans Conzelmann' [xix-xxxiii]), both of which were delivered at the academic memorial celebration on 20 June 1990. Last but not least, the 'Bibliography' (343–78) has been enlarged and updated.

At this point reference should also be made to Paula Fredriksen, *From Jesus to Christ. The Origins of the New Testament Images of Jesus* (1988), which is excitingly and sensitively written. The book consists of three parts: I. 'The World of the New Testament' (1–64), II. 'The World of Judaism' (65–130), and III. 'The Christs of the Churches' (131–215). Fredriksen treats her topics with great learning and fairness. She puts Judaism and Christianity side by side almost seamlessly, without going into the question of truth. Jesus is discussed on four pages within Part II (127–30); Part III concludes with Chapter 10, 'Jesus of Nazareth in Christian Tradition' (205–15). The book is a thorough introduction to early Christianity and deserves almost unqualified commendation.

Two points of criticism: 1 Thess. 2.14–16 is said not to be authentic (122). The reason Fredriksen gives first is Rom. 9 –11. Furthermore, 'God's wrath has come upon them at last' (1Thess. 2.16) 'most readily calls to mind the Temple's destruction in 70' (122). But the strongest and most important argument against Pauline authorship of 1 Thess. 2.14–16, according to Fredriksen, is the statement in 1 Cor. 2.8, which certainly comes from Paul: 'None of the rulers of this age understood this [wisdom]; for if they had understood, they would not have crucified the Lord of glory.' According to Fredriksen, the rulers of this world are to be understood as astral, non-human figures. But if Paul is here referring to human agents of the death of Jesus, the rulers of this world must be Romans (and not Jews, as 1 Thess. 2.14–16 says). For Paul the logic behind these sentences does not hold; for him different groups caused the death of Jesus: the Jews in 1 Thess. 2.14–16, God himself (Rom. 8.32), but also Jesus, who delivered himself up (Gal. 2.10). Moreover Fredriksen does not ask at all whether in 1 Thess. 2.14–16 Paul did not adopt a tradition corresponding to Mark 12.

Fredriksen bases her thesis that the Jesus of the Gospel of Mark is a 'man of hurry' (44) on the repeated use of *kai euthys*. That is a very strange view, unless further reasons are given. The expression evidently refers to a chronological sequence and must not be understood in a psychological way.

Eleven years after the publication of *From Jesus to Christ*, in her new work *Jesus of Nazareth, King of the Jews: A Jewish Life and the Emergence of Christianity* (New York 1999), Paula Fredriksen tackles the question of Christian origins by dealing with the issue of how the Jewish life of Jesus was developed into Christianity. Whereas in her earlier work '(t)he actual person whose Jewish life and Roman death stood at the source of the ... later (New Testament) Christian images ... proved more elusive' (xv), Fredriksen 'felt that I needed to know more before I could say more' (ibid.). The book has five chapters. After an introduction with the title 'The History of the Historical Jesus' (3–17) there follow Chapter I, 'Gospel Truth and Historical Innocence' (18–50); Chapter II, 'God and Israel in Roman Antiquity' (51–73); Chapter III, 'Trajectories: Paul, the Gospels, and Jesus' (74–154); Chapter IV, 'Contexts: Galilee, Judea, and Jesus' (155–234); Chapter V, 'The Days in Jerusalem' (235–59). An 'Afterword: Jesus, Christianity, and History' (261–70) offers a conclusion suggesting with

Albert Schweitzer that Jesus should be allowed 'the irreducible otherness of his own antiquity' (270). So far, so good. How does Fredriksen explain the emergence of Christianity, something which she proposed to do? At this point we get nothing but vague answers. She says that after Jesus' death the disciples proclaimed 'that Jesus lived again. God, they said, had raised him from the dead' (261). She cautions, however: 'What those disciples actually saw or experienced is now impossible to say' (ibid.). She continues: 'Paul, whose testimony is late (some twenty years after the events) and admittedly secondhand ('I delivered to you as of first importance what I also received') teaches that the Risen Christ appeared in a *pneumatikon soma*, a 'spiritual body' (261f.).

So Fredriksen leaves the origin of Christianity unexplained,[185] for she does not deal with the links between Jesus and Christianity, meaning (a) the Pre-Pauline traditions, (b) the Hellenists as precursors of Paul, and (c) the question of what is the difference between a disciple of Jesus and a Christian. She has admittedly done important work on the historical Jesus whom she sees, along with Ed Sanders and Albert Schweitzer, as an apocalyptic thinker. But the work on the emergence of primitive Christianity, its history and development, seems still to lie ahead of her.

Paul-Gerhard Müller's book *Der Traditionsprozess im Neuen Testament* ('The Process of Traditions in the New Testament', 1981) does not really fall into the historical sphere, but is nevertheless important for the history of primitive Christianity. The introduction is by Cardinal Joseph Ratzinger (3f.). Müller offers a new way of relating the historically frayed and contradictory traditions about Jesus to each other. Thus his Thesis 4 states: 'The Easter experience led into the sphere of the linguistic interaction of the Jesus tradition with the total christologization of the Jesus phenomenon, in which the pre-Easter Jesuology had already taken on christological colouring' (316). This would be a possible key to the understanding and ordering of such contradictory historical phenomena if Müller could say precisely what the Easter experience is. But here his work fails to give an historical answer. Nevertheless, there are still some important things in the book, e.g. the remarks on Luke 1.1–4 (175–90). Müller does not see the reference to the attempts of the many (Luke 1.1) as a disparaging remark. Rather, Luke knows and estimates 'their quality as language of the impressions gained closer to the phenomenon of Jesus' (177).

Conclusion

In conclusion I will mention some overall perspectives that have emerged as the result of my report.

(a) The description of primitive Christianity should begin with an analysis of the authentic letters of Paul. They remain primary sources, which are strictly to be distinguished from secondary sources like Acts. Many of the works presented in this report depart from this methodological principle and thus a priori stand on shaky ground.[186] Here in general we note an increasing rehabilitation of the historical information in Acts, which is constructive as long as the above-mentioned distinction between primary and secondary sources is observed. But often this no longer happens. On the other hand, one-sidedly negative estimation of Acts is accompanied by a complete neglect of its data in some North American contributions (e.g. Crossan and Mack). I shall not go into them here. At all events, it needs to be noted that Acts is an important source for the first century, even if one must read it critically.

(b) The depiction of primitive Christianity must time and again be made conscious of its own presuppositions. That applies not only to more recent approaches like those of so-called feminist theology or the analysis of the social history of primitive Christianity, but also to historical criticism generally.

145

Anyone who exaggerates historically or theologically generally does so at the expense of the sources.

(c) At the same time, despite the need to be conscious of one's own presuppositions and methods, method is only a preliminary to the scholar's task at hand. As Wilfred Cantwell Smith succinctly remarked about academic method: 'A good academic learns it, assimilates it, forgets it – in the sense that it is taken so much for granted that he moves on from there to the substance of his work. Ideally, he absorbs it to the point where he is unconscious of it, not self-conscious about it.'[187] Ultimately, everything depends on the scholar's eyes and their ability to see. 'The real voyage of discovery consists not in seeking new landscapes but in having new eyes' (Marcel Proust).

(d) The description of primitive Christianity should initially orientate itself on its Jewish roots and learn to evaluate its creative force and multiplicity. As Hengel incisively observes: 'The predicate "Old Testament–Jewish" is often combined with a more "conservative" attitude, and the preference for everything "Hellenistic" with a more "liberal" or "critical" attitude ... This has not furthered the impartiality of the discussion.'[188] From the beginning, the whole fabric of Christianity must be grounded in the whole fabric of Judaism. Thus any history of primitive Christianity should contain an introductory part on Judaism in the Mediterranean world.[189]

APPENDIX I

On the Problem of Pre-Christian Gnosticism

Introduction

For the New Testament scholar, the term 'Gnosticism' derives largely from the work of Rudolf Bultmann and his pupils. Building on the results of the history-of-religions school,[190] Bultmann interpreted the early Christian proclamation against the background of Gnosticism,[191] which he regarded as a religious movement of pre-Christian origin,

> invading the West from the Orient as a competitor of Christianity. Since it appropriated all sorts of mythological and philosophical traditions for its expression, we may call it a synthetic phenomenon. ... In general, we may call it a redemptive religion based on dualism. This is what gives it an affinity to Christianity, an affinity of which even its adherents were aware. Consequently, Gnosticism and Christianity have affected each other in a number of different directions from the earliest days of the Christian movement.[192]

The related *Gnostic myth* can be described as follows. It

> depicts the cosmic drama by which the imprisonment of the sparks of light came about, a drama whose end is already beginning now and will be complete when they are released. The drama's beginning, the tragic event of pri-

147

meval time, is variously told in several variants of the myth
... The demonic powers get into their clutches a person
who originates in the light-world either because he is led
astray by his own foolishness or because he is overcome in
battle ... *Redemption* comes from the heavenly world. Once
more a light-person sent by the highest god, indeed the son
and the 'image' of the most high, comes down from the
light-world bringing Gnosis. He 'wakes' the sparks of light
who have sunk into sleep or drunkenness and 'reminds'
them of their heavenly home.[193]

It is in this sense that I will use the term 'Gnosticism'. First, it
is the designation of a specific myth. Secondly, it provides us
with the name of a movement that was a rival of the early
Christian groups.

Let me now test these two assumptions, commencing with
the latter.

Was Gnosticism a rival movement to Christianity?

In §15 of his *Theology of the New Testament*, mentioned above,
Rudolf Bultmann, under the heading 'Gnostic Motifs', sets
'forth connectedly the extent to which the understanding of
the Christian message in Hellenistic Christianity was unfolded
by means of Gnostic terminology'.[194] The reason for such an
approach is evident: 'For Christian missions, *the Gnostic movement* was a competitor of the most serious and dangerous sort
because of the far-reaching relatedness between them.'[195]
Where did Gnosticism originate? Bultmann is certain that 'the
Gnostic movement did take a concrete form in various baptizing sects in the regions of the Jordan; these also drew certain Jewish groups into their orbit'.[196] As far as the
transmission of Gnostic ideas is concerned Bultmann
remarks: 'Naturally Gnosticism, just like Christianity, is also
spread by wandering teachers.'[197]

Bultmann's pupil Walter Schmithals took great pains to
analyse the penetration of Gnostic teachers into the Pauline
churches, thereby putting historical flesh on the bones of
his teacher's general hypothesis of Gnosticism as a rival

movement of early Christianity.[198] Against Ferdinand Christian Baur's thesis of a Jewish Christian anti-Pauline mission,[199] Schmithals denies any significant influence of Jewish Christianity in the Pauline communities, and actually replaces Jewish Christianity by Gnosticism. Indeed, Paul himself constantly attacked these Gnostic rival missionaries and at the same time quite ironically had a good deal in common with them. According to Schmithals, the Christ-party in Corinth (cf. 1 Cor. 1.12), which for Baur was the focal point of Jewish Christian opposition to Paul, constituted the centre of Gnosticism in Corinth. Its characteristics, to mention the most important ones, were an ascetic detachment from the world (1 Cor. 7.1), a spiritualized eschatology (cf. 1 Cor. 15.12), and a docetic christology (cf. 1 Cor. 2.8; 12.3).

In general, Schmithals' bold reconstruction, also based on an elaborate partition theory of the Pauline letters,[200] has found little assent in scholarship. To mention only a few objections: In order to be able to defend a unified Gnostic opposition to Paul, Schmithals has to argue against the view that 1 Thessalonians (or its parts) is the oldest extant letter of Paul. Instead he places it after 1 Corinthians during the so-called third missionary journey (= Acts 18.23–21.15).[201] But the traditional view on the early place of 1 Thessalonians in Paul's career has solid support to offer, as it is based on the apostle's remarks in the letter itself. In 1.5 and 2.1 (cf. 3.1) Paul refers to the initial preaching in Thessalonica which cannot have happened long before, and the combination of this with Acts 17 leads to the generally accepted view that 1 Thessalonians was written during the so-called second missionary journey (Acts 15.36–18.22). However, if 1 Corinthians was written after 1 Thessalonians, there is not enough time for Gnostic teachers of the type mentioned in that letter to intrude into the Thessalonian community. Hence Schmithals had to twist the historical evidence to uphold his preconceived theory.

Let me hasten to add that not a single text in 1 Thessalonians itself gives rise to the suspicion that there were Gnostics in Thessalonica. At no point is there even a trace of disappointment over the relationship between the congregation and the apostle. How could Paul have said that he had no need to write to them regarding brotherly love (1 Thess. 4.9) if incidents similar to those in Corinth had occurred in their congregation?

I argue thus despite Wolfgang Harnisch's attempt to establish the view that the same Gnostic group is involved in 1 Cor. 15 and 1 Thess. 4,[202] for Harnisch fails to account for the different responses to the allegedly identical situation. Paul in 1 Corinthians strongly emphasizes the future resurrection of Christians: if one denies this resurrection, then Christ has not been raised (1 Cor. 15.16). This polemic may indeed be directed against a Gnostic point of view (see below). Yet in 1 Thess. 4.13–18 we find the argument that Christians who have died suffer no disadvantage when compared with the living, for the dead too will be caught up to participate in everlasting fellowship with Christ. This means, however, that in contrast to 1 Cor. 15, 1 Thess. 4.13–18 does not make the resurrection of Christians a major point of discussion. (It is only an auxiliary thought to ensure the future union of the minority of deceased Christians.) For this reason Harnisch's assumption that the resurrection of the Christians had become a controversial point in Thessalonica is open to serious question. Hence a Gnostic point of view as the target of Paul's statements remains unlikely.

To formulate a preliminary conclusion: the thesis of a Gnostic movement that systematically invaded the Pauline communities finds little or no support in the earliest extant letter of Paul, 1 Thessalonians. Studies of the other Pauline communities (Corinth, Philippi, Galatia) do not yield any different result.[203] Scholarship must in all likelihood abandon the hypothesis that a cohesive Gnostic movement[204] is reflected in Paul's letters. 'The plain truth is that you could not have found anyone in Corinth to direct you to a Gnostic church; the overwhelming probability is that there was no such thing.'[205] Indeed, the same negative statement applies to the suggestion that there were Gnostic churches in Philippi, Thessalonica, Ephesus or in the province of Galatia. Yet there seems to have been at least one case of a Gnostic group that extended in the first and second century from Samaria to

Rome: the Simonians. They worshipped Simon as the first God Zeus while at the same time telling the myth about his (first) thought for whose salvation Simon Zeus, the highest god, had appeared. Moreover, there must have been some contact between them and the Hellenist Philip (see Acts 8.9–13).[206] But this does not rehabilitate the hypothesis of a unified Gnostic front in the Pauline communities.

Gnosticism as a designation of a specific myth

If in all likelihood, with the possible exception of the Simonians, there was no such thing as a rival Gnostic movement within or competing with Pauline Christianity, the question arises whether there ever was a specific Gnostic myth as an entity of its own. Having dismissed the notion of a general Gnostic movement in early Christianity, should we also abandon the category 'Gnosticism' altogether?[207]

At this point I will insist that the existence of a Gnostic myth as outlined following Rudolf Bultmann's description at the beginning of my essay can be demonstrated on the basis of Paul's letters. For the sake of further clarification, here is the proposal made at the 'Messina Colloquium on the Origins of Gnosticism'. The participants propose the following formulations as regards 'gnosticism': It

> involves a series a coherent series of characteristics that can be summarized in the idea of a divine spark in man, deriving from the divine realm, fallen into this world of fate, birth and death, and needing to be awakened by the divine counterpart of the self in order finally to be reintegrated. Compared with other conceptions of a 'devolution' of the divine, this idea is based ontologically on the conception of a downward movement of the divine whose periphery (often called Sophia or Ennoia) had to submit to the fate of entering into a crisis and producing – even if only indirectly – this world, upon which it cannot turn its back, since it is necessary for it to recover its pneuma – a dualistic conception on a dualistic background, expressed in a double movement of devolution and reintegration ...

Not every *gnosis* is Gnosticism, but only that which involves
in this perspective the idea of the divine consubstantiality
of the spark that is in need of being awakened and reintegrated.[208]

The first text that fits in with or at least does not contradict
such a conclusion is:

1 Cor. 2.6–8

[6] Yet we speak wisdom among the perfect, although it is
not a wisdom of this age or of the rulers of this age, who
are doomed to perish. [7] But we speak God's wisdom in a
mystery, the hidden (wisdom), which God decreed
before the ages for our glory. [8] None of the rulers of this
age understood this; for if they had, they would not have
crucified the Lord of glory.

In this text Paul is using a unique motif with respect to the
subject of the killing of Jesus, the Lord of glory. In general
Paul speaks of Jesus giving himself to be killed (Gal. 1.4; 2.20)
or God handing over his son Jesus to be put to death (Rom.
8.32) or accuses the Jews of murdering God's son (1 Thess.
2.15).[209] In contrast, 1 Cor. 2.8 attributes the killing to the
ignorance of the rulers who would *not* have committed the
killing had they recognized the identity of the victim who in
reality is the wisdom of God. By hiding his/her own identity
the redeemer is able to overthrow the hostile powers of this
world. The logic behind the text obviously presupposes that
the rulers were doomed because they attempted a killing that
in reality was impossible.[210] Given the logic behind Paul's
christological statement, one has to conclude that he 'is
picking up a theme widely used in Gnosticism[211] and applying
it to the passion and death of Jesus. Christology is being
expressed . . . in terms borrowed from the syncretistic religious
milieu'.[212] The theme behind 1 Cor. 2.8 can now be amply
documented in the Nag Hammadi Library in contexts that are
independent of the New Testament.

Here are two examples. The first is from the Paraphrase of
Shem (= Paraph. Shem [NHC VII, 1]) [213] and the second
from the Apocalypse of Adam (= Apoc. Adam [NHC V, 5]).[214]

Both texts reflect a gnosticism that shows no influence by Christianity.[215] While thus witnessing to the existence of a pre-Christian Gnostic myth, in chronological terms the texts still do not predate the beginnings of Christianity. But this is not a valid reason to regard Gnosticism as chronologically younger than Christianity. Bluntly put, unless one can show that Christian elements were removed from these and other texts only at a later stage,[216] they can serve as a witness to the existence of a pre-Christian Gnostic myth.

Paraph. Shem 36.2–24

(The heavenly redeemer Derdekeas says:)

It is I who opened the eternal gates which are shut
    from the beginning.
 – To those who long for the height of life, and
    those who are worthy of the repose he revealed
    them. –
I granted perception to those who are perceptive.
I disclosed to them all the thoughts and the
    teaching of the righteous ones.
And I did not become their enemy at all.
But I – having endured the <u>wrath</u> of the world –
    was victorious.

There was not one of them who knew me.
The gates of fire and endless smoke opened
    against me.
All the winds *rose up against me.*
The thunderings and the lightning-flashes for a
    time will *rise up against me.*
And they will bring their <u>wrath</u> upon me.
And on account of me as far as the flesh is
    concerned, they will rule over them according to
    race.[217]

A similar topic is dealt with in 'The Apocalypse of Adam'. The third coming of the 'Illuminator' leads to persecution, for the 'powers' are unaware of his identity.

Apoc. Adam 77.4–18

Then the god of the powers will be disturbed, saying,
'What is the power of this man who is higher than we?'
Then he will arouse a great wrath against that man. And
the glory will withdraw and dwell in holy houses which it
has chosen for itself. And the powers will not see it with
their eyes nor will they see the illuminator either. Then
they will punish the flesh of the man upon whom the
holy spirit has come.[218]

How should we explain Paul's use of a Gnostic motif in his
discussion of God's wisdom? I would suggest that it was, simply
put, part of Paul's own world-view. One has to take into
account that the aforementioned instruction about God's
wisdom was part of Paul's teaching to the mature (1 Cor. 2.6).
Evidently in his instruction the apostle distinguishes between
two levels: (a) basic teaching for the converts, (b) advanced
teaching for the initiated. Such a distinction has a parallel in
Hebrews 5.13 and resembles the Gnostic differentiation
between three groups of human beings: the spiritual, the
psychic and the earthly.[219]

Does my analysis make Paul a Gnostic? By no means! I wish
only to stress that his writings sometimes presuppose or come
close to a Gnostic myth. It is, however, no integral part of his
own deliberative thinking, for he himself excludes a total
dualism. At the same time, Gnostic motifs are not confined to
one passage in Paul's authentic letters. There are plenty of
others.

In 2 Cor. 4.4 Paul again comes very close to a dualism
reminiscent of that in 1 Cor. 2.6–8. This time he uses the
expression 'the god of this world', which resembles 'the rulers
of this age' (1 Cor. 2.8). The whole passage reads as follows:

2 Cor. 4.4–6

[4] In their case (= those who are perishing) the god of
this age has blinded the minds of the unbelievers, to
keep them from seeing the light of the gospel of the
glory of Christ, who is the likeness of God. [5] For we do
not proclaim ourselves, but Jesus Christ as Lord, and

ourselves as your servants for Jesus' sake. [6] For it is God who said, 'Let light shine out of darkness,' who has shone in our hearts to give the light of the knowledge of the glory of God in the face of Christ.

After the discussion of letter and spirit in 2 Cor. 3 Paul defends himself and describes the devil as the god of this world in a rather bold way in order to explain the unbeliever's refusal to accept the gospel. After speaking so audaciously Paul obviously sees the danger of such a language and in v. 6, which in form parallels v. 4, adds a reference to Gen. 1.3. By doing so he excludes any real dualism at the outset, but even here he cannot avoid the language of Gnosticism, since in the complicated construction of the sentence, 'light', 'knowledge' and 'glory' continue to have a Gnostic ring.[220]

So far we have discussed two examples from the Pauline letters which in all likelihood reflect a Gnostic myth and therefore attest Gnosticism as an ingredient of Paul's world-view. The same conclusion can be drawn with respect to Paul's view of human beings. Of course, it is obvious that the Old Testament is the basis for Paul's remarks about human beings. When the apostle talks about 'all flesh' (1 Cor. 1.29; Gal. 2.16) he is simply reiterating the Jewish point of view. And when speaking of the weakness of the flesh (Rom. 6.19) or designating the nature of man as 'flesh and blood' (1 Cor. 15.50; Gal. 1.16) the same foundation is evident.[221] However, there are also other passages that are strongly reminiscent of Gnostic anthropology.

Gal. 5.17

The desires of the flesh are opposed to the spirit, and the desires of the spirit are opposed to the flesh; for these are against each other, to prevent you from doing what you want.

To be sure, this is an explanation serving to exhort the Galatians to remember that they are under the spirit and not under the law that Paul associates with the flesh. But the dualism between flesh and spirit remains without any basis in the Old Testament tradition. Paul's 'treatment and evaluation of the flesh is more congenial to the Gnostic context'[222] than to anything else (including Philo). His 'perception of the flesh as the entry point for the sinful desires that ultimately bring death to humans unless they receive the Spirit of Christ comes very close to what one finds in Gnostic mythology'.[223]

Having investigated these various Gnostic elements as part of Paul's world-view, we must now turn our attention to other texts which never belonged to Paul's language or thought, but derive from the members of his own community.

1 Cor. 12.1–3

[1] Now concerning spiritual gifts, brothers, I don't want you to be ignorant. [2]You know that when you were Gentiles you were led astray and carried away to dumb idols. [3] Therefore I want you to understand that no one speaking by the Spirit of God ever says, 'Jesus be cursed!' and no one can say, 'Jesus is Lord!' except in the Holy Spirit.

In this text the apostle sets out to deal with the Corinthians' question (indicated by v. 1) concerning spiritual gifts. After looking back in v. 2 to their Gentile past which was characterized by being 'led astray and carried away to dumb idols,' i.e. by moments of ecstasy experienced in heathen religions, Paul in v. 3 proceeds to answer the question about spiritual gifts: 'Therefore I want you to understand that no one speaking by the Spirit of God ever says, "Jesus be cursed!" and no one can say, "Jesus is Lord" except in the Holy Spirit.'

Two explanations have been offered to shed light on the strange exclamation, 'Jesus be cursed!' (a) Paul made up the curse against Jesus as a counterpart to the formula 'Jesus is Lord'. (b) Some Corinthians spoke the curse against Jesus in ecstasy during worship.

Suggestion (a) is highly unlikely for two reasons. First, the curse against Jesus precedes the sentence 'Jesus is Lord'. One would have expected a reverse order if the curse were purely rhetorical. Secondly, the curse against Jesus is highly offensive.

Suggestion (b) is probably correct. Some Christians in Corinth during worship *did* curse Jesus.[224] This cursing has affinities to Gnosticism, being based on a sharp distinction between Jesus, who is irrelevant for salvation, and Christ, who really matters. Furthermore, the cursing of Jesus was actually practised by the Gnostic group of the Ophites that the church father Origen described early in the third century. In *Contra Celsum* he refers to a ritual of the Ophites, namely that 'they do not admit anyone into their congregation unless he has first pronounced curses against Jesus' (VI 28).[225] This ritual had as its goal the exclusion of anyone with a belief in the divinity *and* humanity of Jesus. In the same way the author of 2 John demands that everyone should confess Jesus' coming in the flesh and not receive those with a different faith into their houses (v. 10). Indeed, he does not accept the belief in the divinity of Jesus if it is not accompanied by a belief in Jesus' full humanity (v. 7; cf. 1 John 4.2). Thus the emphatic confession of Jesus' coming in the flesh served the purpose to exclude anybody who solely believed in the heavenly Jesus.

Certainly we should not postulate a genetic connection between the Ophites and the persons behind 2 John or the Corinthians who cursed Jesus. But this much is certain: '*both* cases of cursing are to be ascribed to the basic tendency of Gnostic Christology, sharply to separate the man Jesus and their heavenly spiritual being Christ, and to regard the former as without significance.'[226]

Finally, there are plenty of other Gnostic texts that derogate (the earthly) Jesus. From the Nag Hammadi documents (a) the docetic hymn from the Second Treatise of the Great Seth (= Treat. Seth [NHC VII, 2]) and (b) a part of a dialogue between Peter and Jesus from the Apocalypse of Peter (= Apoc. Peter [NHC VII, 3]) are especially interesting.

Treat. Seth 55.9–57.7

And I was in the jaws of lions.
And the plan which they devised about me (led) to
    the dissolving of their deception and their lack
    of understanding.

I did not give myself up to them as they had
    planned.
And I was not disturbed in any way, although they
    tormented me.
And I did not really die but only in semblance,
so that they would (not) put me to shame through
    them because these are a part of me.
I was removed from any shame,
and I was not anxious in the face of what had
    happened to me through them.
I was only apparently to become a slave of fear,
but I suffered pain (only) in their sight and
    thought, so that a word will never be found to
    speak about them.
For my death, which they think happened,
    (happened) to them only in their deception and
    their blindness, when they nailed their man unto
    their death.
For their minds did not see me.
For they were deaf and blind.
And in doing this, they condemn themselves.
Yes, they saw me; they punished me.
It was another, their father, who drank the gall and
    the vinegar; it was not I.
They struck me with the reed.
It was another, who bore the cross on his shoulder,
    Simon.
It was another upon whose head they placed the
    crown of thorns.
But I was rejoicing in the height over all the
    (apparent) wealth of the archons and the seed
    of their deception, of their vain glory.
And I was laughing at their ignorance.
And I subjected all their powers.
For when I came downward, no one saw me.
For I was altering my shapes, changing from one
    appearance to an(other) appearance.
And therefore, when I was at their gates, I assumed
    their likeness.

For I passed them by quietly, and I saw the places,
and I did not fear and was not ashamed, for I was
undefiled.

And I was speaking with them, mingling with them
through those who are mine, and I trod on those
who were strict on them in envy,

and I quenched the fire.

And I did all these things out of my will to
accomplish what I desired by the will of the
Father above.[227]

Apoc. Peter 81.15–82.16

The Saviour said to me, 'The one whom you see above
alongside the cross, joyful and **laughing**, is the living
Jesus. But the one into whose hands and feet nails are
driven is his bodily part, which is the substitute. *They put
to shame* this, which came into being in his likeness. But
look at him and me.'

And after I had looked, I said, 'Lord, no one sees you.
Let us flee from this place.'

But he said to me, 'I have told you that they are blind.
Depart from them. And see, they do not know what they
are saying. For the son of their glory *they have put to shame*
instead of my servant.'

And I saw how someone was about to approach us,
who resembled him, and how the one who was by the
cross **laughed**. And he was *full* of the Holy Spirit, and
he is (was) the Saviour. And there was a great, *ineffable*
light around them, and the multitude of *ineffable* and
invisible angels praising them. And it was I who saw
when he was revealed as the one to whom praise was
given.[228]

Given these parallels, which could easily be multiplied, one
cannot but assume a Gnostic background for the curse against
Jesus in 1 Cor. 12.3.

But now several questions have to be asked. Did the Corinthians who cursed Jesus already share a Gnostic viewpoint
before they joined the Pauline community? Or did Paul

impart a Gnostic world-view to them? If the latter should be the case, why does Paul attack a Gnostic view not only in 1 Cor. 12.3 but also in 2 Cor. 4.4–6? Before trying to answer these questions, I would like to analyse another Pauline text that relates to the problem discussed so far.

1 Cor. 15.12

Now if Christ is proclaimed as having been raised from the dead, how can some of you say that there is no resurrection of the dead?

In the rest of chapter 15 Paul develops his idea of a bodily resurrection which according to the apostle can be deduced directly from the proclamation 1 Cor. 15.3b–5: 'Christ died for our sins in accordance with the scriptures, [4] he was buried, he has been raised in accordance with the scriptures, [5] he appeared to Cephas, then to the Twelve.'

Paul's statement in v. 12 that some in the Corinthian church rejected the resurrection, implying that the dead perish, seems not to be quite correct. First, such a conclusion by Paul is improbable, for all the Corinthians had accepted the proclamation of 1 Cor. 15.3b–5 as Paul himself acknowledges (v. 12a). Secondly, the Corinthians who were under attack by Paul practised baptism on behalf of the dead (v. 29). This is a point which Paul himself made against the total denial of the resurrection by those who practise such a baptism. But it could also be used in favour of the so-called deniers of a resurrection. Thirdly, the major difference between the Corinthians and Paul was most likely the issue of a bodily resurrection which Paul defended and which the Corinthians, who came from a Gentile background, did not understand. Probably the Corinthians thought of the resurrection as a spiritual experience which had already happened and which continued in the present. With respect to Jesus they simply could not believe in his bodily resurrection and interpreted the tradition of Christ's resurrection (1 Cor. 15.4) differently from Paul. Thus it is most likely that they already held a docetic christological view and separated Christ who matters from Jesus who was rotting away in the tomb.[229] When

Paul in v. 12 bases his thesis of Christ's and the Christians' future bodily resurrection on the creed of the resurrection of Christ as preached during the founding mission (v. 4), the Corinthians were not impressed. Unable to share Paul's interpretation of the creed, instead they read a distinction between Jesus and Christ into it and could do without a future bodily resurrection.

Summary and outlook

Let me summarize the result of my study. (a) Among other elements, Paul's world-view presupposes Gnosticism, i.e. a sort of Gnostic myth. (b) Paul nowhere fully endorses this myth in order to interpret the basic proclamation of Jesus being the lord and the one who died and rose again. (c) Paul's Gentile Christian pupils were more open to this myth than Paul, and used and/or developed it further to express their faith. (d) While there is not enough evidence to postulate a Gnostic movement within primitive Christianity, there are many reflections of Gnostic thought in the earliest extant documents of the New Testament, i.e. in the letters of Paul.

Is it possible to find the origin(s) of this myth and to determine how old it is? Whatever the answers to these questions will be, the issue of a pre-Christian Gnosticism is still an important subject that should not be resolved by denying Gnosticism altogether. (From the outset, such a thesis would come to grief in view of the Gnostic Simonians, anyway.) The New Testament itself remains one of the most fertile fields in which to search for the existence and nature of Gnosticism, the more so, since in 1 Tim. 6.20–1 ('Avoid the godless chatter and contradictions of what is falsely called knowledge, for by professing it some have missed the mark as regards the faith') there is obviously evidence for Gnostic myth in the New Testament itself. Bishop Irenaeus may not have been so wrong after all when he used 'knowledge falsely so called' from 1 Tim. 6.20–1 as an umbrella term for 'a wide range of heresies for which the modern scholars have supplied the category "Gnosticism".'[230] Even so outspoken a critic of a pre-

Christian Gnosticism as Martin Hengel grants that 1 Tim. 6.20–1 has Gnostic teachings in mind.[231] Yet he fails to realize that by dating the Pastorals around 110–120 CE he has at least granted a beginning of Gnosticism roughly at the same time as Christianity, because the origin of teachings hardly coincides with their first attestation.

In view of the available evidence presented in this appendix there can be no doubt about the existence of a Gnostic myth in the first century, though apart from what we know about the Simonians little can be said about Gnosticism as a movement. Given the nature of the Gnostic religion it may be worthwhile exploring the question whether Gnosticism is possibly a structure or a specific stage that various religions in antiquity went through. But with these remarks I have opened another page of the mysterious book that is commonly called Gnosticism.

APPENDIX 2

Gerd Theissen's A Theory of Primitive Christian Religion

At the beginning of the 1970s Gerd Theissen gave a whole generation of theological students in Germany and beyond a new fascination with the historical reconstruction of primitive Christianity by his sociological and exegetical works. Having incurred the hostility of officials of the Protestant church, who for example prevented him from being called to a chair at the University of Kiel, and professors of New Testament theology, who initially made it impossible for him to be called to Heidelberg, to begin with he was denied an appointment to a German university. He had to earn his living as a school teacher and later taught New Testament abroad, at the University of Copenhagen.[232] Once he had shown by his *On Having a Critical Faith* (1978, ET 1979) that he was a confessing theologian who explicitly identified himself with the Christian traditions (see the Preface), things turned in his favour. Since 1980 Theissen has been probably the best-known German New Testament scholar internationally, as Ordinarius Professor in Heidelberg. His scholarly achievements have been rewarded not only by calls to other universities but also by several honorary doctorates.

This appendix examines Gerd Theissen's *A Theory of Primitive Christian Religion* to see whether it advances our knowledge of the origin and history of primitive Christianity. I shall deal with it in precisely the same way as in the criticisms of other contributions presented in my book. In other words, I shall measure Theissen's work exclusively by 1. whether it does justice to the criteria of historical criticism; 2. whether and to what degree it enriches our historical knowledge of primitive Christianity; and 3. whether it can fit individual results plausibly into the overall development of primitive Christianity.

However, first of all I must describe the purpose of Theissen's book, since its aim is not quite a description of the history of primitive Christianity. Theissen wants to develop a theory of primitive Christianity (see the title of his book), to present a 'decidedly undogmatic analysis of primitive Christianity' (248), 'a theoretical depiction of primitive Christianity' (252). He writes:

> A theory of primitive Christianity seeks to describe in general religious categories the dynamic of primitive Christian belief which governs the whole of life. It seeks to make possible a twofold reading of this faith: a view from inside and a view from outside – and above all to mediate between these two perspectives (1).

Laudably Theissen puts his definition of 'religion' at the beginning. He writes: *'Religion is a cultural sign language which promises a gain in life by corresponding to an ultimate reality'* (2). Here he deliberately leaves open the question 'whether and in what way there is an ultimate reality' (2).

At the same time the author is pursuing missionary aims with his book. Right at the beginning he makes this clear in the form of a confession:

> I am a Christian. I teach theology in a theological faculty. I am an ordained minister. I preach. I love primitive Christianity and its texts (xviii).

Theissen understands primitive Christian religion as 'sign-language – a "semiotic cathedral"– which has been erected in the midst of history: not out of stones but out of signs of various kinds' (17). He sees himself as more than a curator of the semiotic cathedral which he has described (18). Rather, this is the place in which he himself preaches and prays.

I would like to show this cathedral to all visitors and communicate to them something of its meaning and significance. I do not mind whether or not the visitors also want to take part in worship, whether they are at home in a different cathedral, or whether they avoid such places. But in my walk round the cathedral it would not be enough for me ... merely to relate historical facts about the history of its buildings or to give aesthetic descriptions of its style. I would also want to communicate something of its religious significance to all the visitors. If I left this out, I would be leaving out the reason why I love my cathedral. Hence this attempt at a theory of primitive (Christian) religion: it is a visit to and an explanation of the primitive Christian sign world which gives everyone the freedom to get to know it, yet leave it without prayer. Of course I would be delighted if the visitors understood why one can pray in such a cathedral and why in the view of those who built it and developed it that is the primary significance of this place (306f).[233]

The book consists of five main parts.

Part One deals with 'Myth and History in Primitive Christianity' (19–60). The section 'The Significance of the Historical Jesus for the Origin of Primitive Christian Religion' describes the revitalization of the Jewish religion by Jesus (21–40) and the section 'How Did Jesus Come to be Deified?' sketches the transformation of the Jewish sign system by post-Easter belief in Jesus (41–60).

Part Two deals with 'The Ethics of Primitive Christianity' (61–117). It has three sections, 'The Two Basic Values of the Primitive Christian Ethic: Love of Neighbour and Renunciation of Status' (63–80), 'Dealing with Power and Possessions in Primitive Christianity. Ethical Demands in the Light of the Two Basic Values: I' (81–99), and 'Dealing with Wisdom and Holiness in Primitive Christianity. Ethical Demands in the Light of the Two Basic Values: II' (100–17).

Part Three deals with 'The Ritual Sign Language of Primitive Christianity' (119–60). It has two sections, 'The Origin of the Primitive Christian Sacraments from Symbolic Actions'

(121–38), and 'The Sacrificial Interpretation of the Death of Jesus and the End of Sacrifice' (139–60)

Part Four deals with 'Primitive Christian Religion as an Autonomous Sign World' (161–206). One section describes from Paul to the Synoptic Gospels, 'The Way from Primitive Christian Religion to an Autonomous Sign World' (163–84), the other 'The Gospel of John: The Internal Autonomy of the Primitive Christian Sign World is Brought into Consciousness' (185–206).

Part Five deals with 'The Crises and Consolidation of Primitive Christianity' (207–307). It has three sections, 'The Crises of Primitive Christianity' (209–48), 'Plurality and Unity in Primitive Christianity and the Origin of a Canon' (249–85), and 'Conclusion: The Construction and Plausibility of the Primitive Christian Sign World' (286–307).

It is often difficult to follow Theissen's arguments. They presuppose a considerable knowledge of the New Testament and also a good deal of knowledge of the theory of religion. Wayne A. Meeks criticizes Theissen on this last point. He remarks that Theissen

> draws upon the most dissonant of theoretical perspectives, ranging from the market-based rational-choice model of Rodney Stark to the semiotic model of Clifford Geertz, from functionalism to conflict theory, from cognitive dissonance to social stigmatization. Theissen is very good at typology and classification. With a few deft strokes, he lines out the major positions on each theoretical position. What one misses is *argument*, a wrestling with the positive and negative features of each system and some clear rationale for dealing with the conflicts among them.[234]

Yet it is evident 'that the really hard problems in the history of ancient Christianity cannot be solved at the theoretical level' [235] and the importance of a book on the religion of the first Christians is to be measured by its proximity to the historical reality of that time. That is what I shall do in connection with the points which follow.

1. The canonical claim of the Synoptic Gospels, the biblical canon and the concept of primitive Christianity

(a) The term 'canonical' appears for the first time in connection with the New Testament Gospels. Theissen writes:

> With the *form* of the Gospel, primitive Christianity gives itself its own basic narrative, and parts company with the narrative community of Judaism. For the Gospels were written *a priori* with a canonical claim (169).

He later makes this claim more specific by stating that the Gospels of Matthew and Luke wanted to replace the Gospel of Mark (267f.). In other words, one canonical claim overtrumped the other. But things were different with the Gospel of John:

> We find an affirmation of different Gospels only in the Gospel of John. In its two conclusions the Gospel emphasizes that it offers only a selection from a much greater Jesus tradition (268).

In view of what the author of the Third Gospel himself says about the purpose of his writing ('so that you [Theophilus] may know the basis of the teaching in which you were instructed'), it is difficult to establish that the Gospel of Luke makes any canonical claim for itself. When Theissen speaks of the Fourth Gospel it is to be regretted that he starts from the final form of the Fourth Gospel (cf. 354f. n. 1), instead of treating John 21 as a secondary appendix. This has consequences for any overall assessment of the Gospel of John (chs 1–20).[236] For historical reconstruction, source criticism has the same function as chronology: they are the 'two eyes of history'. We must neglect neither to the detriment of critical work.

(b) Theissen claims that the canon of the Old and New Testaments is intended 'as a confession of plurality' (261). It 'is the great achievement of early catholic primitive Christianity, which I would prefer to call "canonical primitive Christ-

ianity"' (270). 'It is decisive that the canon did not suppress
the inner plurality of primitive Christianity, but preserved it.
That is the only reason why it was accepted so quickly and
without conflicts in a pluralistic primitive Christianity' (270).
Heikki Räisänen has rightly criticized these harmonizing
judgements:

> Such a reading is plausible from the perspective of the
> subsequent history of its effect, and it may be beneficial to
> use the New Testament canon in such a manner in a
> church today. But to interpret the situation in the second
> century in this way runs the risk of anachronism. On the
> contrary, patristic authors took great efforts to deny diver-
> sity, as e.g. the numerous attempts to explain away the
> differences between the gospels show.[237]

(c) Theissen links the formation of the canon to the end of
primitive Christianity and claims that the exegetes only come
later.

> This formation of the canon is the *end of primitive Christ-
> ianity*. The history of primitive Christianity is the history of
> the origin of a religious system. Its origin is completed and
> concluded the moment that this sign system is no longer
> developed by the composition of new writings but is
> regarded as closed. From now on the further development
> of the religion is carried on by interpretation of a sign
> system which is regarded as closed – by exegesis. To exag-
> gerate: primitive Christianity dies with the exegetes. The
> productive phase of the formation of a new symbolic lan-
> guage comes to an end. The formation of the canon
> separates primitive Christianity from the early church
> (251).

While the end of primitive Christianity may very well coincide
with the formation of the canon, there were certainly exegetes
before its final formation. As early as the beginning of the
second century the Christian Gnostic Basilides wrote a 20-
volume commentary on the Gospel. In the words of Hans
Lietzmann:

Basilides was the first to expound a Christian book, and indeed nothing less than 'the gospel'. We cannot say whether one of our four gospels, or a selection, prepared by Basilides himself, of a gospel-harmony, constituted the text. That it was not apocryphal is shown by all the extant citations of the gospel which the Basilidians quoted. The most significant fact is that this book, written to expound gnostic doctrine, is the very first commentary on a gospel. No Christian who was a member of the church catholic, had, up to that date, made a gospel a subject of a continuous exegesis ... Further, Basilides dealt with the gospel as sacred scripture, and therefore explained it allegorically, in exactly the same way as the Church was accustomed to explain the Old Testament. On this point, the Church had not yet gone so far as to put the gospels on a similar level to the traditional book, i.e. the Old Testament, and so treat it as itself Holy Scripture; the New Testament canon was still at the prenatal stage. In this respect, again, gnosticism stimulated the Church and called forth new activity just because it had gone on ahead.[238]

2. Jesus – A member of two religions, Judaism and Christianity?

Theissen writes:

One of the most important results of 200 years of modern research into Jesus is that he belongs to two religions: to Judaism, to which he was attached with all his heart, and to Christianity, whose central point of reference he became after his death – on the basis of interpretations of his person which his Jewish followers gave (22).

As the historical Jesus was not a Christian, he cannot belong to Christianity. The research into Jesus carried out for 250 years has demonstrated that Jesus is a part of Jewish religion.[239] Rudolf Bultmann takes account of this clear finding in his *Theology of the New Testament* by including the 'message of Jesus' in the presuppositions of his theology of the New Testament. The introductory sentences of his book run:

> The message of Jesus is a presupposition for the theology of the New Testament rather than a part of that theology itself. For New Testament theology consists in the unfolding of those ideas by means of which Christian faith makes sure of its own object, basis and consequences. But Christian faith did not exist until there was a Christian kerygma.[240]

Precisely because of this anti-Judaistic misuse of the figure of Jesus of Nazareth we should not surreptitiously make the historical Jesus an adherent of Christianity. Taking up a remark of Alfred Loisy, one could say that Jesus expected the kingdom of God; Christianity came and commandeered Jesus against his will.

3. The resurrection of Jesus – an objective event?

Criticizing the hypothesis of subjective visions, according to which the Easter visions were exclusively products of the psychological processes in the disciples, Theissen writes:

> It completely depends on our construction of reality whether we think it possible that an objective message can also be communicated to people through internal psychological processes. To take an analogy: in my view there can be no doubt about the 'objectivity', i.e. the factual correctness, of some transfer of information after the death of people (of which stories are told above all in time of war), even if we cannot fit them into our scientific constructions of reality. We cannot exclude them (334 n. 5).

This view recalls the hypothesis of objective visions which in recent times has been associated with Hans Grass. Grass had remarked:

> Where ... historical criticism is taken seriously ... so that even the most critical possibilities are taken into account,

i.e. in the case of the resurrection that no empty tomb and no appearances of the Risen Christ can be demonstrated in the 'spatial bodily world', but only visions of the disciples; and where on the other hand we cannot surrender the belief that Christ lives as the exalted Lord, because faith and the church would no longer have any right to existence without a living exalted Lord, the attempt must be made to think of the two together. The hypothesis of objective visions has made this attempt and done so theologically; for unlike the hypothesis of subjective visions it is a theological and not an historical hypothesis, because it maintains the trans-subjective origin of the Easter visions and the Easter faith and the transcendent reality of what is seen and believed in these visions.[241]

Grass's attempt to rescue the foundation of the Christian proclamation of the resurrection has rightly not met with approval. The introduction of the hypothesis of objective visions must be regarded as an apologetic ploy, since a 'vision is by definition something which cannot be examined inter-subjectively'.[242] However much Grass deserves sympathy for taking historical criticism seriously, his *theology* is contra-dictory, because with the vision hypothesis he presupposes ' a this-worldly subject as an unchanged fixed entity'.[243]

First, the arguments that can be advanced against Grass's view can also be advanced against Theissen. Secondly, it is to be doubted whether in fact an approach can be made to the primitive Christian confession of the resurrection by means of parapsychology. After all, spirits of dead people likewise appear, and in spiritism there are messages from the beyond which we cannot exclude despite our scientific construction of reality.

Apologetic theologians of the present day like Theissen are fond of pointing out that the scientific understanding of reality rests on a particular picture of the world, and may not unquestioningly be presupposed in a treatment of the Easter texts. But here what Alexander Bommarius said in a debate on the resurrection of Jesus applies:

Even if we are aware of the relativity of our own pictures of the world – that we in fact have only our 'picture' – in life we must rely on the conditions of finitude. However, how long we can continue to rely on this picture of the world is another question, a question which we cannot answer, since how long is something that will simply emerge.[244]

At all events, it does not automatically follow from a recognition that the scientific picture of the world is not without its presuppositions that Jesus left his tomb with a new body created by God or that God sent down a light for Peter with a 'telegram from heaven'.

4. The Judaistic crisis in the first century – a consequence of the Edict of Claudius in the year 49?

Theissen bases his remarks on the occasion for the Judaistic crisis of the first century on a dubious chronology of the Edict of the emperor Claudius against the Jews.[245] He writes:

> The recognition of the Gentile mission at the Apostolic Council gave great impetus to the Gentile mission. The disturbances in the community in Rome shortly after the Apostolic Council (46/48), because the message of Christ was being actively presented there, could be a remote effect of the Apostolic Council. Christianity would already have been present in Rome. However, a Jewish community could only provoke unrest if it accepted uncircumcised Gentiles as members on an equal footing. This unrest led to the edict of Claudius in AD 49 and the expulsions of those who had played a prominent part in the unrest. The expulsion affected Jews (221).

The date of the Edict of Claudius allows Theissen to describe the reaction of Jewish communities in the Roman empire to the Christian communities coming into being in the Pauline mission sphere.

> After the Edict of Claudius the Jewish communities attempted even more strongly to prevent the new move-

ment from gaining a footing in the places where they lived
(221)

Theissen then cites as examples of the effects of the Edict of
Claudius the actions of the local Jewish community against
Paul described in Acts 17.5–9 and 18.12–17.[246]

> At all events, the Jews did not want to risk being expelled
> from Thessaloniki, like (some of) the Roman Jews. By cont-
> rast, in Corinth the Jewish community appeared before the
> governor Gallio with the direct accusation, in order to dis-
> tance itself from the Christians (221).

Claudius' Edict on the Jews also gives Theissen the key for
deriving the demand for circumcision by Jewish Christians in
the Pauline communities from the new political situation.

> In both letters with an anti-Judaistic theme, Galatians and
> Philippians, Paul is combating a Judaistic counter-mission
> which in order to avoid conflict with its environment wants
> to integrate the newly-formed Christian groups into Juda-
> ism. Directly, it wants to reduce the conflict with the Jewish
> communities, and indirectly also (in the interest of the
> Jewish communities) the conflict with the pagan environ-
> ment and the state authorities, which threatened to inter-
> vene in disturbances of the 'peace'. We have to recognize
> the integrity of the motives of these 'opponents' of Paul.
> Peace between religious groups is a great good.[247]

First, Theissen overestimates the significance of the Jerusalem conference for the Gentile mission (he keeps speaking
anachronistically of the Apostolic Council. How many people
took part? Perhaps 20 or 25?) This meeting was certainly not
convened as a council; Paul forced a discussion with the Jerusalem apostles and in Galatians blows this up into a special
event. Secondly, the Edict of Claudius against the Jews was
probably issued in 41 (and not 49),[248] so that the Judaistic
crisis in the first century may not be derived from this decree.
It is also doubtful whether Paul's opponents in Galatia and
Philippi travelled to the Pauline communities and worked in

them only in order to avoid a political conflict. Rather, they were associated with the anti-Paulines in Jerusalem who regarded Paul as an apostate from the law (Acts 21.21), and for whom hostility to Paul had become second nature.[249] They were not concerned to adapt to political conditions but to safeguard their own existence as Jews, their Jewish identity. They could no longer see Paul as an adherent of Israel. So they did not want to build on his preaching in his own communities, nor could they. For that reason, too, it is wrong to say that the Jewish-Christian missionaries in Galatia had not attacked Paul. Certainly, Theissen writes:

> Paul's opponents did not attack him, but commandeered him. In contrast to I and II Corinthians ... there are no indications of personal attacks against which Paul had to defend himself (222).

Yet in Gal. 1–2 Paul defends himself against the claims of his opponents that he is dependent on the Jerusalem apostles, does not have the same rank as they do and has had conditions imposed on him by them. These statements, which are contrary to the truth, amount to a personal attack. The controversy in Galatia is therefore a continuation of the attack at the Jerusalem conference.[250] However, Theissen sees this also as a possibility when he writes: 'In Galatia and Philippi the mission (against Paul) has Judaistic traits. Here it could have been made up of groups close to the "false brethren" of the Apostolic Council (Gal. 2.4)' (259).

5. The Gnostic crisis in the second century – caused by the precarious situation of the Christians at that time?

According to Theissen, in view of the persecutions of Christians under Pliny at the beginning of the second century the need arose within the church 'for forms which privatized religion. Gnosticism was such a religion' (236). Theissen wants to demonstrate this by three points: the need for public confession, martyrdom, and food laws. All three were rejected by the Gnostics. He writes:

(S)ome gnostics taught that one need not make a confession before the state archon ... many Gnostics denied the crucifixion of Jesus with the help of a deception theory ... Here no doubt we find a portrait of the Gnostic: he stands unmolested and unrecognized alongside the martyrs ... many Gnostics taught that one could eat meat offered to idols without coming into any harm' (236).

The first two points are not appropriate as distinguishing marks between Gnostics and church Christians. First we must be clear that the Valentinian Gnostic Ptolemy is the first identifiable Christian martyr in Rome.[251] The examples in Koschorke's book[252] to which Theissen refers should have prevented him from drawing over-hasty conclusions about the Gnostics' fear of martyrdom. And eating meat offered to idols? Paul already allowed that, and it did not make him a Gnostic.

Theissen makes a careless association where he constructs a parallel between the crises in the first and second centuries:

In the second century, Gnostic forms of primitive Christianity avoided conflicts in the same way as did the development of Judaistic forms of Christianity in the first century. Christianity could have more easily come to terms with its environment both as a part and extension of Judaism and as a variant of universal symbolic language (239).

As I have demonstrated above, given the historical evidence, such a theory is clumsy.

These historical soundings into Gerd Theissen's *A Theory of Primitive Christian Religion* make me have considerable reservations about his book. Equal restraint, indeed blunt rejection, seems to me to be appropriate when it comes to Theissen's attempt to let missionary appeals enter his account in such a way that he confuses the professor's desk with the preacher's pulpit. Unfortunately this happens strikingly frequently with him.[253] It perplexes me as much as the value judgements which are constantly scattered over his work.[254]

Nevertheless Theissen remains a great New Testament scholar, even if his earliest works are more important to me than
for example his *A Theory of Primitive Christian Religion*.

To conclude with, let me sketch out now what I imagine to be
an appropriate scholarly theology.[255]

Theology is a scholarly discipline when it observes the
scholarly norms of the modern university and bids farewell to
epistemological principles of any kind – including the privi-
lege of knowing God. Theology is a historical discipline in so
far as it investigates Christianity with the help of the historical-
critical method. And the historical method has three presuppositions: causality, a consideration of analogies, and a
recognition of the reciprocal relationship between historical
phenomena. Its way of working follows the methodological
atheism of modernity ('as if God did not exist'), though this is
to be distinguished from a dogmatic atheism. Freed from
supernatural presuppositions and equipped with the instru-
ments of historical criticisms, theology understood in this way
as an academic discipline produces what amounts to a
Copernican shift for *all* churches and religious communities.
It has asserted itself in the humanities and offered completely
new insights.

The historical method is part of the emancipatory process
of scientific curiosity. It seeks to find meanings, i.e. to
understand, but if it is to strive for objectivity and disenchant
the world, it must emancipate itself from all the alien claims
that it encounters:

(a) from the claim to canonical status or the holiness of
    particular writings;
(b) from the claim to a revelation, since revelation is not a
    scientific concept;
(c) from the claim to be able to distinguish between
    orthodoxy and heresy in a sense which goes beyond
    the reconstruction and perception of *historical claims*.
    For here dogmatic and theological judgments on
    which it is essentially impossible to make a decision
    stand over against each other.

The historical method[256] refuses to give an answer to the religious question of truth and can only compare different claims to truth with one another. In this respect it is critical of ideologies. As a scientific historical and philological instrument it is obliged to use the methods of the humanities in all its manifestations. In its adoption of new methods from neighbouring disciplines like sociology, psychology and ethnology, the way in which it can be examined and can prove fruitful in illuminating historical phenomena is decisive. Its presuppositions must remain open to revision and can always only be validated by its effect in providing explanations and interpretations, not by the church's will for power.

On the question of the spiritual life of such an academic theologian I would like to recall some remarks by Émile M. Cioran. He is writing about specialists in the history of religion. If such a person

> in fact prays, he is betraying his teaching, he is contradicting himself, he is damaging *what he writes,* in which there is no *true* God, as all gods are treated as being of equal worth. It is pointless to describe them and make acute comments on them; he cannot breathe life into them once he has sucked the marrow from them, compared them with one another and, to complete their misery, rubbed them and polished them so long that all that is left are bloodless symbols which are useless for believers. It is pointless to go on assuming that at this stage of scholarship, disillusionment and irony there is still anyone there who truly believes. We are all ... *would-be* believers, we are all religious spirits without religion.[257]

Notes

1. From the foundation of *Theologische Rundschau* in 1898 there had previously been accounts of literature on 'Acts and the Apostolic Age' at regular intervals. Carl Clemen started these in Vol. 1, 371–7.

2. See also Hans Windisch's account of research, 'Literature on the New Testament', *HThR* 15, 1922, 115–216; *HThR* 19, 1926, 1–114. On Windisch see Marinus de Jonge, 'Hans Windisch als Neutestamentler an der Universität Leiden (1914–1929)', in *Text und Geschichte: Facetten theologischen Arbeitens aus dem Freundes- und Schülerkreis. Dieter Lührmann zum 60. Geburtstag*, MThSt 50, Marburg 1999, 47–65.

3. On Kümmel's work on 'Primitive Christianity' in general see Otto Merk, 'Das Urchristentum im Werk von Werner Georg Kümmel. Ein Überblick', in Ulrich Mell and Ulrich B. Müller (eds), *Das Urchristentum in seiner literarischen Geschichte. Festschrift für Jürgen Becker zum 65. Geburtstag*, BZNW 100, Berlin/New York 1999, 543–54.

4. Other individual themes, like Acts as a source for primitive Christianity, had been given a separate report. Cf. Erich Grässer, 'Die Apostelgeschichte in der Forschung der Gegenwart', *ThR* NF 26, 1960, 93–167; id., 'Acta-Forschung seit 1960', *ThR* NF 41, 1976, 141–94, 259–90; *ThR* NF 42, 1977, 1–68 (Grässer's four articles have been reprinted in id., *Forschungen zur Apostelgeschichte*, WUNT 137, Tübingen 2001, 59–287); Eckhard Plümacher, 'Acta-Forschung 1974–1982', *ThR* NF 48, 1983, 1–56; *ThR* NF 49, 1984, 105–69. The question of Peter and Rome was likewise excluded from the account, as it had been treated separately; cf. Erich Dinkler, 'Die Petrus-Rom-Frage', *ThR* NF 25, 1959, 189–230, 289–335; ThR NF 27, 1961, 33–64; *ThR* NF 31, 1965/66, 232–53.

5. Hans Hübner, 'Kreuz und Auferstehung im Neuen Testament', *ThR* 54, 1989, 262–306; 57, 1992, 58–82.

6. Windisch, 258.

7. Windisch, 326.

8. Kümmel 1983, 114.
9. Kümmel 1983, 115.
10. German original *Einführung in das Neue Testament im Rahmen der Religions- und Kulturgeschichte der hellenistischen und römischen Zeit*, Berlin 1980; ET *Introduction to the New Testament Vol. I, History, Culture, and Religion of the Hellenistic Age; Vol. II, History and Literature of Early Christianity*, New York and Berlin 1982. The second edition of Vol. I was published in 1995 and the second edition of Vol. II in 2000. Koester writes about Vol. I of the second edition: 'While the first American edition of this book ... was a revised translation of my German book, *Einführung in das Neue Testament*, this second edition of the first volume of the *Introduction to the New Testament* is no longer dependent upon a previously published German work' (I, xxi). See the similar remark about the second edition of Vol. II that was published five years later (II, xix). At the same time, Koester has 'not been persuaded that ... (he) should change its perspective, approach, and overall structure' (ibid.). He continues: 'I remain committed to the methods of historical criticism, and to an interpretation of the Early Christian writings and of the traditions that preceded them in the context of their own unrepeatable historical, theological, and social situations' (ibid.). Both the German and the American editions of the book were dedicated to the memory of Koester's teacher Rudolf Bultmann, who had encouraged Koester to 'deal more intensively with the extra-canonical writings from the early Christian period'. Koester continues: 'His unwavering insistence upon the consistent application of the historical-critical method and his emphasis upon the investigation of early Christian literature in the context of the history of religions must remain basic commitments of New Testament scholarship' (I, xxv). See on this further Helmut Koester, 'New Testament Introduction: A Critique of a Discipline', in Jacob Neusner (ed.), *Christianity, Judaism, and Other Greco-Roman Cults (Festschrift for Morton Smith)*, SJLA 12.1, Leiden 1975, 1–20. On the *religionsgeschichtliche Schule* roots of Koester's approach that were mediated to him through Bultmann see my remarks in *RSR* 10, 1984, 116–20.
11. Cf. Kümmel, 123f.
12. Kümmel, 348.
13. Cf. Jacob Burckhardt, *Reflections on History*, London 1943, ch. I, 15–32.
14. Alkier does not include in his section 'Hermann Samuel Reimarus: The Radical Challenge to the Credibility of Biblical Historiography' (81–9) Reimarus' *Apologie oder Schutzschrift für die vernünftigen Verehrer Gottes*, which was first published complete in 1972 in an edition by Gerhard Alexander. Instead he cites the fragments edited by Lessing on the grounds that they were 'in fact influential' in the history of the reception of the work (81 n. 131). I do not find this way of proceeding helpful. When writing a history of research you cannot leave out what was *really* written. Otherwise the history of research turns into a history of winners. I suspect that Alkier's procedure is based on misgivings

about the old-fashioned way of writing history by trying to come as close as possible to what really happened. See further his new book *Wunder und Wirklichkeit in den Briefen des Apostels Paulus: Ein Beitrag zu einem Wunderverständnis jenseits von Entmythologisierung und Rehistorisierung,* WUNT 134, Tübingen 2001. Significantly enough the book ends with a sort of sermon. Cf. the following example from the last paragraph: 'No general answer can be given to the question whether the letters of Paul are a basis for or against miracles in the sense of "paranormal" phenomena. But they do express the certainty and (interpreted) experience that God the creator has acted, acts and will act in a miraculous way. They promise us the possibility of turning to him and to his Son our Lord Jesus Christ' (307).

15. Even after the appearance of Alkier's work cf. e.g. still the article by Hans Dieter Betz, 'The Birth of Christianity as a Hellenistic Religion: Three Theories of Origins', *JR* 74, 1994, 1–25. Betz works out three different theories: (a) Theories of Fulfilment (3–10: Semler, Tindal, Lessing, Herder); (b) The Theory of Original Fraud (10–15: Reimarus); (c) The Theory of Original Betrayal (15–24: Nietzsche). According to Betz the consequence for present-day research is: 'The main difficulty, then, for understanding historical origins lies with the critical distinctions to be made between what is reality and what is theory' (25).

16. On Locke and Toland see now Henning Graf Reventlow, *Epochen der Bibelauslegung, Band IV: Von der Aufklärung bis zum 20. Jahrhundert,* Munich 2001, 57–78.

17. *Das Urchristentum als gegliederte Epoche,* SBS 155, Stuttgart 1993. Despite its title, however, the book is not a study of the historical division of primitive Christianity but more an account of the main stages of primitive Christian theology. See below pp. 30ff. on the composite volume *Christian Beginnings* edited by J. Becker (1987, ET 1993), and Ulrich Mell and Ulrich B. Müller (eds), *Das Urchristentum in seiner literarischen Geschichte. Festschrift für Jürgen Becker* (n. 3). The term 'Urchristentum' is part of the title of the volume because in his work Becker has paid special attention 'to the whole of primitive Christianity as an epoch which manifests itself in many different literary forms and can be understood as a phenomenon divisible into different periods of history' (V). This obviously alludes to the title of Becker's 1993 book on primitive Christianity.

18. 'Zur Wissenschaft vom Urchristentum und der Alten Kirche – ein methodischer Versuch', *ZNW* 68, 1977, 200–30 (= id., *Zur Literatur und Geschichte des frühen Christentums, Gesammelte Aufsätze,* ed. Ute Eisen, WUNT 99, 1997, 365–95).

19. Cf. my *Heretics: The Other Side of Early Christianity,* London and Louisville 1996, 11.

20. This work is not considered in Becker's article (n. 17) (see the relevant criticism by Petr Pokorný, review of Becker, *Urchristentum,* *ThLZ* 120, 1995, cols 517f.: 518).

21. See my *Heretics* (n. 19), 242–6 (nn. 82–8). Not surprisingly Helmut Koester (*Ancient Christian Gospels: Their History and Development*, Philadelphia and London 1990) praises Bauer's book thus: 'The appearance of a second edition of this epochal work thirty years (1964) after its original publication (1934) and four years after the death of its author (1960) as well as a publication of an English translation (1971) signified a fundamental change in scholarship. It seemed as if almost two millennia of discrimination against those whom the Fathers of the church had labelled as "heretics" would come to an end ... (T)hese "heresies" were not simply secondary deviations from an already established orthodoxy, but resulted from developments in the Christian communities that occurred as early as the time of Paul's mission to the Gentiles' (xxx). Yet Koester's enthusiasm very seldom received a positive reaction in German-speaking countries. Cf. only the closing sentence in a review of *Ancient Gospels* by Ulrich Luz of the University of Bern in Switzerland (Luz had previously taught at Göttingen): 'Koester's book is not so much an introduction into the Gospels as an introduction into Koester, and as such, it definitely has its great merits' (*Interpretation* 47, 1993, 87–8: 88).

22. Cf. the three volumes *Jewish and Christian Self-Definition*: Vol. I, *The Shaping of Christianity in the Second and Third Centuries*, ed. E. P. Sanders, London 1980; Vol. II, *Aspects of Judaism in the Graeco-Roman World*, ed. E. P. Sanders with A. I. Baumgarten and Alan Mendelson, London 1981; Vol. III, *Self-Definition in the Graeco-Roman World*, ed. Ben F. Meyer and E. P. Sanders, London 1982.

23. See further the contribution to Bauer by Frederik Wisse, 'The Use of Early Christian Literature as Evidence for Inner Diversity and Conflict', *Nag Hammadi, Gnosticism, and Early Christianity*, ed. Charles W. Hedrick and Robert Hodgson, Jr, Peabody, MA 1986, 177–90: 182–90. In his study *Polycarp and the New Testament: The Occasion, Rhetoric, Theme, and Unity of the Epistle to the Philippians and its Allusions to New Testament Literature*, WUNT II/134, Tübingen 2002, Paul Hartog points to an important aspect of the history of the reception of Walter Bauer's book in the English-speaking world: 'Bauer's major theme of the early and widespread presence of heresy has been generally accepted in modern scholarship, with an accompanying stress upon the diversity of early Christianity' (219 n. 24). In passing I may point out that the late Morton Smith (1915–91) saw 'his own work as complementary to that of Walter Bauer on early Christianity and Erwin Goodenough on early Judaism' (thus Shaye J. D. Cohen, 'In memoriam Morton Smith: Morton Smith and his Scholarly Achievement', in *Josephus and the History of the Greco-Roman Period: Essays in Memory of Morton Smith*, edited by Fausto Parente and Joseph Sievers, Studia Post-Biblica 41, Leiden 1994, 1–8: 7).

24. One must note, however, that present German patristic research does not pay much attention to Walter Bauer's approach. E.g., Winrich A.

Löhr, in a brilliant survey ('Das antike Christentum im zweiten Jahrhundert – neue Perspektiven seiner Erforschung', *ThLZ* 127, 2002, 247-62), suggests 'that by all means the unreflected use of the heresiology of the church fathers must be avoided' ('*dass die unbesehene Fortschreibung der altkirchlichen Häresiologie unbedingt zu vermeiden ist*'). Yet he does not once mention Walter Bauer nor does he discuss the importance of the Nag Hammadi texts for the second century. It is also noteworthy that Christoph Markschies (*Between Two Worlds: Structures of Earliest Christianity*, London 1999), after 'the extensive debate ... about Walter Bauer's book *Orthodoxy and Heresy in Earliest Christianity* ... seeks to draw attention to structures which despite sometimes very different theological options bound together the most different Christian communities. These structures, which shaped identity, allow us despite all the plurality to speak of *one* early Christianity' (ix-x). Yet, since in his study Markschies leaves out the most notorious 'heretics' of primitive Christianity Marcion and the anti-Pauline Ebionites – to name only these two – , his introductory statement is unsatisfactory and does not lead us any further.

25. In my view, this verdict holds even if Paul is not discussed at all in the flourishing Jesus research of every day, since there he is usually regarded as someone who corrupted the message of Jesus.

26. *Gemeindebildung*, meaning, the community has created the preaching.

27. Chapters 10 ('Worship in Early Christianity' [180–213]) and 15 ('The Old Testament in the New' [278–311]) have been added to the English edition. Yet neither the English publisher nor the translator has intervened to reduce the structural deficiencies of this book.

28. It should be remarked in passing that in a not very convincing way Schmithals excludes 1 Thess. 2.14–16 as an un-Pauline text, and also 1 Thess. 4.15–18 (109; cf. 242f.).

29. Thus, however, Jürgen Roloff in his review, *ThLZ* 120, 1995, 666–9: 666.

30. Reference should also be made to Schmithals' insistence that F. C. Baur's Judaist thesis is also historically erroneous in any historical variation. Thus he argues that the false brethren in Gal. 2.4 are representatives of the Jewish supervisory authorities (116, cf. 120). As I have gone into this at another point (*Opposition to Paul in Jewish Christianity*, Minneapolis 1989, 113f. and index, 359 s.v. Schmithals), I need not reject his thesis once again. J. Roloff, *ThLZ* 1995, 668, also opposes Schmithals' view that Paul's opponents in Galatians were not Judaizers.

31. Cf. the affirmation by Klaus Berger, *Darf man an Wunder glauben?*, Stuttgart 1996. The first paragraph of this book reads: 'Miracles are by no means incidental to Christianity. No, the future of Christian belief depends on whether we can rediscover the charms of these sensual demonstrations of God's love ... As the resurrection, too, is a miracle, it can be said that doing away with miracles would make Christianity just any religion' (11).

32. Cf. only Heikki Räisänen, *Beyond New Testament Theology. A Story and a Programme*, London 1990, [2]2000.

33. Cf. *ThR* 17, 1914, 79–90; *ThLZ* 52, 1927, 80–3; 'Literaturgeschichte, Biblische', in *RGG*² III, 1675–7, 1680–2.
34. Kurt Flasch, Professor Emeritus of Philosophy at the Universtiy of Bochum, is best known for his work on Augustine. Cf. id., *Was ist Zeit? Augustinus von Hippo. Das XI. Buch der Confessiones. Historisch-philosophische Studie. Text – Übersetzung – Kommentar*, Frankfurt 1993.
35. The result of Berger's analysis is considered to be at least possible by his pupil Axel von Dobbeler, *Der Evangelist Philippus in der Geschichte des Urchristentums: Eine prosopographische Skizze*, TANZ 30, Tübingen and Basel 2000, 63–4. This Heidelberg Habilitationsschrift has a strange tendency to assume that everything that Berger has written is proven and consists of little more than a paraphrase of the Philip traditions of primitive Christianity. Indeed, as its subtitle indicates, Dobbeler's book is only a sketch.
36. The second edition of the work, from the same year (1995), expands the book by a further 90pp. I do not doubt that with this way of working one could write several hundred pages more.
37. See my *Heretics* (n. 19), 143–6, 223–4.
38. See *New Testament Apocrypha*, revd edn of the collection initiated by Edgar Hennecke, ed. Wilhelm Schneemelcher, ET ed. R. McL. Wilson, Vol. II, *Writings Related to the Apostles. Apocalypses and Related Writings*, Cambridge and Louisville 1991, 493–503.
39. It is important to note that in 1 Cor. 15.3–5 the statements about Jesus' death, burial, and appearance to Cephas are in the aorist tense. Hence the translation must take this into account, the more so since Paul's use of the perfect tense 'has been raised' throughout 1 Cor. 15, i.e. vv. 4, 12, 13, 14, 16, 17, 20, has a specific goal, namely to emphasize the importance of Jesus' resurrection for the present. Paul similarly uses the perfect tense when speaking about 'Christ crucified' so that the cross and the crucified Christ directly impinge on the present (1 Cor. 1.23; 2.2; Gal. 3.1; 6.14).
40. There is a quite positive evaluation of Vouga's book by Heikki Räisänen: '"Theologie des Neuen Testaments" und ihre Alternativen heute', *Das Urchristentum in seiner literarischen Geschichte* (n. 3), 517–42, 533–40. I remain unconvinced, the more so since in the same volume (*Das Urchristentum*) Vouga continues his confusing ways of argument under the title 'Das Problem der Selbstdefinition und der theologischen Einheit des frühen Christentum' (487–515).
41. Vögtle's last major work is *Die 'Gretchenfrage' des Menschensohnproblems. Bilanz und Perspektive*, QD 152, Freiburg 1994; in it, taking up theses from his unpublished Habilitationsschrift, he argues that the title Son of man appears only after Easter.
42. Cf. only A. Vögtle and R. Pesch, *Wie kam es zum Osterglauben?*, Freiburg 1975; Lorenz Oberlinner (ed.), *Auferstehung Jesus – Auferstehung der Christen. Deutungen des Osterglaubens*, QD 105, Freiburg 1986.
43. According to the principle of difference only what is neither characteristic of primitive Christianity nor universally Jewish can come from Jesus (30).

44. *Das Reich Gottes ist mitten unter euch. Neuorientierung an Jesu Lehre und Leben,* Düsseldorf 1986. For example, the interpretation of the parable of the sower in the first book mentioned (212ff.) corresponds to the interpretation in the second book (85ff.); for the parable of the leaven cf. 74ff./218ff.; for the parable of the grain of mustard seed, 72ff./215ff.

45. While it is true that Bruce's book *The Defence of the Gospel in the New Testament* is aimed at a popular audience and therefore might not seem appropriate for a scholarly critique, it is also correct to say that all the items which I criticize in the text are repeated in his larger works. Cf. *The Acts of the Apostles,* London ²1952; *A Mind for What Matters: Collected Essays,* Michigan 1990 (this book contains a list of references for the other books and articles by Bruce). At the same time, it must be said that Bruce's knowledge of the Greek and Roman literature is enormous. Thus his work is and will remain worth considering.

46. Cf. also Burchard's article 'Jesus' in *Der kleine Pauly* II, Munich 1975, cols 1344–54, which unfortunately is not mentioned in the bibliography.

47. On one point I would like to disagree, however: Burchard considers it 'questionable whether a Johannine movement existed after John's death' (24).

48. For both points cf. my *Paul, Apostle to the Gentiles. Studies in Chronology,* London and Philadelphia 1984, 64–77.

49. Jürgen Becker, *Paul: Apostle to the Gentiles,* Louisville 1993. A Foreword to the English edition by Marion L. Soards (ix-xii) introduces the author and the work to the English-speaking reader. The subtitle *Apostle to the Gentiles* is a strange translation of the German *Apostel der Völker* (which of course should have been translated as *Apostle to the Nations*).

50. Cf. p.74 below.

51. On the collection cf. also Becker, *Paul* (n. 49), 259f.

52. In *The Social Teaching of the Christian Churches,* Vol. I, New York 1931, Troeltsch speaks of the '*type of Christian patriarchalism* founded upon the religious recognition of and the religious overcoming of earthly inequality. There was a certain preparation for this in Judaism but it receives special colour from the warmth of the Christian idea of love, through the inclusion of all in the Body of Christ ... It only attained its full development certainly in the Middle Ages ...' (78). Becker takes the term from Gerd Theissen, *Social Reality and the Early Christians: Theology, Ethics and the World of the New Testament,* Minneapolis 1992, 56 n. 67, according to whom the term 'love patriachalism' in substance derives from Troeltsch.

53. Cf. Peter Schäfer, 'Der Flucht Johanan b.Zakkais aus Jerusalem und die Gründung eines Lehrhauses in Jabne', *ANRW* II 19, 2, Berlin 1979, 43–101.

54. Cf. also U. B. Müller, 'Apokalyptik im Neuen Testament', in Friedrich Wilhelm Horn (ed.), *Bilanz und Perspektiven gegenwärtiger Auslegung des*

Neuen Testaments. Symposium zum 65. Geburtstag von Georg Strecker, BZNW 75, Berlin 1995, 144–69.

55. Cf. 1 Thess. 4.13–17 with SyrBar 29f., to come to the conclusion that form-critically, too, in Paul we have a miniature apocalypse.

56. Jacob Burckhardt, *Reflections on History*, London 1943, 74.

57. See five photographs of the pioneers in investigating Slavonic Enoch (248f.): N. A. Popov (1833–91), S. Novakovic (1842–1915), R. H. Charles (1855–1931), G. N. Bonwetsch (1848–1925) and M. I. Sokolov (1855–1906).

58. *The Gospel according to John*, London and Philadelphia 1955, [2]1978.

59. See the analyses by Wilhelm Pratscher, *Der Herrenbruder Jakobus und die Jakobustradition*, FRLANT 139, Göttingen 1987, 13–27 ('Die Distanz zum irdischen Jesus'). I do not think that the otherwise excellent and comprehensive monograph by John Painter, *Just James: The Brother of Jesus in History and Tradition*, Minneapolis 1999, 11–41 (cf. id., 'Who Was James?', in: Bruce Chilton and Jacob Neusner [eds.], *The Brother of Jesus: James the Just and His Mission*, Louisville 2001, 10–65: 24–27) has succeeded in disproving the hypothesis of James' and his family's negative attitude to Jesus during the latter's lifetime. It is remarkable that studies on James are thriving today though we do not have a single writing from his own pen or much historically reliable information about him. Apart from the two books just mentioned cf. further Bruce Chilton and Jacob Neusner (eds), *James the Just and Christian Origins*, NT.S 98, Leiden 1999.

60. By comparison see Eusebius, *Church History* V 13, 2: Apelles is said to follow the sayings of a possessed woman. His work *Phaneroseis* consists of notes of the revelation of the seer Philoumene (cf. Tertullian, *Praescr.* 30). All that tells against Hamman's view. On Apelles see now the important book by Katharina Greschat, *Apelles und Hermogenes: Zwei theologische Lehrer des zweiten Jahrhunderts*, VigCh.S 48, Leiden 2000, 17–134.

61. Reference should be made to the book by the sociologist Rodney Stark, *The Rise of Christianity: A Sociologist Reconsiders History*, Princeton 1996, which has attracted much notice in North America (cf. the second volume of the *Journal of Early Christian Studies* 6, 1998, which is devoted to the discussion of Stark's book). Stark's assessment also corresponds to that of Frend, whose book *The Rise of Christianity* we shall consider next. On Stark see further Birger A. Pearson, 'On Rodney Stark's Foray into Early Christian History', *Religion* 29, 1999, 171–6; Jack T. Sanders, *Charisma, Converts, Competitors: Societal and Sociological Factors in the Success of Early Christianity*, London 2000, 135–59. On the circumstances of the expansion of primitive Christianity see the Göttingen Habilitationsschrift by Wolfgang Reinbold, *Propaganda und Mission im ältesten Christentum. Eine Untersuchung zu den Modalitäten der Ausbreitung der frühen Kirche*, FRLANT 188, Göttingen 2000. (The hostile review of Reinbold's book by Karl-Wilhelm Niebuhr, *ThLZ* 127, 2002, 187–9, demonstrates strikingly that at some theological faculties in Germany

there are still — or dare I say again — theological prejudices against historical criticism and reconstruction.)

62. Cf. above all Frederick Wisse, 'The "Opponents" in the New Testament in the Light of the Nag Hammadi Writings', in B. Barc (ed.), *Colloque international sur les textes de Nag Hammadi*, Quebec and Louvain 1981, 99–120.

63. Cf. Lüdemann, *Heretics* (cf. n.19), 159, with nn. 517, 518.

64. As a further example of Frend's stupendous erudition I would simply mention his report on archaeological research into early Christianity, William H. C. Frend, *The Archaeology of Early Christianity. A History*, Minneapolis 1996 (412 pp.).

65. This is argued in even more recent exegesis by Reinhard Feldmeier (*Die Krisis des Gottessohnes. Die Gethsemaneerzählung als Schlüssel der Markuspassion*, WUNT II/21, Tübingen 1987), though his argument is questionable. On the objection to the historicity of the scene that the sleeping disciples will not do as historical witnesses, Feldmeier writes: 'It is hardly believable that after Jesus' lament and his call to keep watch all (three) disciples should have fallen asleep (not to mention the several repetitions of such an occurrence)' (137). Later he continues that it is not improbable that Jesus 'revealed his grief to his disciples and afterwards withdrew to pray. As the Jews usually prayed aloud and Jesus was not far away from the disciples … there is no reason to dispute that the disciples could have heard Jesus' prayer. We can also well imagine that the disciples fell asleep during the night hours, especially if before and including the Passover meal they had drunk at least four cups of wine. Jesus will then have awakened them at some point, perhaps at first Peter with his remark in 14.37b, which sounds very personal' (137).

66. For criticism cf. my *Opposition to Paul* (n. 30), 25–7; Daniélou's demonstration of Jewish thought-forms in the Christian church in the time between the New Testament and the beginnings of Hellenistic apologetic theology is an ideal which never existed in history.

67. Against this see Carsten Claussen, *Versammlung, Gemeinde, Synagoge: Das hellenistisch-jüdische Umfeld der frühchristlichen Gemeinden*, StUNT 27, Göttingen 2002; see further Anders Runesson, *The Origins of the Synagogue: A Socio-Historical Study*, CB.NT 37, Stockholm 2001.

68. This is clearly overstated, since Christianity did not exist at the time of the Maccabees.

69. For the chronological questions see the mammoth account by Alfred Suhl, 'Paulinische Chronologie im Streit der Meinungen', *ANRW* II 26.2, Berlin 1995, 929–1188, and recently Rainer Riesner, *Paul's Early Period: Chronology, Mission Strategy, Theology*, Grand Rapids, Michigan 1998.

70. Cf. Niels Hyldahl, *Die paulinische Chronologie*, Leiden 1986.

71. In passing, it should be pointed out that the two new major monographs on Paul by Jerome Murphy O'Connor, *Paul. A Critical Life*, Oxford 1996, and Joachim Gnilka, *Paulus von Tarsus. Apostel und Zeuge*, HThK, Suppl. XI, Freiburg 1996, also start from this.

72.   Cf. the analysis by C. Hill (see below, pp. 58f), which comes to a similar conclusion.

73.   Cf. e.g. Johannes Munck, *Paul and the Salvation of Mankind*, London 1959 (for criticism cf. my *Opposition to Paul* [n. 30], 24–5).

74.   Cf. Eusebius, *Church History* II 23, 4–6. However, Berger, *Theologiegeschichte* (see above, pp. 13f.) thinks that reports of this are credible (159).

75.   Cf. also M. D. Goulder, 'The Jewish-Christian Mission 30–130', *ANRW* II 26.3, Berlin 1996, 1979–2037; id., *Paul and the Competing Mission in Corinth*, Peabody, MA 2001 (this is the first volume of the planned larger work).

76.   Goulder has given comprehensive reasons for not following scholarly trends – for example in not assuming the existence of Q and supposing that Matthew used Luke – so this is not just a whim; cf. *Luke. A New Paradigm*, JSNT.S 20, I, II, Sheffield 1989.

77.   In a recently published letter to A. von Harnack of 2 January 1905, W. Wrede withdrew his view of an 'unmessianic' life of Jesus. Cf. Hans Rollmann and Werner Zager, 'Unveröffentlichte Briefe William Wredes zur Problematisierung des messianischen Selbstverständnisses Jesu', *JHMTh* 8, 2001, 274–322.

78.   See my *Heretics* (n. 19), 91–3.

79.   In view of Daniel 12.2–3 and Jubilees 23.30–31 I would cautiously agree. See my *Die Auferweckung Jesu von den Toten. Ursprung und Geschichte einer Selbsttäuschung*, Lüneburg 2002, 53–4. But cf. also the different view of Martin Hengel, 'Das Begräbnis Jesu bei Paulus und die leibliche Auferstehung aus dem Grabe', in Friedrich Avemarie and Hermann Lichtenberger (eds), *Auferstehung – Resurrection*, WUNT 135, Tübingen 2001, 119–83.

80.   On 2 Thessalonians as a forgery see my *Paul: The Founder of Christianity*, Amherst, NY 2002, 247–52.

81.   See Andreas Lindemann, *Paulus im ältesten Christentum. Das Bild des Apostels und die Rezeption der paulinischen Theologie in der frühchristlichen Literatur bis Marcion*, BHTh 58, Tübingen 1979, 174–7.

82.   However, it is nonsense to describe Ernst Troeltsch as a 'social scientist'.

83.   Burtchaell, 351.

84.   See also a little known article by Ernst Bammel, 'Die Anfänge des Sukzessionsprinzips im Urchristentum', *Studia Ephemeridis Augustinianum* 31, 1990, 63–72.

85.   Yet Martin Hengel thinks that 'the historical importance of James . . . is more contingent on his personal charisma and his own authority . . . than on his close kinship with Jesus' ('*die historische Bedeutung des Jakobus . . . noch mehr durch sein persönliches Charisma und seine ihm eigene Autorität . . . als durch seine enge Verwandtschaft mit Jesus bedingt ist*'), id., 'Jakobus der Herrenbruder – der erste Papst?' (1985), in id., *Paulus und Jakobus. Kleine Schriften III*, WUNT 141, Tübingen 2002, 549–82: 580 n. 86.

86.   *Peter. Disciple – Apostle – Martyr*, London and Philadelphia 1953. See now Christian Grappe, 'Kirche II. Urchristentum', *RGG*[4], IV, 1000–4.

87. Bargil Pixner, *Wege des Messias und Stätten der Urkirche* (ed. Rainer Riesner), Giessen 1991. For a devastating criticism of Pixner see Jörg Frey, 'Die Bedeutung der Qumranfunde für das Verständnis des Neuen Testaments', in *Qumran – Die Schriftrollen vom Toten Meer*, ed. Michael Fieger, Konrad Schmid, Peter Schwagmeier, NTOA 47, Freiburg and Göttingen 2001, 129–208 ('A "Quarter of the Essenes" as Germ-Cell of the Primitive Community?' ['Ein "Essenerviertel" als Keimzelle der Urgemeinde?']).

88. On Baur see my *Opposition to Paul* (n. 30), 1–7.

89. See now my *Paul: The Founder of Christianity* (n. 80), 259–82 ('The Hellenists as Precursors of Paul').

90. For Hill cf. also Heikki Räisänen, 'Die "Hellenisten" der Urgemeinde', *ANRW* II 26.2, 1995, 1468–514: 1476. See also the criticism of Hill by C. Marvin Pate, *The Reverse of the Curse*, WUNT II/114, Tübingen 2000, 429–34.

91. Henning Paulsen, 'Sozialgeschichtliche Auslegung des Neuen Testaments', in: id., *Zur Literatur und Geschichte des frühen Christentums*, WUNT 99, Tübingen 1997, 462–7: 462f.

92. See now David G. Horrell (ed.), *Social-Scientific Approaches to New Testament Interpretation*, Edinburgh 1999. The book contains a collection of 13 influential essays by authors who are proponents of a broadly social-scientific approach to the New Testament (from Bruce J. Malina to John H. Elliott) and a valuable introduction by the editor David G. Horrell, 'Social-Scientific Interpretation of the New Testament: Retrospect and Prospect' (3–27). According to Horrell 'the wide variety of social-scientific approaches to the Bible retains a close link with the aims of historical criticism' (3).

93. Cf. Henry Chadwick, *Origen: Contra Celsum*, translated with an Introduction and Notes, Cambridge [2]1965.

94. Cf. Joseph R. Hoffmann, *Porphyry's 'Against the Christians'*, edited and translated with Introduction and Epilogue, Amherst, NY 1994.

95. Gerd Theissen, *Social Reality and the Early Christians* (n. 52), esp. 35–6.

96. Schmeller also criticizes the fact that in Theissen's view of the development of the Jesus movement, Easter plays no role in this reconstruction. He maintains, rather, that 'Easter has decisive significance for the development of the Jesus movement' (74).

97. Cf. G. Theissen, *ThLZ* 118, 1993, cols. 516f., in a review of the German translation *Das soziale Umfeld des Neuen Testaments*, Göttingen 1991. According to Theissen some statements in the sphere of Palestinian Judaism need to be corrected.

98. See similarly John Dominic Crossan, *The Birth of Christianity: Discovering What Happened in the Years Immediately After the Execution of Jesus*, San Francisco 1998, xxx: 'There is only one Jesus, the *historical* Jesus who incarnated the Jewish God of justice for a believing community committed for continuing such incarnation even afterward.' Cf. xxi: '(T)he birth of Christianity is the interaction between the historical

Jesus and his first companions and the continuation of that relationship despite his execution.' Crossan's thesis begs the question of the origin of the Gentile mission. One cannot and should not reconstruct the birth of Christianity without dealing with Paul, the more so since his mission among the Gentiles was already in full swing in the 30s. Crossan is unaware of the possibility, if not the likelihood, that 1 Thessalonians was written in the early 40s: see my *Paul: The Founder of Christianity* (n. 80), 22–64 for details. Even if the traditional date for this letter – 50 CE – should stand, there is a lot of evidence that allows us on the basis of the extant letters to reconstruct Paul's preaching in the 30s.

99. As the authors explain elsewhere, they retain the term 'early Christian' ('*urchristlich*') for pragmatic reasons and equate it with 'New Testament' (1).

100. *Das Charisma des Gekreuzigten*, WUNT 45, Tübingen 1987.

101. Martin Hengel, *The Charismatic Leader and His Followers*, Edinburgh and New York 1981, already takes us further here. Cf also Sanders, *Charisma* (n. XX), 16–18.

102. A great deal of notice has been taken of this work in North America since its appearance. See only the review symposium in *Horizons. The Journal of the College Theology Society* 10, 1983, 352–65 (with contributions by Gerard S. Sloyan, Howard Clark Kee, Joseph A. Grassi, Pheme Perkins and Wayne A. Meeks).

103. 'Was wissen wir über die Sozialstruktur der paulinischen Gemeinden? Kritische Anmerkungen zu einem neuen Buch von W. A. Meeks', *NTS* 34, 1988, 71–82.

104. Karl Holl, 'Der Kirchenbegriff des Paulus in seinem Verhältnis zu dem der Urgemeinde' (1921), in id., *Gesammelte Aufsätze zur Kirchengeschichte II. Der Osten*, Tübingen 1928, 44–67.

105. The most recent valuable study of the collection by Stephan Jaubert (*Paul as Benefactor: Reciprocity, Strategy and Theological Reflection in Paul's Collection*, WUNT II/124, Tübingen 2000) rightly stresses: 'The role and impact of the collection within the early Christian movement could scarcely be overestimated' (218).

106. Cf. Jaubert, *Paul as Benefactor* (n. 105), 210–15.

107. Cf. now her in-depth commentary, *Colossians and Ephesians*, Sacra Pagina Series, Vol. 77, Collegeville, Minnesota 2000.

108. Cf. my *Heretics* (n.19), 138ff.

109. See the two collections of articles edited by E. Schüssler Fiorenza, *Searching the Scriptures. Volume One: A Feminist Introduction*, New York and London 1993; *Volume Two: A Feminist Commentary*, New York and London 1994.

110. A 'Tenth Anniversary Edition' appeared in 1994 with a supplementary new introduction 'Remember the Struggle' (xiii-xlii). Here we learn among other things that Schüssler Fiorenza would now prefer to speak of 'beginnings' rather than 'origins' (xxxvii n. 10). Otherwise she

reports reactions to her contribution, but says nothing substantially new, so I shall not go further into the new preface.

111. Wolfgang Stegemann's benevolent review of Schüssler Fiorenza's book (*EvTh* 51, 1991, 383–95) strikes the same tone. He writes that she 'opposes . . . the claim to historical objectivity, *which in any case only veils other epistemological interests*' (387: his italics). For the reasons given above in the text I cannot endorse Stegemann's compliment to Schüssler Fiorenza, that 'in her real area of research, New Testament exegesis, her discussion is at the highest level and in precise detail, and at the same time always understandable' (383).

112. These linguistic contortions need not be commented on further here.

113. Here I shall mention only as particularly blatant her view that the 'elect lady' of 2 John 1, like the 'elect sister' of 2 John 13, is the female leader of a house church (300) and not the symbolic name for a church in Asia Minor of which the writer was a member. But as the two-part prescript (2 John 1–3) which recalls the letters of Paul shows, 2 John is not a personal letter like 3 John but a letter to a community. Verse 13 contains the greetings of the members ('children') of the sister church to which the Elder belongs. See further Martin Hengel, 'Die "auser-wählte Herrin", die "Braut", die "Mutter" und die Gottesstadt', in id., Siegfried Mittmann and Anna Maria Schwemer (eds.), *La Cité de Dieu. Die Stadt Gottes*, WUNT 129, Tübingen 2000, 245–85.

114. Reference should be made to a continuation of the work discussed above: *Jesus. Miriam's Child, Sophia's Prophet. Critical Issues in Feminist Christology*, New York 1994 and London 1995. However, this book brings no new insights; for example, it repeats the superficial exegesis of the story of the tomb (121–8; cf. now even talk of 'the proclamation of the empty tomb') and disparages attempts to distinguish between authentic and inauthentic sayings and actions of Jesus (86–8 [on the Jesus Seminar]), an approach which takes up the best insights of earlier form criticism. The book is more interested in (feminist) theology than in a reconstruction of history. It only remains to add that subsequently Schüssler Fiorenza has produced a wealth of works of feminist theology: their titles give the impression of asking historical-critical questions, but for the reasons mentioned above they do not answer them.

115. On Herbert Braun see the account by Willy Schottroff, 'Herbert Braun – eine theologische Biographie. Zu Grösse und Grenze einer liberalen Theologie', in id., *Das Reich Gottes und der Menschen. Studien über des Verhältnis der Christlichen Theologie zum Judentum*, Munich 1991, 195–229.

116. Ute E. Eisen, 'Wie ungeduldig waren die frühchristlichen Frauen? Zu Luise Schottroffs feministischer Sozialgeschichte des frühen Christentums', *EvTh* 56, 1996, 377–87: 387.

117. For both cf. esp. Luise Schottroff, *Befreiungserfahrungen. Studien zur Sozialgeschichte des Neuen Testaments*, ThB 82, 1990, 96–133 ('Women Disciples of Jesus in New Testament Times').

118. Cf. pp. 126f. below. Peter Pilhofer, *Philippi, Band 1: Die erste christliche*

Gemeinde Europas, WUNT 87, Tübingen 1995. But note Pilhofer's *caveat* when using the expression 'Europe' (154f.).

119.   See my article 'Heidenchristen', *RGG⁴*, III, 1516–20.

120.   Cf. Kathleen E. Corley, *Private Women, Public Meals: Social Conflict in the Synoptic Tradition*, Peabody 1993, 86.

121.   See above, pp. 85 and 90.

122.   Cf. Gerd Lüdemann, *The Resurrection of Jesus: History, Experience, Theology*, London and Minneapolis 1994, *passim*.

123.   Cf. the survey in A.-J. Levine, 'Second Temple Judaism, Jesus, and Women. Yeast of Eden', *Biblical Interpretation* 2, 1994, 8–33. Cf. the trilogy by Tal Ilan, *Jewish Women in Greco-Roman Palestine*, TSAJ 44, Tübingen 1995; ead., *Mine and Yours Are Hers: Retrieving Women's History from Rabbinic Literature*, AGAJU XLI, Leiden, New York and Cologne 1997; ead., *Integrating Women into Second Temple History*, TSAJ 76, Tübingen 1999, and Angela Standhartinger, *Das Frauenbild im Judentum der hellenistischen Zeit. Ein Beitrag anhand von 'Joseph und Asenath'*, AGAJU XXVI, Leiden, New York and Cologne 1995. From the older literature see especially the work by Günter Mayer, *Die jüdische Frau in der hellenistisch-römischen Antike*, 1987, which remains important because of the wealth of material that it contains. Cf. now also E. W. Stegemann and W. Stegemann, *The Jesus Movement: A Social History of Its First Century*, Minneapolis 1999, 353–407 ('The Social Roles and Social Situation of Women in the Mediterranean World and in Early Christianity'). For this work see also above, pp. 65–70 and a major forthcoming work by Kathleen E. Corley (*Women and the Historical Jesus: Feminist Myths of Christian Origin*, Santa Rosa, CA 2002). For the moment see ead., 'Feminist Myths of Christian Origins', in *Reimagining Christian Origins. A Colloquium Honoring Burton L. Mack*, ed. E. A. Castelli and H. Taussig, Valley Forge 1996, 51–67.

124.   *Jerusalem in the Time of Jesus*, London 1969, 359–76.

125.   Cf. Ferguson's remark: '(T)he variety can be emphasized to the neglect of the extent of the central cure of faith, and the diversity can be taken as normative in such a way as to make unintelligible the sense of an apostolic norm, the history of the canon, and the development toward "orthodox"' (490/²575). To me this seems just playing with words.

126.   A correction needs to be made to the history of research: the history-of-religions school started by investigating 'late Judaism' and not the non-Jewish religions of antiquity (thus 3f.). Cf. the retrospect by Wilhelm Bousset, 'Religion und Theologie' (1919) = id., *Religionsgeschichtliche Studien, Aufsätze zur Religionsgeschichte des Hellenistischen Zeitalters*, ed. Anthonie S. Verheule, NT.S 50, 1979, 29–43: 41; also the very critical review of Klauck's book by David Frankfurter, *JR* 82, 2002, 439–40.

127.   Friedrich Avemarie (*Die Tauferzählungen der Apostelgeschichte. Theologie und Geschichte*, WUNT 139, Tübingen 2002) regards my suggestion as 'attractive' ('*reizvoll*'). But he thinks 'that a secret hint in Acts 8 to Ennoia-Helen does not make any sense, for it is only Simon who is

being blamed in 8.20–23' ('*dass in Act 8 ein versteckter Hinweis auf jene Ennoia-Helena keinen Sinn ergäbe, denn allein Simon ist es, der in 8,20–23 zurechtgewiesen wird'* [226 n. 79]). Yet since the *epinoia* is *Simon's* thought, the logic of Avemarie's argument is rather doubtful. Let me hasten to add that it is equally questionable that the historical Simon ever received Christian baptism (*pace* Avemarie, *Tauferzählungen*, 243–54). Acts 8.13 is clearly redactional and Simon's baptism is needed in order to demonstrate Philip's superiority over Simon. This aim should not be translated into a factual statement. Equally unsatisfactory is Christoph Markschies' treatment of the story in Acts 8 about Simon. He remarks: 'If the author of the New Testament Acts is not concealing anything important (and we have no occasion to assume this), then the "Simonian system" came into being only after the death of Simon, who was merely a magician, and also only after the New Testament book was written' (*Gnosis,* London and New York 2003, 75). Markschies seems to be almost relieved that Simon 'was merely a magician' without realizing that Luke had good reasons to degrade Simon as a mere magician in order to make him compete with Philip.

128.   Contra Martin Hengel, 'Die Ursprünge der Gnosis und das Urchristentum', in Jostein Adna, Scott J. Hafemann und Otfried Hofius (eds), *Evangelium Schriftauslegung Kirche. Festschrift für Peter Stuhlmacher zum 65. Geburtstag,* Göttingen 1997, 190–223: 212; id., 'Paulus und die Frage einer vorchristlichen Gnosis', in id., *Paulus und Jakobus. Kleine Schriften III,* WUNT 141, Tübingen 2002, 473–510: 'In Justin's report Simon appears as a semi-pagan heretic' (478). Hengel obviously misses the chief question, namely whether Justin in his report presupposes a Simonian gnostic myth. There can be little doubt that he does.

129.   Ugo Bianchi (ed.), *Le Origini dello Gnosticismo,* Leiden 1967, XXVI-XXIX (English text).

130.   See also the 'Authoritative Teaching' (NHC VI, 3), where the soul, enslaved in the body and abused, seeks knowledge of its roots which will bring it redemption (31.24ff).

131.   Translation on the basis of Gerd Lüdemann and Martina Janssen, *Suppressed Prayers: Gnostic Spirituality in Early Christianity,* London 1998, 135–6.

132.   Cf. as a further parallel to the Simonian myth from the Nag Hammadi Library 'The Thunder: Perfect Mind' (NHC VI, 2). This writing largely consists of the self-revelation of a revelation entity in 'I am' sayings, the majority of which have an antithetical formulation. Not only does the Gnostic revelation entity give itself the title *epinoia* in this writing (14.12), but here too there are numerous elements from the soul-Helen myth. For example the motive of the holy prostitute can be clearly grasped (13.15ff; 14.26ff; 15.1ff; 16.20ff; 17.15ff). The revealer appears as a prostitute in the lowest places; she is caught in shamelessness – just like Helen or the soul – yet she is the holy one, who even becomes the redeemer (cf. e.g. 21.29ff.).

133. In the following the first page reference refers to the German original, the second to the English edition.
134. Cf. my *Jesus After Two Thousand Years: What he really said and did*, London 2000 and Amherst, NY 2001.
135. For bibliography I would refer only to Friedrich Wilhelm Horn, *Das Angeld des Geistes. Studien zur paulinischen Pneumatologie*, FRLANT 154, Göttingen 1992.
136. Unfortunately Horn's work does not undertake this task.
137. To remedy the defect of the failure to take account of Gnosticism it must be remarked that a possible docetic background to 1 Cor. 2.8 should have been illustrated from the Nag Hammadi texts. Cf. only 'The Second Logos of the Great Seth', NHC VII, 2, 55,9–57,6.
138. For Elkesai see most recently F. Stanley Jones, 'The Genre of the Book of Elkasai: A Primitive Church Order, Not an Apocalypse', in Alf Özen (ed.), *Historische Wahrheit und theologische Wissenschaft*, Frankfurt, etc. 1996, 87–103.
139. See also the following works on the same problem which have appeared since Hurtado: Michael Mach, *Entwicklungsstadien des jüdischen Engelglaubens in vorrabbinischer Zeit*, TSAJ 34, Tübingen 1992; Loren T. Stuckenbruck, *Angel Veneration and Christology*, WUNT II/70, Tübingen 1995; Darrell D. Hannah, *Michael and Christ. Michael Traditions and Angel Christology in Early Christianity*, WUNT II/109, Tübingen 1999 (see the review by Jürgen Wehnert, *ThR* 66, 2001, 498–501); Samuel Vollenweider, 'Zwischen Monotheismus und Engelchristologie. Überlegungen zur Frühgeschichte des Christusglaubens', *ZThK* 99, 2002, 21–44, reprinted in id., *Horizonte neutestamentlicher Christologie*, WUNT 144, Tübingen 2002, 3–27.
140. Reprinted in Nikolaus Walter, *Praeparatio Evangelica. Studien zu Umwelt, Exegese und Hermeneutik des Neuen Testaments*, WUNT 98, Tübingen 1997, 383–404.
141. The reason given: 'Basically, apart from some inscriptions, no texts have come down to us from other centres of Jewish Diaspora in the Hellenistic-Roman sphere (not to mention Babylonia), so we can hardly know how Jews e.g. in Antioch or Tarsus, in Ephesus or Athens or even Rome may have thought' (42).
142. Cf. also Nikolaus Walter, 'Paulus und die Gegner des Christusevangeliums in Galatien', in *Praeparatio Evangelica* (n. 140), 273–80.
143. See Adela Yarbo Collins, *The Beginning of the Gospel: Probings of Mark in Context*, Minneapolis 1992, 119–49 ('The Empty Tomb and Resurrection according to Mark').
144. Ludwig Bieler, ΘΕΙΟΣ ANHP. Das Bild vom Göttlichen Menschen in Spätantike und Christentum, 2 vols, Vienna 1935/36, here Vol. I, 4. Cf. the recent massive study by David S. du Toit, *THEIOS ANTHROPOS: Zur Verwendung von ΘΕΙΟΣ ANHP und sinnverwandten Ausdrücken in der Literatur der Kaiserzeit*, WUNT II/91, Tübingen 1997 (on Bieler: 18–24).
145. A bizarre detail in passing: in his contribution 'Christian Prophecy and

the Messianic Status of Jesus' (404–22), D. E. Aune thinks he can say that Acts 7.56 is an indirect polemic against the Simonians (419 n. 55).

146. See now *Qumran-Messianism: Studies on the Messianic Expectation in the Dead Sea Scrolls*, edited by James H. Charlesworth, Hermann Lichtenberger and Gerbern S. Oegema, Tübingen 1998.

147. But see Gerd Theissen, *The Social Setting of Pauline Christianity: Essays on Corinth*, Philadelphia 1982.

148. It is well known that Walter Bauer, *Orthodoxy and Heresy in Earliest Christianity*, London and Philadelphia 1971, 44–60, thought that the earliest recognizable form of Christianity in Egypt was Gnostic. The state of research is open here. See esp. Birger Albert Pearson, *Gnosticism, Judaism, and Egyptian Christianity*, Minneapolis 1990, 194–213 ('Gnosticism in Early Egyptian Christianity'); id., *The Emergence of the Christian Religion: Essays on Early Christianity*, Harrisburg, PA 1997, 178–85 ('Early Christian Diversity in Egypt'). For the Christian Gnostic Basilides, who was active in Alexandria at the beginning of the second century, cf. the comprehensive study by Winrich A. Löhr, *Basilides und seine Schule: Eine Studie zur Kirchen- und Theologiegeschichte des zweiten Jahrhunderts*, WUNT 83, Tübingen 1996, esp. 331–5 ('Basilides und sein Schülerkreis im alexandrinischen Kontext').

149. See my *Heretics* (n.19), 27–30 with n. 133 ('The state of research', 250–2).

150. Cf. especially Richard Bauckham, *James: Wisdom of James, Disciple of Jesus the Sage*, London and New York 1999 (lit.); id., 'James and Jesus', in Bruce Chilton and Jacob Neusner (eds.), *The Brother of Jesus: James the Just and His Mission*, Louisville 2001, 100–37; Martin Hengel, 'Der Jakobusbrief als antipaulinische Polemik', in id., *Paulus und Jakobus. Kleine Schriften III*, WUNT 141, Tübingen 2002, 511–48.

151. See my *Opposition to Paul* (n. 30), 140-9 and *passim*. On the pseudepigraphical character of the letter of James see now Christoph Burchard, *Der Jakobusbrief*, HNT 15/1, Tübingen 2000, 5.

152. See my *Early Christianity according to the Traditions in Acts*, London and Minneapolis 1989, *passim*.

153. Burton L. Mack, *The Christian Myth: Origin, Logic, and Legacy*, New York 2001, 210.

154. See Wayne A. Meeks and Robert L. Wilken, *Jews and Christians in Antioch in the First Four Centuries of the Common Era*, SBL Sources for Biblical Study 13, Missoula 1978.

155. But see Fredrick W. Norris, 'Antiochien I', *TRE* 3, 1978, 99–103; Frank Kolb, 'Antiochia in der frühen Kaiserzeit', in *Geschichte – Tradition – Reflexion. Festschrift für Martin Hengel zum 70.Geburtstag*, ed. H. Cancik, H. Lichtenberger and P. Schäfer, *Band II: Griechische und Römische Religion*, ed. H. Cancik, Tübingen 1996, 97–118; Anna Maria Schwemer, 'Paulus in Antiochien', *BZ* 42, 1998, 161–80.

156. Schwemer, 'Paulus' (n. 155), thinks that the incident at Antioch took place only at the point in time of Acts 18.22 (161).

157. Cf. recently Wolfgang Reinbold, 'Die Hellenisten. Kritische Anmerkungen zu einem Fachbegriff der neutestamentlichen Wissenschaft', B*Z* 42, 1998, 96–102.

158. Cf. Georg Schöllgen, 'Probleme der frühchristlichen Sozialgeschichte. Einwände gegen Peter Lampes Buch über "Die stadtrömischen Christen in den ersten beiden Jahrhunderten", *JAC* 32, 1989, 23–40: 36.

159. 'At any rate, we know at least two points (*plerique pauperes* [viz., in Minucius Felix, *Octavius*, 36.3]; the increases in the number of the socially more elevated in the second century), at which Christianity reflects the social development of society as a whole' (second edition, 113).

160. Suetonius, *Life of Caesars, Claudius* 25.

161. There can be no doubt about 41 CE as the date of this command; see my 'Das Judenedikt des Claudius (Apg 18, 2)', in Claus Bussmann and Walter Radl (eds.), *Der Treue Gottes trauen. Beiträge zum Werk des Lukas. Für Gerhard Schneider*, Freiburg 1991, 289–98: 292

162. Dio Cassius, *Roman History* 60.6.6.

163. Harry J. Leon, *The Jews of Ancient Rome*, New York 1960, 24.

164. Dio Cassius, *Roman History* 57.18.5a. Cf. Suetonius, *Life of Caesars, Tiberius* 36. Cf. David Alvarez Cineira, *Die Religionspolitik des Kaisers Claudius und die paulinische Mission*, Freiburg 1999, 188–93 (bibl.).

165. See my analysis in 'Das Judenedikt des Claudius' (n. 161), 293–6.

166. Helga Botermann, *Das Judenedikt des Kaisers Claudius*, Hermes-Einzelschriften 17, Stuttgart 1996, 56. The most recent illustration of Botermann's observation is Gerd Theissen, 'Die Verfolgung unter Agrippa I und die Autoritätsstruktur der Jerusalemer Gemeinde. Eine Untersuchung zu Act 12,1–4 und Mk 10,35–45', in Ulrich Mell und Ulrich Müller (eds), *Das Urchristentum in seiner literarischen Geschichte. Festschrift für Jürgen Becker zum 65. Geburtstag*, BZNW 100, Berlin and New York 1999, 263–289: 275 n. 21.

167. See further H. Dixon Slingerland, *Claudian Policy Making and the Early Imperial Repression of Judaism at Rome*, USF Studies in the History of Judaism 160, Atlanta 1997.

168. See Leon, *Jews* (n. 163), 25. Yet Alvarez, *Religionspolitik* (n. 164), writes: 'It cannot be concluded from Tacitus' silence, as is often done, that Dio's report has priority over that of Suetonius' (195 n. 172). For one thing, Alvarez underestimates the weight of the silence of Tacitus on this point. Moreover, the question of priority between Dio's and Suetonius's account is a moot point, because they do not contradict one another here (see above, p. 123).

169. Agrippa I, who was present in Rome in 41, the point in time at which Claudius was proclaimed emperor, may have played an important role in working out the edict on the Jews. For example he could have clarified for the new emperor the difference between Jews and Jewish Christians. Shortly afterwards he himself took action against the Jewish Christians in Jerusalem (Acts 12). See Daniel R. Schwartz, *Agrippa I: The Last King of Judaea*, TSAJ 23, Tübingen 1990, 94–6, 119–24.

170. This chronological naivety is, alas, not limited to Lampe. Indeed, it is shared by many learned New Testament scholars. A recent example is Friedrich Avemarie (*Die Tauferzählungen der Apostelgeschichte. Theologie und Geschichte*, WUNT 139, Tübingen 2002). He writes about the relevance of the Gallio inscription for the absolute chronology of Paul: this inscription would be useless for research on Paul if this research were to base itself 'solely on the letters of Paul. The fact that Acts knows him (Gallio) and furthermore classifies him correctly as the *proconsul Achaiae* is enough reason for assuming that Paul's founding proclamation chronologically overlapped with the time of Gallio's tenure in office' (10). This conclusion is too hasty, as it (a) simply refuses to look at the evidence for a founding of the Corinthian community before the Jerusalem conference and (b) fails to take into account that Luke – though several times reporting on visits by Paul to a given locality – presents detailed information about the apostle's activity there in only *one* report (see above, p.123). Hence the chronology of the other traditions in Acts 18.1-11 cannot be naively based on the Gallio inscription.

171. See further on this the remark by Carolyn Osiek, 'The Oral World of Early Christianity in Rome. The Case of Hermas', in Karl P. Donfried and Peter Richardson (eds), *Judaism and Christianity in First-Century Rome*, Grand Rapids and Cambridge 1998, 151–72: 'Even if the *Shepherd* stands in marked contrast to *1 Clement* by way of literary quality, for example, nothing can be directly concluded about the relative social status of the authors, though Clement may in fact have represented the interests of the ruling classes in a way that Hermas did not' (170). Cf. Carolyn Osiek, *Shepherd of Hermas: A Commentary*, Hermeneia, Minneapolis 1999.

172. Jeffers' essay 'Jewish and Christian Families in First-Century Rome', in Donfried and Richardson, *Judaism and Christianity* (see n. 171), 128–50, seeks to show that 'family life among the Jews and Christians in first-century Rome did not differ much from family life among pagan Romans among the lower class at that time' (129). His new book, *The Greco-Roman World of the New Testament Era: Exploring the Background of Early Christianity*, Downers Grove, Ill. 1999, is highly useful for its presentation of specific background material. Let me hasten to add that there never was a New Testament era. It is misleading to equate the 'New Testament era' with the 'first century AD' (*pace* 13).

173. For the insight into the point of reference of Phil. 4.15 which Pilhofer misses in research cf. my *Paul, Apostle to the Gentiles* (n. 48), 105–7.

174. See now the report by Eckhard J. Schnabel, 'Die ersten Christen in Ephesus: Neuerscheinungen zur frühchristlichen Missionsgeschichte', *NT* 41, 1998, 349–82. While Schnabel among other things reviews some of the books that are discussed also in my report, his own approach is marred by an uncritical use of Acts, and he nowhere tries to relate the information in Paul's authentic letters to the data of Acts. Yet Schna-

bel's work has some value because like so many other evangelically orientated books it is well acquainted with the secondary literature and the archaeological work in question.

175. See my *Heretics* (n. 19), 137f.

176. It should be noted that three years later Helmut Koester edited another collection of essays of a similar scope, *Pergamon, Citadel of the Gods: Archaeological Record, Literary Description, and Religious Development*, Harrisburg, PA 1998. The article which directly bears on ancient Christianity at Pergamon was written by Adela Yarbro Collins, 'Pergamon in Early Christian Literature' (163–84). Her general summary statement on Pergamon comes close to Steven Friesen's thesis on Ephesus (see above, p.134). She writes: 'The Book of Revelation ... stands the propaganda of the current ruler on its head: Roman imperial power represents the forces of chaos that threaten to dissolve the order intended by the divine ruler of all' (184). So far so good. One wishes that she had addressed the specific question whether the Nicolaitans (Rev. 2.6, 15) had anything to do with the Hellenist Nicolaus (Acts 6.5), all the more so since Irenaeus *(Haer.* I 26 3) claims a genetic relationship between the two. Such a relationship seems to be probable or at least possible for two further reasons. (a) A move from Palestine to Asia Minor is attested for another Hellenist, Philip (cf. Eusebius, *Church History* III 31 3). (b) The eating of sacrificial meat by the Nicolaitans, which the author of Revelation (2.14) attacks, fits in well with the liberal spirit of the Hellenists and of Paul (cf. 1 Cor. 10.25), which was introduced into Christianity by the Hellenists.

    If the above considerations are sound, we have an important tool for reconstructing an historical link between Jerusalem and Pergamene/ Ephesine Christianity. Before engaging in theories of the relationship between the imperial power and the faith of the author of Revelation, we need to reconstruct an *Ereignisgeschichte* (history of events) to put texts in the proper and specific context. See now Heikki Räisänen, 'The Nicolaitans: Apoc. 2; Acta 6', in id., *Challenges to Biblical Interpretation: Collected Essays* 1991–2001, Leiden 2001, 141–89 (bibl.).

177. See also Jozef Verheyden, 'The Flight of the Christians to Pella', *EThL* LXVI, 1990, 368–84. For criticism of Verheyden's monograph see Jürgen Wehnert, 'Die Auswanderung der Jerusalemer Christen nach Pella – historisches Faktum oder theologische Konstruktion?', *ZKG* 102, 1991, 231–55; Marco Frenschkowski, 'Galiläa oder Jerusalem? Die topographischen und politischen Hintergründe der Logienquelle', in Andreas Lindemann (ed.), *The Sayings Source Q and the Historical Jesus*, BEThL CLVIII, Louvain 2001, 535–59: 551–6.

178. Cf. also Wehnert, 'Auswanderung', 237.

179. See also my *Heretics* (n. 19), 27–30.

180. Andreas Lindemann, *Paulus im ältesten Christentum. Das Bild des Apostels und die Rezeption der paulinischen Theologie in der frühchristlichen Theologie bis Marcion*, BHTh 58, Tübingen 1979. This influential book with an

extent of more than 400 pages devotes less than 20 to Marcion and does not even concede him a theology of grace. On such a caricature see my *Heretics* (n. 19), 162f. Cf. also id., 'Paul in the Writings of the Apostolic Fathers', in William S. Babcock (ed.), *Paul and the Legacies of Paul*, Dallas 1990, 25–45.

181. 'Paulus in den Nag-Hammadi-Texten. Ein Beitrag zur Geschichte der Paulusrezeption im frühen Christentum', *ZThK* 78, 1981, 177–205.

182. While Dehandschutter's assumption that Polycarp was 'not unoriginal' (291) is a necessary correction of earlier negative scholarly views (see the examples, 275), his claim that Polycarp's letter as we have it (chapters 1–14) is a literary unity seems to be indefensible. One has rather to assume that two letters were made into one (cf. the scholarly hypothesis that 2 Corinthians is a composition of at least two Pauline letters). Koester, *History and Literature of Early Christianity II*[2] (n. 10) formulates the scholarly consensus thus: 'The first (letter), consisting of chapters 13–14, was a cover letter for the sending of copies of the Ignatian letters to the Philippians upon their request. Here Polycarp refers to Ignatius as being still alive. In Phil. 9.1, however, Polycarp refers to Ignatius and two of his associates as blessed martyrs of the past, whose examples must be recalled. Thus the letter to which this remark belongs must have been written much later; Phil. 1–12 is therefore a different letter, which belongs to a later time' (308–9). See also Thomas Lechner, *Ignatius adversus Valentinianos? Chronologische und theologiegeschichtliche Studien zu den Briefen des Ignatius von Antiochien*, VigCh.S 47, Leiden 1999, 12–18, for an impressive critique of attempts to harmonize PolPhil 9 and 13–14.

183. See the continuation of his 1985 study: Graydon F. Snyder, *Inculturation of the Jesus Tradition: The Impact of Jesus on Jewish and Roman Cultures*, Harrisburg, PA 1999, esp. Part 3 ('Trajectories of Inculturation' [91–213]), where Snyder deals with 'Symbols', 'Representation Art', 'Architecture', etc. Note also the 428 photographs following 88.

184. See the translator's comments on the possible reasons for the limited response to the book (ix). My further guess is that the confessional statements have alienated readers who are interested only in history. See the statement of John G. Gager in a book that covers the same topic, *The Origins of Anti-Semitism: Attitudes Toward Judaism in Pagan and Christian Antiquity*, New York 1983: 'Some very recent publications, most notably H. Conzelmann's *Heiden — Juden — Christen* ... receive no attention here. The bearing of my own work on such publications will be clear to any who care to read them. Conzelmann's work makes it painfully clear just how difficult it is to change the course of long-established conversations' (vi). See further Peter Schäfer, *Judeophobia: Attitudes toward the Jews in the Ancient World*, Cambridge and London 1997; René S. Bloch, *Antike Vorstellungen vom Judentum. Der Judenexkurs bei Tacitus im Rahmen der griechisch-römischen Ethnographie*, Historia Einzelschriften 160, Stuttgart 2002. As the three books cited, by Gager,

Schäfer and Bloch, are extremely distinguished works, the failure to take account of Conzelmann's work in them is all the more regrettable, not least also because Conzelmann's perspective was broader and his historical knowledge more comprehensive than that of Schäfer, Gager and Bloch. Having had numerous conversations with Hans Conzelmann I have to add that of all his publications the book *Gentiles – Jews – Christians* was closest to his heart.

185. A note of precision is appropriate here. I do not think that we will ever fully explain the origins of Christianity. Fredriksen, however, makes no attempt at explanation except to paraphrase the texts and to subtract their supernatural claim.

186. See also the 875 page commentary on Acts by Ben Witherington III, *The Acts of the Apostles. A Socio-Rhetorical Commentary*, Grand Rapids 1998, 88: 'I would suggest that the Pauline evidence deserves only a slight preference over the Acts data where they both mention the same subject.'

187. Wilfred Cantwell Smith, 'Methodology and the Study of Religion: Some Misgivings', in *Methodological Issues in Religious Studies*, ed. R. D. Baird, Chico, CA 1974, 1–25: 3–4.

188. Martin Hengel, *Judaica et Hellenistica, Kleine Schriften* I, WUNT 90, Tübingen 1996, 5.

189. The following studies are especially helpful: Martin Hengel, *The 'Hellenization' of Judaea in the First Century after Christ*, London 1989; John M. G. Barclay, *Jews in the Mediterranean Diaspora: From Alexander to Trajan (323 BCE –117 CE)*, Edinburgh 1996; E. P. Sanders, 'Jesus' Galilee', in Ismo Dunderberg, Christopher Tuckett and Kari Syreeni, *Fair Play: Diversity and Conflicts in Early Christianity. Essays in Honour of Heikki Räisänen*, NT.S 103, Leiden 2002, 3–41 (bibl.).

190. Cf. Wilhelm Bousset, *Hauptprobleme der Gnosis*, FRLANT 10, Göttingen 1907; Richard Reitzenstein, *Hellenistic Mystery Religions*, Pittsburgh 1978. Cf. also the critical assessment by Carsten Colpe, *Die religionsgeschichtliche Schule. Darstellung und Kritik ihres Bildes vom gnostischen Erlösermythos*, FRLANT 78, Göttingen 1961, and Gerd Lüdemann and Alf Özen: 'Religionsgeschichtliche Schule', *TRE* XXVIII, Berlin 1997, 618–24. Unfortunately Colpe's book has been used in some circles, contrary to his intentions, to challenge the existence of a pre-Christian gnosis.

191. See especially Rudolf Bultmann, *Theology of the New Testament*, Vol. I, New York and London 1951; Vol. II, New York and London 1955.

192. Rudolf Bultmann, *Primitive Christianity In Its Contemporary Setting*, New York and London 1959, 162.

193. Bultmann, *Theology* I, 166–7.

194. Bultmann, *Theology* I, 164.

195. Bultmann, *Theology* I, 165.

196. Bultmann, *Theology* I, 167.

197. Bultmann, *Theology* I, 171.

198. Walter Schmithals' relevant two books are *Gnosticism in Corinth: An Investigation of the Letters to the Corinthians*, Nashville 1971, and *Paul and*

the Gnostics, Nashville 1972. His results are summarized in the monograph: *Neues Testament und Gnosis*, Darmstadt 1984. There is a fair
treatment of Schmithals in English by Pheme Perkins, *Gnosticism and the
New Testament*, Minneapolis 1993, 74–80.

199. On Baur cf. my *Opposition to Paul* (n. 30), 1–7.

200. Cf. his latest book on the subject, which gives the text of 27(!) letters of
Paul: Walter Schmithals, *Die Briefe des Paulus in ihrer ursprünglichen
Gestalt*, Zürich 1984. I shall not discuss these theories because they have
no direct relevance for my criticism.

201. See the discussion in my *Paul, Apostle to the Gentiles* (n. 48), 206–9.

202. See Wolfgang Harnisch, *Eschatologische Existenz: Ein exegetischer Beitrag
zum Sachanliegen von 1. Thessalonicher 4,13–5,11*, FRLANT 110, Göttingen 1973.

203. Cf. my *Opposition to Paul* (n. 30).

204. Bultmann's view that Gnosticism took hold in Gnostic baptismal groups
such as the Mandaeans is open to serious doubts. Cf. the recent contribution to the Mandaean hypothesis by Roald Zellweger, 'Das Man-
däerproblem im Lichte des frühen syrischen Christentums', in Gerd
Lüdemann (ed.), *Studien zur Gnosis*, ARGU 9, Frankfurt 1999, 261–87.

205. Arthur Darby Nock, *Essays on Religion and the Ancient World* II, Oxford
1972, 957.

206. See my *Untersuchungen zur simonianischen Gnosis*, GTA 1, Göttingen 1975;
'The Acts of the Apostles and the Beginnings of Simonian Gnosis', *NTS*
33, 1987, 420–6. Roland Bergmeier, *Das Gesetz im Römerbrief und andere
Studien zum Neuen Testament*, WUNT 121, Tübingen 2000, 238–46 ('Die
Gestalt des Simon Magus in Act 8 und in der simonianischen Gnosis –
Aporien einer Gesamtdeutung' [1986]) is a thorough review article of my
1975 monograph; Bergmeier thinks that the evidence for a Gnostic
'Simon' is not sufficient. In my 1987 article I have identified *epinoia tes
kardias* in Acts 8.22 as an ironical reference to Simon's female companion
Helen. I hope that this suggestion puts to rest the objection to a Gnostic
'Simon' in Acts 8 for the lack of the appearance of his female *syzygos*, who
is mentioned explicitly only by Justin (I *Apol.* 26. 3) around 150 CE. 'Luke'
had no reason to mention Simon's companion Helen, as in Acts he also
fails to refer to Peter's wife, who, as we may conclude from Paul
(1 Cor.9.5), accompanied her husband on his missionary trips. Alasdair
H. B. Logan's article 'Simon Magus', *TRE* 31, Berlin 2000, 272-6, fails to
recognize that Simon's adherents came from the Gentile population of
Samaria as Justin Martyr, himself a former Gentile from Flavia Neapolis,
attests (*Dial.* 120. 6).

207. Cf. Michael Allen Williams, *Rethinking 'Gnosticism': An Argument for Dis-
mantling a Dubious Category*, Princeton 1996.

208. Ugo Bianchi (ed.), *Le Origini dello Gnosticismo*, Leiden 1967, XXVI-
XXVII. To be sure, the participants limit 'gnosticism' to the second
century and speak of 'proto-gnosticism' if the same type of myth occurs
in the first century or earlier. But this distinction should not keep us

from using the above description of a Gnostic myth and the term 'gnosticism' for a myth from the first century.

209. On the polemic against the Jews in 1 Thessalonians see my *Paul: The Founder of Christianity* (n. 80), 151–3.

210. Otherwise the text makes little sense. Unless they knew the attempt would prove disastrous, why should the rulers have desisted from their plan to kill Jesus?

211. Cf. AscJes 10.8–12; IgnEph 19.1; Gospel of Philip §26. See further Rudolf Bultmann, *Exegetica: Aufsätze zur Erforschung des Neuen Testaments*, Tübingen 1967, 75–80.

212. George MacRae, 'Nag Hammadi and the New Testament', in Barbara Aland (ed.), *Gnosis. Festschrift für Hans Jonas*, Göttingen 1978, 144–57: 155.

213. See Frederik Wisse, in Birger A. Pearson (ed.), *Nag Hammadi Codex VII*, NHMS 30, Leiden 1996, 15–23.

214. Cf. Birger A. Pearson, T*he Emergence of the Christian Religion: Essays on Early Christianity*, Harrisburg 1997, 135–44.

215. MacRae, 'Nag Hammadi and the New Testament' (n. 212), 153–5.

216. See e.g. Jörg Büchli, *Der Poimandres – ein paganisiertes Evangelium: Sprachliche und begriffliche Untersuchungen zum 1. Traktat des Corpus Hermeticum*, WUNT II/27, Tübingen 1987. Büchli tries to make the case for CH I being a paganized Christian text. Yet despite the applause by Martin Hengel ('Paulus und die Frage einer vorchristlichen Gnosis', id., *Paulus und Jakobus: Kleine Schriften III*, WUNT 141, Tübingen 2002, 473–510: 482–3), his attempt has failed. See Jens Holzhausen, *Der 'Mythos vom Menschen' im hellenistischen Ägypten*, athenäums monografien Theophaneia 33, Bodenheim 1994, 7–79 (bibl.).

217. Translation on the basis of Wisse, *Nag Hammadi Codex VII*, 99–101. I have indicated in the printing that the passage is poetical and must be divided into two parts. See also the underlining and italics in the text. Line two is a parenthesis possibly added by a later reader of the text.

218. Translation following George MacRae, in Douglas M. Parrott (ed.), *Nag Hammadi Codices V, 2–5 and VI with Papyrus Berolinensis 8502, 1 and 4*, NHS 11, Leiden 1979, 177–9.

219. Cf. Kurt Rudolph, *Gnosis: The Nature and History of an Ancient Religion*, San Francisco 1983, 91f.

220. On the analysis of 2 Cor. 4.4 and its relationship to Gnosticism cf. George MacRae, 'Why the Church Rejected Gnosticism', in E. P. Sanders (ed.): *Jewish and Christian Self-Definition I: The Shaping of Christianity in the Second and Third Centuries*, London 1980, 126–133, esp. 130f.

221. For the Jewish basis of Paul's anthropology see Bultmann, *Theology I* (n. 191), 190–227 and *passim.*

222. Perkins, *Gnosticism and the New Testament* (n. 198), 34.

223. Perkins, *Gnosticism and the New Testament* (n. 198), 80. See also Jörg Frey, 'Die paulinische Antithese von "Fleisch" und "Geist" und die palästinisch-jüdische Weisheitstradition', ZNW 90, 1999, 45–77. Yet Frey does not even discuss the possibility of a Gnostic background at this point.

224. Cf. Schmithals, *Gnosticism in Corinth* (n. 198), 127–8. See further Gerd Theissen, *Psychological Aspects of Pauline Theology*, Philadelphia 1987, 309. Theissen explains the factual cursing of Jesus from the perspective of depth psychology. He writes: 'In the "Anathema Jesus", attitudes that had been repressed in the converts as a result of a "postdecisional" conflict are revealed ... In the postdecisional conflict, they had suppressed the judgment "Jesus is cursed!" which corresponded to the general system of values, in order not to fall into contradiction with themselves. But under reduced self-control, the value stance that had been excluded by the decision in favour of Christianity and that had been suppressed again broke through and led to the cry "Jesus is cursed!"' (311). I am not as certain as Theissen seems to be that the pre-Christian Corinthians had a real reason to *curse* Jesus.

225. Birger A. Pearson, 'Did the Gnostics curse Jesus?' *JBL* 86, 1967, 301–5, has questioned whether the passage from Origen can be used as evidence of a Gnostic cursing of Jesus. Against this see Norbert Brox, 'ANATHEMA IHΣOYΣ (1 Kor 12,3)', *BZ* 12, 1968, 103–11: 107. Referring to C. Jenkins, 'Origen on I Corinthians', *JThSt* 10, 1909, 30, lines 30–34, Brox points out that in his exegesis of 1 Cor. 12.3 Origen does refer to the Ophites' curse as a fact.

226. Schmithals, *Gnosticism in Corinth* (n. 198), 128.

227. Translation on the basis of Gerd Lüdemann and Martina Janssen: *Suppressed Prayers: Gnostic Spirituality in Early Christianity*, London 1998, 72–3. Cf. further Klaus Koschorke, *Die Polemik der Gnostiker gegen das kirchliche Christentum*, Leiden 1978, 44–48 ('Gnostische Polemik gegen die Verkündigung des Gekreuzigten').

228. Translation on the basis of Lüdemann and Janssen, *Suppressed Prayers* (n. 227), 160.

229. I am aware that 'docetism' is not automatically identical with Gnosticism. Yet Gnosticism always includes docetism. See the survey by Winrich A. Löhr, 'Doketismus', *RGG⁴* II, 925–7 (bibl.).

230. Birger A. Pearson, 'Early Christianity and Gnosticism in the History of Religions', *Studia Theologica* 55, 2001, 81–106: 97. Pearson later remarks: 'To be sure Irenaeus regards this Gnosis as a Christian heresy, and church historians have traditionally taken the same approach. Even now, in the face of all the new evidence ... notably the Nag Hammadi texts, some scholars persist in finding a heretical Christian origin for Gnosticism. Historians of religions take a different tack, however, arguing that Gnosis and Gnosticism arose independently of Christianity, and can be regarded as a religion in its own right' (98).

231. Martin Hengel, 'Die Ursprünge der Gnosis und das Urchristentum', *Evangelium Schriftauslegung Kirche: Festschrift für Peter Stuhlmacher zum 65. Geburtstag*, Göttingen 1997, 190–223: 190–1.

232. Cf. the hints given by Gerd Theissen, *Studien zur Soziologie des Urchristentums*, WUNT 19, Tübingen 1979, IV; id., *Psychological Aspects of Pauline Theology*, Philadelphia 1987, xi.

233.　At least in passing I should indicate a criticism here. I find it difficult to see prayer as the primary significance of cathedrals. That was not even their significance when they were built, since their architects had massive clerical and political interests (though the workers employed to build them must certainly have addressed many spontaneous prayers to heaven as they risked their lives). Today cathedrals offer even less space for prayer. They are cold, lofty, and as beautiful and impersonal as the statues of gods in Greek temples. By using the image of a cathedral Theissen makes precisely the opposite effect to what he intends on many secular people whom he wants to missionize. This is hardly the way in which they can sense his love of the Christian religion.

234.　Wayne A. Meeks, *Interpretation* 55, 2001, 77–80: 78.

235.　Wayne A. Meeks, *In Search of the Early Christians: Selected Essays*, New Haven and London 2002, 256. The sentences that follow are worth quoting: 'There is still considerable confusion in the ways that humanists and social scientists talk about theory and in the ways they use models derived from their theories. One of the goals of interdisciplinary discussion ought to be to try to clear up as much of that confusion as we can' (ibid.). Later Meeks points that it 'has become popular to malign the naiveté of the Enlightenment's pretensions to rationality, objectivity, and universality in perspective' (259). He replies: 'Objectivity may be beyond our grasp, but the attempt to be resolutely honest about our own past remains, however inevitable its shortcomings, a noble endeavor' (ibid.).

236.　The impossibility of taking in all the source-critical theories about the Gospel of John does not relieve one of the need to offer one's own solution, since the Fourth Gospel could not have been written in its present form. Cf. Frank Schleritt, in Gerd Lüdemann, *Jesus After Two Thousand Years: What He Really Said and Did*, London 2000 and Amherst, NY 2001, 406–588.

237.　Heikki Räisänen, *Beyond New Testament Theology: A Story and a Programme*, 2nd edn, London 2000, 145.

238.　Hans Lietzmann, *The Beginnings of the Christian Church*, London [3]1953, 286. Cf. also Martin Hengel, *The Four Gospels and the One Gospel of Jesus Christ: An Investigation of the Collection and Origin of the Canonical Gospels*, London 2000, 57f. Remarkably, Helmut Koester (*Ancient Christian Gospels: Their History and Development*, Philadelphia and London 1990) does not investigate Basilides. He had devoted only six lines to him in his *Einführung in das Neue Testament im Rahmen der Religionsgeschichte und Kulturgeschichte der hellenistischen und römischen Zeit*, Berlin 1980, 669; the remarks on Basilides in the second edition of *History and Literature of Early Christianity. Volume Two: Introduction to the New Testament*, New York 2000, are more extensive (237f). But even here there is no reference to his role as an exegete. Instead, Koester writes enigmatically: '(H)is *Commentaries* perhaps show the influence of Christian writings' (237). For Basilides cf. Winrich A. Löhr; *Basilides und seine Schule: Eine Studie zur Theologie- und Kirchengeschichte des zweiten Jahrhunderts*, WUNT 83, Tübingen 1996 (for his commentary on the Gospels see esp.11f.).

239. Theissen has shed impressive light on Jesus' Jewish identity (e.g., 27, 33, etc.).

240. Rudolf Bultmann, *Theology of the New Testament*, Vol. I (n. 191), 3.

241. Hans Grass, *Ostergeschehen und Osterberichte*, Göttingen ⁴1970, 248.

242. Dietz Lange, *Glaubenslehre: Band II*, Tübingen 2001, 138.

243. Joachim Ringleben, *Wahrhaft auferstanden: Zur Begründung der Theologie des lebendigen Gottes*, Tübingen 1998, 99.

244. Alexander Bommarius, in id. (ed.), *Fand die Auferstehung wirklich statt? Eine Diskussion mit Gerd Lüdemann*, Düsseldorf 1995, 122. Previously he had aptly remarked: 'Even if it is quite clear to us that our "technological rationalism" is not the ultimate wisdom, we prefer to cross by a bridge which engineers have constructed in accordance with the scientific, and not the mythological, picture of the world' (121f).

245. He bases his judgement on the published dissertation of his pupil David Alvarez Cineira, *Die Religionspolitik des Kaisers Claudius und die paulinische Mission* (n. 164). At another point (Theissen, 'Verfolgung unter Agrippa I' [n. 166]), Theissen explicitly refers to the chronological agreement between Orosius and Acts 18.2 (275 n. 21). I have made the necessary comments on this on p. 124 above.

246. I shall leave aside here the well-known arguments on the historicity of the two episodes.

247. Gerd Theissen, *Die Religion der ersten Christen: Eine Theorie des Urchristentums*, Gütersloh 2000, 303. These sentences have been added in the German edition. Theissen comments on the relationship between the German and the English editions: 'The German version has been revised once again and important additions have been made in the text and the notes' (14).

248. See above, p. 124.

249. Cf. my *Paul: The Founder of Christianity* (n. 80), 88–91.

250. See my *Heretics* (n. 19), 40–9 for details.

251. See my 'Zur Geschichte des ältesten Christentums in Rom', *ZNW* 70, 1979, 86–114. This thesis, which goes back to Adolf Harnack, has by now become the almost universal consensus.

252. Klaus Koschorke, *Die Polemik der Gnostiker gegen das kirchliche Christentum*, NHS 12, Leiden 1978.

253. Cf. the positive review of Theissen's book by Andreas Lindemann ('Zur "Religion" des Urchristentums', *ThR* 67, 2002, 238–61: 246–61); he remarks that Theissen's book is 'over wide stretches a kind of cautious "apologia"' (260).

254. Cf. Theissen's remark about the narcissistic Gnostic view (301), which I can understand only as a value judgement. See also 284: 'One can only guess that in these Jewish Christian Gospels we have lost the voices of a very impressive Christianity which was no less valuable than the Christianity close to Judaism in the Letter of James or in Matthew.'

255. Cf. the contributions in Jacob Neusner (ed.), *Faith, Truth, and Freedom: The Expulsion of Professor Gerd Lüdemann from the Theological Faculty of Göttingen University. Symposium and Documents*, Binghamton, NY 2002 (bibl.) cf. *Religion* 32, 2002, 87–142.

256. Morton Smith, 'Historical Method in the Study of Religion' (1968), in id., *Studies in the Cult of Yahweh. Volume One: Studies in Historical Method, Ancient Israel, Ancient Judaism*, edited by Shaye J. D. Cohen, Religions in the Graeco-Roman World 130/1, Leiden 1996. 3–11.

257. Émile M. Cioran, 'Anfänge einer Freundschaft', in Hans Peter Duerr (ed.), *Die Mitte der Welt: Aufsätze zu Mircea Eliade*, Frankfurt 1984, 183–91: 191.

Bibliography of Works Discussed

Stefan Alkier, *Urchristentum. Zur Geschichte und Theologie einer exegetischen Disziplin*, BHTH 83, Tübingen 1993

Léonie J. Archer, *Her Price is Beyond Rubies. The Jewish Woman in Graeco-Roman Palestine*, JSOT, Suppl. Ser. 60, Sheffield 1990

William Baird, *History of New Testament Research. Volume One: From Deism to Tübingen*, Minneapolis 1992

Ernst Bammel, *Jesu Nachfolger. Nachfolgeüberlieferungen in der Zeit des frühen Christentums*, Studia Delitzschiana, Dritte Folge 1, Heidelberg 1988

Jürgen Becker (ed.), *Die Anfänge des Christentums. Alte Welt und neue Hoffnung*, Stuttgart 1987; ET *Christian Beginnings: Word and Community from Jesus to Post-Apostolic Times*, Louisville, Ky 1993

—, *Das Urchristentum als gegliederte Epoche*, SBS 155, Stuttgart 1993

Klaus Berger, *Theologiegeschichte des Urchristentums. Theologie des Neuen Testaments*, UTB für Wissenschaft, Tübingen and Basel 1994

— and Carsten Colpe (eds), *Religionsgeschichtliches Textbuch zum Neuen Testament*, TNT 1, Göttingen 1987; ET M. Eugene Boring, Klaus Berger and Carsten Colpe (eds), *Hellenistic Commentary to the New Testament*, Nashville 1995

Alan E. Bernstein, *The Formation of Hell. Death and Retribution in the Ancient and Early Christian Worlds*, Ithaca 1993

Hans Dieter Betz, *Hellenismus und Urchristentum. Gesammelte Aufsätze* I, Tübingen 1990

Peder Borgen, *Early Christianity and Hellenistic Judaism*, Edinburgh 1996

— and Soren Giversen (eds), *The New Testament and Hellenistic Judaism*, Aarhus 1995

Lukas Bormann, *Philippi. Stadt und Christengemeinde zur Zeit des Paulus*, NT.S LXXVIII, Leiden 1995

Christfried Böttrich, *Weltweisheit. Menschheitsethik. Urkult. Studien zum slavischen Henochbuch*, WUNT II/50, Tübingen 1992

Christoph vom Brocke, *Thessaloniki – Stadt des Kassander und Gemeinde des Paulus. Eine frühe christliche Gemeinde in ihrer heidnischen Umwelt*, WUNT II /125, Tübingen 2001

Raymond E. Brown and John P. Meier, *Antioch and Rome. New Testament Cradles of Catholic Christianity*, New York and Ramsey 1983

Frederick F. Bruce, *The Defence of the Gospel in the New Testament*, revd edn, Leicester 1977

James Tunstead Burtchaell, *From Synagogue to Church: Public Services and Offices in the Earliest Christian Communities*, Cambridge 1992

James H. Charlesworth (ed.), *The Messiah. Developments in Earliest Judaism and Christianity*, Minneapolis 1992

Bruce Chilton and Craig A. Evans (eds), *James the Just and Christian Origins*, NT.S XCVIII, Leiden, Boston and Cologne 1999

Michel Clévenot, *Von Jerusalem nach Rom. Geschichte des Christentums im 1.Jahrhundert*, Freiburg (Switzerland) 1987

Carsten Colpe, *Das Siegel der Propheten. Historische Beziehungen zwischen Judentum, Judenchristentum, Heidentum und frühem Islam*, ANTZ 3, Berlin 1990

Hans Conzelmann, *Heiden – Juden – Christen. Auseinandersetzungen in der Literatur der hellenistisch-römischen Zeit*, BHTH 62, Tübingen 1981; *ET Gentiles – Jews – Christians. Polemics and Apologetics in the Greco-Roman Era*, Minneapolis 1992

Anton Dauer, *Paulus und die christliche Gemeinde im syrischen Antiochia. Kritische Bestandsaufnahme der modernen Forschung mit einigen weiterführenden Überlegungen*, BBB 106, Weinheim 1996

Everett Ferguson, *Backgrounds of Early Christianity*, Grand Rapids 1987 (^{2}1983)

Christopher Forbes, *Prophecy and Inspired Speech in Early Christianity and its Hellenistic Environment*, WUNT II/75, Tübingen 1995

Paula Fredriksen, *From Jesus to Christ. The Origins of the New Testament Images of Jesus*, New Haven and London 1988

—, *Jesus of Nazareth, King of the Jews: A Jewish Life and the Emergence of Christianity*, New York 1999

W. H. C. Frend, *The Rise of Christianity*, London and Philadelphia 1984

Marlis Gielen, *Tradition und Theologie neutestamentlicher Haustafelethik. Ein Beitrag zur Frage einer christlichen Auseinandersetzung mit gesellschaftlichen Normen*, BBB 75, Frankfurt am Main 1990

Michael Goulder, *A Tale of Two Missions*, London 1994 (US title *St Paul versus St Peter. A Tale of Two Missions*, Louisville, Ky 1995)

Christian Grappe, *D'un Temple à l'autre. Pierre et l'Eglise primitive de Jérusalem*, Paris 1992

—, *Images de Pierre aux deux premiers siècles*, Paris 1995

Matthias Günther, *Die Frühgeschichte des Christentums in Ephesus*, ARGU 1, Frankfurt am Main 1995 (^{2}1998)

Ferdinand Hahn, Karl Kertelge and Rudolf Schnackenburg, *Einheit der Kirche. Grundlegung im Neuen Testament*, QD 84, Freiburg 1979

Adalbert Hamman, *Die ersten Christen*, Stuttgart 1985

Craig C. Hill, *Hellenists and Hebrews. Reappraising Division within the Earliest Church*, Minneapolis 1992

Pieter W. van der Horst, *Essays on the Jewish World of Early Christianity*, NTOA 14, Freiburg (Switzerland) and Göttingen 1990

Larry W. Hurtado, *One God, One Lord. Early Christian Devotion and Ancient Jewish Monotheism*, Minneapolis and London 1988

Niels Hyldahl, *The History of Early Christianity*, Studies in the Religion and History of Early Christianity 3, Frankfurt am Main 1997

James J. Jeffers, *Conflict at Rome. Social Order and Hierarchy in Early Christianity*, Minneapolis 1991

Martin Karrer, *Der Gesalbte. Die Grundlagen des Christustitels*, FRLANT 151, Göttingen 1991

Hans-Josef Klauck, *Die religiöse Umwelt des Urchristentums, I. Stadt- und Hausreligion, Mysterienkult, Volksglaube; II. Herrscher- und Kaiserkult, Philosophie, Gnosis*, Kohlhammer Studienbücher Theologie 9,1 + 2, Stuttgart 1995 + 1996; ET, *The Religious Context of Early Christianity: A Guide to Graeco-Roman Religions*, Edinburgh 2000

Helmut Koester (ed.), *Ephesos, Metropolis of Asia: An Interdisciplinary Approach to its Archaeology, Religion, and Culture*, Harvard Theological Studies 41, Valley Forge, PA 1995

Peter Lampe, *Die stadtrömischen Christen in den ersten beiden Jahrhunderten*, WUNT II/18, Tübingen 1987, ²1989; ET London and Minneapolis 2003

Christian Link, Ulrich Luz and Lukas Vischer, *Sie aber hielten fest an der Gemeinschaft ... Einheit der Kirche als Prozess im Neuen Testament und heute*, Zurich 1988

Hermann von Lips, *Weisheitliche Traditionen im Neuen Testament*, WMANT 64, Neukirchen-Vluyn 1990

Gerd Lüdemann, *Heretics. The Other Side of Early Christianity*, London and Louisville, Ky 1996

Margaret Y. MacDonald, *The Pauline Churches. A Socio-historical Study of Institutionalization in the Pauline and Deutero-Pauline Writings*, Cambridge 1988 (reprinted 1990)

—, *Early Christian Women and Pagan Opinion. The Power of the Hysterical Women*, New York 1996

Wayne A. Meeks, *The First Urban Christians. The Social World of the Apostle Paul*, New Haven and London 1983

Mary E. Mills, *Human Agents of Cosmic Power in Hellenistic Judaism and the Synoptic Tradition*, JSNTS 41, Sheffield 1990

Helmut Mödritzer, *Stigma und Charisma im Neuen Testament und seiner Umwelt. Zur Soziologie des Urchristentums*, NTOA 28, Freiburg (Switzerland) and Göttingen 1994

Karlheinz Müller, *Studien zur frühjüdischen Apokalyptik*, SBAB 11, Stuttgart 1991

Paul-Gerhard Müller, *Der Traditionsprozess im Neuen*

Testament. Kommunikationsanalytische Studien zur Versprach-lichung des Jesusphänomens, Freiburg 1982

Ulrich B. Müller, *Zur frühchristlichen Theologiegeschichte. Judenchristentum und Paulinismus in Kleinasien an der Wende vom ersten zum zweiten Jahrhundert n.Chr*, Gütersloh 1976

Peter Pilhofer, *Philippi. Band I: Die erste christliche Gemeinde Europas*, WUNT 87, Tübingen 1995

—, *Philippi. Band II: Katalog der Inschriften von Philippi*, WUNT 119, Tübingen 2000

Eckhard Plümacher, *Identitätsverlust und Identitätsgewinn. Studien zum Verhältnis von kaiserzeitlicher Stadt und frühem Christentum*, Biblisch-Theologische Studien 11, Neukirchen-Vluyn 1987

Eckhard Rau, *Von Jesus zu Paulus. Entwicklung und Rezeption der antiochenischen Theologie im Urchristentum*, Stuttgart 1994

Reinhold Reck, *Kommunikation und Gemeindeaufbau. Eine Studie zu Entstehung, Leben und Wachstum paulinischer Gemeinden in den Kommunikationsstrukturen der Antike*, SBB 22, Stuttgart 1991

Thomas A. Robinson, *The Bauer Thesis Examined. The Geography of Heresy in the Early Christian Church*, Studies in the Bible and Early Christianity 11, Lewiston and Queenston 1988

Ludger Schenke, *Die Urgemeinde. Geschichtliche und theologische Entwicklung*, Stuttgart 1990

Thomas Schmeller, *Brechungen. Urchristliche Wandercharismatiker im Prisma soziologisch orientierter Exegese*, SBS 136, Stuttgart 1989

—, *Hierarchie und Egalität. Eine sozialgeschichtliche Untersuchung paulinischer Gemeinden und griechisch-römischer Vereine*, SBS 162, Stuttgart 1995

Walter Schmithals, *Theologiegeschichte des Urchristentums. Eine problemgeschichtliche Darstellung*, Stuttgart 1994; ET *The Theology of the First Christians*, Louisville, Ky 1997

Luise Schottroff, *Befreiungserfahrungen. Studien zur Sozialgeschichte des Neuen Testaments*, ThB 82, Munich 1990

—, *Lydias ungeduldige Schwestern. Feministische Sozialgeschichte des frühen Christentums*, Gütersloh 1984 ([2]1986); ET *Lydia's Impatient Sisters. A Feminist Social History of Early Christianity*, Louisville, Ky and London 1995

Elisabeth Schüssler Fiorenza, *In Memory of Her: A Feminist Theological Reconstruction of Christian Origins*, New York and London 1983 (²1994); German *Zu ihrem Gedächtnis . . . Eine feministisch-theologische Rekonstruktion christlicher Ursprünge*, Munich and Mainz 1988

Daniel R. Schwartz, *Studies in the Jewish Background of Christianity*, WUNT 60, Tübingen 1992

Jean-Marie Sevrin (ed.), *The New Testament in Early Christianity. La réception des écrits néotestamentaires dans le christianisme primitif*, Leuven 1989

Walter Simonis, *Jesus von Nazareth. Seine Botschaft vom Reich Gottes und der Glaube der Urgemeinde. Historischkritische Erhellung der Ursprünge des Christentums*, Düsseldorf 1985

—, *Das Reich Gottes ist mitten unter euch. Neuorientierung an Jesu Lehre und Leben*, Düsseldorf 1986

Graydon F. Snyder, *Ante Pacem. Archaeological Evidence of Church Life Before Constantine*, Macon 1985

John F. Stambaugh and David L. Balch, *The Social World of the First Christians*, London 1986 (US title *The New Testament in its Social Environment*, Philadelphia 1986)

Ekkehard W. Stegemann and Wolfgang Stegemann, *Urchristliche Sozialgeschichte. Die Anfänge im Judentum und die Christusgemeinden in der mediterranen Welt*, Stuttgart 1995; ET *The Jesus Movement: A Social History of Its First Century*, Minneapolis 1999

Rick Strelan, *Paul, Artemis, and the Jews in Ephesus*, BZNW 80, Berlin 1996

Nicholas H. Taylor, *Paul, Antioch and Jerusalem. A Study in Relationships and Authority in Earliest Christianity*, JSNT.S 66, Sheffield 1992

Gerd Theissen, *A Theory of Primitive Christian Religion*, London and Minneapolis 1999 (published in the US as *The Religion of the Earliest Churches: Creating a Symbolic World*); revised and expanded German edition *Die Religion der ersten Christen: Eine Theorie des Urchristentums*, Gütersloh 2000

Werner Thiessen, *Christen in Ephesus. Die historische und theologische Situation in vorpaulinischer und paulinischer Zeit und zur Zeit der Apostelgeschichte und der Pastoralbriefe*, TANZ 12, Tübingen and Basel 1995

Paul Trebilco, *Jewish Communities in Asia Minor*, SNTS Mon. Ser. 69, Cambridge 1991

Jozef Verheyden, *De vlucht van de Christenen naar Pella. Onderzoek van het getuigenis van Eusebius en Epiphanius*, Verhandelingen van de Koninklijke Academie voor Wetenschappen, Letteren en Schone Kunsten van Belgie, jg. 50, Nr. 127, Brussels 1988

Anton Vögtle, *Die Dynamik des Anfangs. Leben und Fragen der jungen Kirche*, Freiburg 1988

Manuel Vogel, *Das Heil des Bundes. Bundestheologie im Frühjudentum und im frühen Christentum*, TANZ 18, Tübingen and Basel 1996

François Vouga, *Geschichte des frühen Christentums*, UTB 1733, Tübingen and Basel 1994

Michael Walsh, *The Roots of Christianity*, London 1986 (US title *The Triumph of the Meek: Why Early Christianity Succeeded*, San Francisco 1986)

Werner Zager, *Begriff und Wertung der Apokalyptik in der neutestamentlichen Forschung*, EH XXIII 358, Frankfurt am Main 1989

Index of Authors

215